Le Petit Journal

Le Petit Journal
CHAQUE JOUR 5 CENTIMES
Le Supplément illustré
CHAQUE SEMAINE 5 CENTIMES

SUPPLÉMENT ILLUSTRÉ
Huit pages : CINQ centimes

ABONNEMENTS

	TROIS MOIS	SIX MOIS	UN AN
PARIS	1 fr.	2 fr.	3 fr 50
DÉPARTEMENTS	1 fr.	2 fr.	4 fr.
ÉTRANGER	1 50	2 50	5 fr.

Sixième année — DIMANCHE 13 JANVIER 1895 — Numéro 217

LE TRAITRE

Dégradation d'Alfred Dreyfus

MARCH TO JUSTICE

GLOBAL MILITARY LAW LANDMARKS

MARCH TO JUSTICE

GLOBAL MILITARY LAW LANDMARKS

Editors
Navdeep Singh
Franklin D Rosenblatt

OCCAM
www.bluone.ink

Title – March to Justice: Global Military Law Landmarks
Editors – Navdeep Singh, Franklin D Rosenblatt
ISBN – 978-81-949547-1-2
Edition – I

Published by – BluOne India LLP

Publisher's Address –
306, Tower-I, Assotech Business Cresterra,
Plot No. 22, Sector 135, Noida.

Website – www.bluone.ink
Email – publisher@bluone.ink

Printed in India at Thomson Press (India) Ltd.

OCCAM

An imprint of BluOne Ink

CONTENTS

Foreword

Diego García-Sayán

United Nations Special Rapporteur on the
Independence of Judges and Lawyers

Mr ***Diego García-Sayán*** *was appointed the United Nations Special Rapporteur on the Independence of Judges and Lawyers in December 2016. He has also served as a judge of the Inter-American Court of Human Rights for two consecutive terms and as Minister of Justice as well as Minister of Foreign Affairs of Peru.*

I have been honored by the invitation to present this book *March to Justice: Global Military Law Landmarks* prepared to promote a necessary discussion on milestone decisions by constitutional courts across jurisdictions that have importantly/positively impacted military justice.

Although unique on its rules, the military justice system should be recognized as a full partner in administering justice for certain matters within its competence alongside the ordinary civilian justice system. Therefore, the principle of judicial independence should become a parameter to assess and study the functioning of military courts too.

Defending the principle of judicial independence and pointing out whenever it is attacked is precisely the *raison d'être* of the mandate of the Special Rapporteur of the United Nations on Independence of Justice, and I am honored to introduce to the reader this rather important perspective of analysis of the independence of justice around the world.

Achieving checks and balances, judicial independence, and improving rights protection are common goals for contemporary democracies. In recent years we have witnessed significant efforts to strengthen this principle in countries transitioning to democracy. This task, however, has not always been easy.

Ideally, a truly independent judiciary should possess at least three features. First, it should be impartial. Second, judicial decisions should not be influenced by any external or personal interest in the outcome of the case and should be respected once issued. Finally, judges, and prosecutors, should be free from interference so neither party to a case, nor other external interest, can influence outcomes or the judicial decision-making process. The same standards are pertinent to the military courts.

However, over the years, we have observed serious attempts to undermine those characteristics. A nation's justice system depends, in a democratic society, upon the adherence to the principle of its independence. This principle is essential to achieve proper judicial processes and to maintain other judicial values, such as impartiality, objectivity, and public trust in the judicial decision-making process.

The role of judiciaries in modern society has increased in recent decades. The judiciary is a social institution that shapes the lives of individuals. There is increasing attention and awareness, as well, on how the relationships between the judiciary and the other branches of government are being established so to promote and protect their independence and checks and balances, as is discussed in this book.

The challenges in terms of safeguarding and defending the principle of judicial independence are growing. As a response to that, in 1994, the then UN Commission on Human Rights (now Human Rights Council), in the resolution of 1994/41, noting both the increasing frequency of attacks on the independence of judges, lawyers, and court officials and the link which exists between the weakening of safeguards for the judiciary and lawyers and the gravity and frequency of violations of human rights, decided to create the mandate of a Special Rapporteur on the independence of judges and lawyers. Since 2016, when the Human Rights Council elected me, I have been honored to be in charge of that crucial responsibility. Over the past years, I have identified and recorded not only attacks on the independence of the judiciary, lawyers, and court officials but also the progress achieved in protecting and enhancing their independence and making concrete recommendations.

As this book indicates, the purpose of military justice has been to ensure that military leadership can maintain discipline, efficiency, and morale. Also, military justice has adapted in several countries to legal, military, and societal changes. While many challenges remain, it becomes relevant to study and analyze the outcome of decisions, impact and scope to better understand the consequential effects on military courts in democratic settings.

The challenges to judicial independence in the twenty-first century are significant in several areas, as I have noted in my reports presented before the UN General Assembly and the Human Rights Council. Also, as several contributors describe in this relevant book, just as the civilian criminal justice system grows and evolves in response to developments in law and society, so does military justice. We cannot disregard the application of the principle of judicial independence in the operation of military courts. Therefore, this book becomes relevant to encourage further discussion on the intersection and application of the principles of judicial independence from the military perspective.

I want to take the opportunity to congratulate Major Navdeep Singh and Colonel Franklin Rosenblatt for coordinating and encouraging an extraordinary dialogue among the contributors on this subject. I do not doubt that this book will turn to be a piece of leading literature to those seeking to understand the most pressing challenges, landmark decisions, and opportunities of military courts around the world in democratic societies.

Diego García-Sayán

Overview

Navdeep Singh

I am not going to take much of your time here, others would speak through their words, and we are in august company.

The idea for this book emanated during an informal conversation with Professor Eugene Fidell. We realised that there was no work available which anthologised the development of military justice and military law over the years in various jurisdictions. I spoke with my friend, Franklin Rosenblatt, about the concept and decided to embark on this journey with his consent immediately. The avowed aim was to chronicle in an anthology those judicial pronouncements, mostly by Constitutional Courts, which changed or altered the course of law related to the military in different nations. We wanted all such decisions and changes and the accompanying commentary to be at one place, and that place now is this book. The essays in this book would also throw light on the systems of law and justice dealing with the military followed in varied jurisdictions and (even if not by design) would probably induce an insightful comparative analysis. An overview of the contents and the methodology followed in this work is detailed in the succeeding paragraphs.

Discipline or Justice or Both

'...fair play and justice cannot always be sacrificed at the altar of military discipline. An unjust decision would be subversive of discipline...', observed the Supreme Court of India, in *Lt Col Prithi Pal Singh Bedi v. Union of India* 1982 AIR 1413.[1]

[1] *Lt Col Prithi Pal Singh Bedi v. Union of India* 1982 AIR 1413 can be accessed at https://indiankanoon.org/doc/278740/

A common string that runs through almost all militaries is the dilemma between discipline and justice. Discipline, no doubt, is the bedrock of any uniformed force, but should it be enforced at the cost of justice? How is a balance to be maintained? How are the two linked? Are they intertwined? The answer may not be too easy to find, but personally, I feel that the need for discipline cannot be allowed to override the concept of justice. Of course, this is not about my opinion, but it was interesting to note that many in the field feel the same. Justice promotes discipline.

It is no exaggeration to say that when the women and men serving our brave forces are assured of just and fair treatment when the occasion so arises, they will give their very best to the uniform that they wear with pride. Any unreasonableness, on the other hand, would dent the morale and confidence of service-members in the system.

These observations of the Delhi High Court on the subject in *Sepoy Durga Prasad v. Union of India* 2004 SCC OnLine Del 1163[2] are even more instructive: '...discipline is highly desirable and is essential for achieving the purpose for which the Armed Forces have been created and set up. However, in order to obtain discipline and obedience, it is essential that the personnel of the Armed Forces are dealt with innate fairness and justice is meted out to the members of the Force. This is necessary to not only ensure discipline but to motivate these brave soldiers who perform their duties in the service of the nation who have to be motivated to lay down their lives to the cause of the nation...'.

To reiterate, this book is not only about military justice and discipline, but also military law, which encompasses a much greater area. More on it later.

Independence

Interestingly, an area of concern with many jurists dealing with the subject all over the globe is the want of proper independence in the system of military justice. In many instances, military trials and tribunals do not quite meet the standards of Article 14 of the International Covenant of

---

[2] *Sepoy Durga Prasad v. Union of India* 2004 SCC OnLine Del 1163, can be accessed at https://www.legitquest.com/case/sepoy-durga-prasad-v-union-of-india/15D6D

Civil and Political Rights[3], which calls for trials by competent, independent and impartial tribunals. This has been the reason for many a litigation, leading to landmark decisions in certain jurisdictions, such as the *Findlay* case leading to breakthrough changes in the United Kingdom and the *Généreux* case, which triggered similar changes in Canada. Needless to state, you can read about these, and more, in this book that you hold.

It is felt by many quarters that most rough edges concerning military justice would be taken care of if true independence is ensured and assured in military trials & appeals, and if command influence is jettisoned. While many nations have taken concrete steps towards independence and offsetting of command influence, certain others are lagging. India, for example, though is known to have vibrant jurisprudence and progressive judicial precedents, till today it does not even have in existence an independent directorate of prosecution or prosecutorial authority within the military.

The concept of an independent prosecution is firmly ensconced in various legal systems, and there is no reason for it not to flourish in a military milieu. Since the nineteenth century, much emphasis has been laid on the fairness and independence of prosecution. In India again, the early twentieth century saw many decisions underlining the preciousness of an independent prosecution. For example, in *Ram Ranjan Roy v. Emperor* (1915) ILR 42 Cal 422,[4] the Calcutta High Court, noting the misconception amongst prosecutors, reiterated that the duty of the prosecution is not to support the police but to assist the Court in determining the guilt or innocence of the accused. In *Ghirrao v. Emperor* AIR 1933 Oudh 265,[5] the following was stated by the Oudh Chief Court regarding the duty of a prosecutor: '...his duty as a public prosecutor is not merely to secure the conviction of the accused at all costs but to place before the Court whatever evidence in possession of the prosecution, whether it be in favour of or against the accused and to leave it to the Court to decide upon all such evidence, whether the accused had or had not committed

---

[3] International Covenant on Civil and Political Rights (ICCPR), can be accessed at https://www.ohchr.org/en/professionalinterest/pages/ccpr.aspx

[4] *Ram Ranjan Roy v. Emperor* (1915) ILR 42 Cal 422, can be accessed at https://indiankanoon.org/doc/1685440/

[5] *Ghirrao v. Emperor* AIR 1933 Oudh 265, can be accessed through SCC Online (subscription based) under the citation 1933 SCC OnLine Oudh CC 63.

the offence with which he stood charged...'.

It is therefore of great concern that what to talk of prosecutorial independence, the value of which was realised more than a century ago, the concept of independence remains hazy even to members of courts-martial (who are not legally qualified) and all other nuts & bolts of the justice dispensation system from top to bottom. We need to work on this. We also need to work on correcting the situation wherein our officers get personally enmeshed with litigation making legal processes a prestige issue, rather than following the ideally expected behaviour as the representatives of a faceless government concerned with justice and not with winning or losing. The pressure on officers performing these roles must be eased. The message must not go out that one has to win 'by hook or crook'. Justice is nobody's personal property. Justice belongs to all of us-to both sides in the judicial process, even in an adversarial system. While penning this, I am reminded of Justice Robert H Jackson's famous words[6] here: 'Although the government technically loses its case, it has really won if justice has been done'.

However, this is not to say that things will remain constant since there is hope that the stakeholders would rise to the occasion and work towards the cause of justice, the first call of which is ensuring independence. A concrete step on the subject in India was taken by the Government when in 2015, the then Defence Minister, Mr Manohar Parrikar, on the directions of the Prime Minister, constituted a *Committee of Experts* to look into the soaring and uncontrolled litigation initiated by the Ministry of Defence against its employees and former employees, and also to resolve long pending service and pension matters which were resulting in litigation, along with improving the system of redressal of grievances. The undersigned was a member of the said *Committee*. One of the most important chapters of the report of the *Committee* was that on Military Justice Reform (Chapter V), which might not only be relevant to India but to any democracy, and which makes an important study for any person dealing with the subject. The report was declassified by Mr Parrikar and is available on the official website[7] of the Ministry of Defence.

[6] Justice Robert H Jackson, Supreme Court of the United States, speech available at https://www.roberthjackson.org/speech-and-writing/the-federal-prosecutor/

[7] Raksha Mantri's Committee of Experts: Review of Service and Pension Matters Including Potential Disputes, Minimizing Litigation and Strengthening Institutional Mechanisms Related To

Though the follow-up on the same has been extremely slow, there is optimism that things would gather some reasonable steam with the 'jointness' modalities of the three defence services experiencing momentum after creating the appointment of Chief of Defence Staff (CDS).

The Yale Draft – A Valuable Global Military Justice Template

A very important facet of the *Yale Draft*,[8] of which both of us (the editors of this book) were participants, was independence and, indeed, many other issues that are touched upon in this book. The *Yale Draft* was the result of the hard work of many professionals, including practitioners, judges, professors, jurists, members of the military, personalities connected with the United Nations and other international bodies, who had gathered at the Yale Law School on 23rd and 24th March 2018 to improve upon the *Decaux Principles* (Issue of the administration of justice through military tribunals/United Nations Economic & Social Council-2006).[9] Professor Fidell was the catalyst of this important milestone in military justice as its convener, and it shall remain a proud piece of collaborative work on the subject for all times to come. The Yale meeting aimed to 'examine the 2006 version of the draft principles and determine whether any changes should be made in them in the interest of (a) resolving the few contentious issues, (b) taking account of intervening developments, and (c) in general clearing the path to formal approval by the Human Rights Council and the General Assembly'. The *Yale Draft*, even as a standalone document, is a valuable resource not only for academia, the bar and the bench but also for policy and lawmakers.

Redressal Of Grievances, 2015, Pp 161-165, accessible at https://www.mod.gov.in/others/measures-reducing-litigation-and-public-grievances

[8] The Yale Draft, can be accessed at https://globalmjreform.blogspot.com/2018/04/decaux-prin ciples-workshop.html

[9] Decaux Principles (Issue of the administration of justice through military tribunals/United Nations Economic & Social Council, 2006), can be accessed at https://www.icj.org/wp-content/uploads/2014/10/Decaux-Principles-military-tribunals.pdf

Writing Style, Methodology and Readership of the Book

Our emphasis while seeking articles for the book was on non-technical, and dare I say it, non-scholarly writing. The reason for this is not far to see – it was to ensure that even the layperson or a non-legal or non-military reader could understand and assimilate the content. Moreover, we wanted it to be simple in the sense that it remains accessible to the general readership rather than restricting it to the legal and military communities. We are confident that the book with this format would appeal to a whole lot of consumers of knowledge, including those from law, the armed forces, the academia and the reader interested in legal and military developments, polity, public policy, human rights and governance.

To retain the originality of the essays and commentaries while editing, we have not tinkered much with the writing styles and arrangements as submitted by our contributors. This has ensured that the pieces remain organic and there is no overarching similarity in writing style. For example, some writers have used diverse headings, some have divided the essays into sub-heads, while others have written in a paragraph form. Even the presentation of footnotes is slightly varied. However, we have not altered the basics of what was submitted, and though the material you see is edited, the essence of writing style, as stated above, is retained. We have also consciously not standardised (or as some of us would say, standardised) the language so that you would find the term 'defence' in a British or Indian contribution and 'defense' in an American one, and that too not strictly enforced but as per the convenience of the contributor! In some chapters, there are recommendations and opinions of the authors which are thought-provoking and provide a model for a nurtured discussion for change. However, needless to state, we might not subscribe to all views expressed by our contributors, which are in any case personal, and not organisational.

Military Law Rather Than Military Justice

While the initial idea was only to cover military justice, that is, law related to discipline, trials and essentially criminal jurisprudence, we decided to broaden the scope of our book to a wider canvas of military law since there are many decisions in many nations which deal with other and ancillary matters, including personnel and staffing matters, which we thought of including. Thus, for example, there are two essays on judicial pronouncements on women in the military, one from the Supreme Court of India and the other from the Supreme Court of the United States.

We hope you enjoy reading this book as much as we relished editing it. To say that it was a fulfilling and delightful experience would be an understatement. It was a pleasure to interact with a host of brilliant contributors, all doing their bit for society, reading dicta of their jurisdictions, being enlightened, and absorbing more knowledge. We shall strive to continue updating future editions of this book with newer important developments in the field. Some of the contributors were known to us from earlier interactions, while some were new friends. This willy-nilly also expands our community of reformers who can work shoulder to shoulder on a global canvas whenever called upon. We are also proud of the overwhelming contribution by many accomplished women to this book, which, to our mind, is also a landmark.

At your service, always.

Navdeep Singh

Advocate, Punjab & Haryana High Court
Chandigarh, India
Twitter: @SinghNavdeep
Email: navdeepsingh.india@gmail.com and Office@NSA.legal

Navdeep Singh is a practising lawyer at the Punjab & Haryana High Court, Chandigarh, India. He is the founder President of the Armed Forces Tribunal Bar Association at Chandigarh. Navdeep has been a national service volunteer-reservist with the Territorial Army in the rank of Major in the past. The Territorial Army is a unique force of volunteers who, while carrying on with their civil vocations, wear the uniform for a few days in a year during their spare time in peace so that they can bear arms for the nation's defence during war and national emergencies. He has been decorated with a record number of 11 Commendations from the Army, Air Force and tri-service institutions for his work for the military community and veterans and other issues confronting the defence services. He has also been operationally deployed, including voluntarily in counterinsurgency operations during vacation periods of the High Court. Besides constitutional and civil & military employment-related matters, he has enthusiastically worked in the fields of rights of disabled soldiers, military widows & kin and for civil & military pensioners. He strongly advocates judicial independence and the freeing of tribunals and quasi-judicial bodies from the tacit control of the executive. Based on the sentiment expressed by the Prime Minister of India for curbing unnecessary litigation initiated by the Ministry of Defence against its employees and former employees, he was made a part (*gratis*) of a High-Level Committee of Experts constituted by the then Defence Minister for reducing such litigation by the Ministry of Defence and the Defence Services in service and pension-related matters, and to strengthen the system of redressal of grievances. He has attended and spoken at multiple international and national level seminars, conferences and meets. He was also a part of the historic Yale Draft (Principles) on Military Justice, an improvement of the existing United Nations document on the same subject, at a meet at the Yale Law School attended by global jurists and representatives of the United Nations. He regularly contributes opinion pieces and articles on law, military-related issues and public policy to newspapers and other media. He has authored five books. He is a member of the International Society of Military Law and the Law of War.

Introduction

Franklin D Rosenblatt

The word 'nationalism' has become unfairly maligned. These days it is most often used as a description for something backward and xenophobic. Us versus Them. It is not usually a positive description. However, 'nationalism' has positive aspects. It can be a word of unity in which disparate and disagreeable parts come together for an overarching purpose.

One mechanism for the promotion of positive nationalism exists through national military service. Such service allows discrete communities to claim a stake in the nation's civic life by demonstrating that their sons and daughters serve in its armed forces. Many communities herald with pride the honorable and sometimes valorous contributions of their members to the nation's military. Such service can also promote civic virtue by providing common ground that can bridge vast divides: soldiers from Boston and Boise serve together, as do soldiers from Kolkata and Chandigarh.

When I think of positive nationalism and the role of national militaries, I think of my friend and co-editor, Navdeep Singh. Navdeep is highly decorated in the Indian military. He is an outspoken and effective advocate for the fairness and basic rights of members and veterans of India's armed forces. Since he lives a hemisphere away from me, most of my interactions with Navdeep these days are online. I take special delight in watching him on social media rebut detractors and calling for harmony in society. His message, delivered with the eloquence of John Adams, is a simple one: service in the Indian armed forces is a common denominator – a source of shared national pride and purpose that can bridge vast differences.

This book originated over several lengthy sessions between Navdeep and me in legal conferences in the USA and other parts of the world. Navdeep and I share similar views about the unifying aspects of military service. We were also curious to learn more about how other highest national courts have performed the delicate balancing of national military prerogatives and individual rights.

The 25 chapters in this book show the variety of experimentation of how national courts from differing legal traditions and differing national security circumstances have achieved this balancing act. We are especially proud of the diversity of our contributors: roughly even between men and women; emerging and established; scholars and practitioners; and a remarkable geographic variance. No such study has ever been undertaken.

While several contributors to the book are highly decorated and have achieved senior ranks in their respective militaries, many others have no military experience. We believe it would be a mistake to limit discussion of the role of military law in national life to just soldiers and veterans. The voices of civilian scholars and activists are just as important in deliberating the proper interrelation of the military to society as are the voices of military members.

Navdeep and I are indebted to our common mentor, **Eugene Fidell,** at Yale Law School. He is rightfully regarded as the world's dean of military law. His *Global Military Justice Reform* blog (https://globalmjreform.blogspot.com/) is essential reading for developments in this topic. We are delighted to lead off this book with his contribution on the US Supreme Court cases of *O'Callahan* and *Solorio*. This essay addresses questions that many countries wrestle with: are military tribunals legitimate? What should be their reach? How can nations guard against encroachments of military authority into the civilian sphere?

Is military justice a real form of justice? As Judge **Jeff Blackett** writes in Chapter 2 about the landmark case *Findlay v. UK* case, military justice must meet certain baselines of fairness:

> The central tenet remains true – no military justice system can be objectively fair without strong guarantees of independence and impartiality. Invariably the military does not wish to relinquish control and fear that a truly independent system will undermine discipline and thus operational effectiveness.

Do basic human rights guarantees apply to military members? General **Jan Peter Spijk** writes about the benchmark case *Engel and Others v. The Netherlands,* in which the European Court of Human Rights determined that the unique nature of military service means that the interpretation of rights is 'not identical' for service members, but a treatment that is a 'clear deviation' from the ordinary treatment of other service members is problematic. Additionally, for any military 'justice' system to be worthy of the name, it must provide fundamental safeguards of fairness and independence.

The subjects of the judicial deliberations in *Findlay* and *Engel* have also been the focus on national courts beyond Europe. **Aditya Puar** writes about the *Prithi Pal Singh Bedi* case in which the Supreme Court of India forcefully asserted that members of the military are entitled to the basic protections of law and due process and are not lesser citizens.

Canada has also addressed these issues. Colonel **Rory Fowler** and **Afton Brooke David** write about the landmark Canadian case *Généreux,* a wide-ranging and impactful decision that ratified the separate system of military justice but demanded basic guarantees of independence in matters such as tenure, financial, and institutional independence of the military justice system's key actors.

As with *O'Callahan* and *Solorio* in the United States, many countries have had to decide what counts as an offense under military law. **Pascal Lévesque** analyzes Canada's approach in the *Stillman* case, which took a more expansive view. Offenses properly before military courts are not just purely military offenses, such as desertion, or even offenses with a military nexus, but are more broadly any criminal offenses enacted under the military code, including those that are also violations of the civilian law.

K Parameshwar and **A Sregurupriya** consider the summary court-martial in India and the effect on rights that follows the curtailment of procedures that are lacking in basic fairness. In the backdrop of decisions of the Supreme Court of India, the essay also prods the reader to think about the evolution of military law systems that are borne from colonial legacies, as with India.

Sometimes the highest courts must delicately balance considerations of both national security and individual rights. Better but rarer are the highest national court decisions that uphold basic rights *and* strengthen national security. Colonel **Katherine K. Stich** writes about the US Supreme Court's *Frontiero* decision that improved the capabilities of the United States military by expanding the right of women to serve.

As further proof that opportunities for women to serve are more likely to come from the highest national courts than from national militaries on their own initiative, **Aishwarya Bhati** writes about impediments to Indian women serving as armed forces officers. Both this and the preceding chapter have much common ground in spirit.

Nations face vexing challenges when addressing allegations of war crimes and other atrocity crimes committed by their own citizens. Should crimes that occurred in other countries be prosecuted domestically? Should the time limits of the ordinary statutes of limitations be waived for such offenses? Do atrocity offenses require their own penal provisions, or can the offenses fit within existing criminal laws? **Kiran Mohandas Menon** presents his insights into the deliberations by the High Court of Australia on these questions in his chapter on the *Polyukhovich* case.

Perhaps no national armed force in the world plays such a prominent role in the public and civic life of its country as the Turkish armed forces. Turkey legal expert **Leslie Esbrook** writes about the efforts of Turkey's highest civilian court to assert itself despite fledgling legitimacy and its limited jurisdiction. Of special importance are the role and weight of decisions of international courts, in this case, the European Court of Human Rights' *Icen v. Turkey* decision, in informing domestic judicial decisions.

Violent crises in a country increase the likelihood that the primacy of civilian legal institutions could be questioned or undermined. Professor **Shruti Bedi** contemplates the resilience of India's highest civilian courts to such challenges. In her chapter, it is discussed how the Supreme Court of India has approached this vexed issue.

National civilian courts must balance fundamental fairness rights with the demands for military discipline. Not all individual rights are lost in military service, as Brazil's Military Superior Court Justice **Maria Elizabeth Guimarães Teixeira Rocha** discusses in her chapter on the individual's right to remain silent under the Brazilian military justice system.

While military tribunals enjoy their strongest sense of legitimacy in ensuring the effective discipline of armed forces, that legitimacy erodes precipitously when military tribunals are used to prosecute civilians in one's own country. Colonel **Manmohan Sood** chronicles Pakistan's highest court's unfortunate endorsement of military trials of civilians.

Preston Lim next considers the limits of military tribunals as a vessel for the progressive development of the law. He writes about the *Martin* case, in which the accused successfully challenged the British military tribunal rules as out of step with the due process requirements of the European Court of Human Rights.

Military force involves the official condonation of violence if it is done in conformance with the law and the advancement of military objectives. A single act may result in either a charge of murder or commendation for valor, depending on one's military status and legitimacy of intention. Colonel **Alok Shukla** analyzes this paradox with an Indian example, *General Officer Commanding v. CBI*. The controversy, variants of which are common in many countries, often plays out, as here, in the determination of primacy when both military and civilian courts have jurisdiction over a matter.

In Denmark, military justice matters are taken up in the regular civilian courts rather than military tribunals. **Lars Stevnsborg** analyzes how this works when national security interests are at stake – in this case, the fallout that resulted when a Danish commando published an unauthorized biography about his military exploits in Afghanistan.

Wing Commander **UC Jha** writes about the dramatic story of Sri Lankan General Sarath Fonseka, a rising political star who was court-martialed in what he alleged was an act of political retribution. The controversy goes to the heart of basic questions posed in many countries, such as: what counts as a 'court'? Do military tribunals qualify?

Many highest national courts must deal with grave threats to national security and balance those needs with basic rights. Georgia is one such country. **Nino Nikolaishvili** guides the reader through the process by which Georgia's highest court balanced the country's need for compulsory military service due to exigent threats with the human rights interest of accommodating conscientious objectors.

Prem Chandra Rai presents a pertinent legal history of his home country, Nepal, and considers the role of the country's highest civilian court in shaping the jurisdiction and reach of military tribunals.

Marialejandra Moreno Mantilla contemplates the role of the highest national courts in enforcing peace in Colombia. There, the civilian courts have acted to create and preserve the peace from years of internal conflicts, including adjudication of atrocity crimes and other efforts to guarantee justice, truth, reparation and non-repetition for victims of armed conflict.

Another country whose courts must contend with grave national security threats is Ukraine. **Kateryna Busol** analyzes the Thunder Road to Justice: that country's Constitutional Court decision from 2001 that rejected accession into an international criminal law treaty regime, a decision that has considerably complicated Ukraine's attempts and initiatives to seek justice at domestic and international levels for the perpetrators of the gravest crimes in the ongoing Russia-Ukraine armed conflict.

For all its prominence on the world stage in the twenty-first century, China still demonstrates remarkable opacity in the interrelation between civilian and military courts. Few scholarly studies or publicly available resources exist on the topic. One prominent legal observer, **Susan Finder**, ably shines a light on this topic and demonstrates the sophisticated legal interplay between Chinese civilian and military courts. This is one rarely touched subject!

Finally, we are pleased to share an exclusive feature about the Israeli soldier, Elor Azaria, also known as 'the Hebron Shooter', with chapters by Professor **Amos Guiora** and Colonel **Maya Heller** (one of the trial judges for the case). This controversy shows why military law topics are often featured in movies & fiction through different lenses. Some view the actions of this soldier as heroic, while others view him as a murderer.

Navdeep and I express our deep appreciation to each of these authors. We believe their expert insights will be of assistance to judges, scholars, policymakers, military members, and civil society activists in countries around the world.

Franklin D Rosenblatt

Mississippi College School of Law
Jackson, Mississippi, USA
Twitter: @frankrosenblatt
Email: frosenblatt@mc.edu

Franklin D Rosenblatt teaches law at the Mississippi College School of Law in Jackson, Mississippi, USA, where his scholarship focuses on criminal law. He is a retired Judge Advocate from the United States Army, where he served for 20 years and attained the rank of Lieutenant Colonel. After his military service, he joined the litigation department at a major law firm, where he headed the firm's Military and National Security Law practise group. He remains active in military cases as a practising lawyer, amicus brief writer, and scholar. While with the US Army, he served in four of the Army's 11 combat divisions as well as two special operations units. He participated in numerous military operations around the globe, including in the Balkans, Southwest Asia, and Southeast Asia. In his final Army assignment, he served as the Deputy Chief of the Army's Trial Defense Service and as lead military defense counsel to Sergeant Bowe Bergdahl in the most publicized court-martial in American history. His military decorations include two awards of the Bronze Star Medal, the Legion of Merit, the Combat Action Badge, the Expert Infantryman Badge, and military parachutist badges of the United States, Japan, and Thailand. He frequently speaks and writes about military law topics and has co-authored two military justice books. Just like the co-editor of this book, he was also a part of the historic Yale Draft (Principles) on Military Justice, an improvement of the existing United Nations document on the same subject, at a Yale Law School conference attended by global jurists and representatives of the United Nations. Franklin also serves as a Court of Appeals Judge with the Mississippi Army National Guard. He serves on the Board of Directors, and as General Counsel for the National Institute of Military Justice, the leading US civil society organization focused on the betterment of military justice. He is also the President of the Criminal and Disciplinary Law Committee for the International Society of Military Law and the Law of War.

Participants – The Yale Draft
Yale Law School, Yale University, New Haven, Connecticut, USA

The Service-Connection Story – from O'Callahan to Solorio

Eugene R Fidell

Solorio, The United States of America

Introduction

One of the most interesting and, in my[1] view, regrettable developments in American military justice in the twentieth century is the willingness of Congress to expand the scope of court-martial subject matter jurisdiction beyond what is necessary, appropriate, or wise. The Supreme Court did not distinguish itself in this respect – *twice*. Overall, it's a discouraging tale and one that reveals both the dark side of American exceptionalism and the need for Congress to pay much more thoughtful attention to military justice. As I shall explain, the current state of affairs tolerates the military's voracious appetite for jurisdiction, reflects the judiciary's uncertain tread in this part of the legal and constitutional forest, misunderstands the Constitution's 'least possible power adequate to the end proposed' standard,[2] reinforces the separatist tendency in relations between the Armed Forces and the American society, and puts the country even further out of step with contemporary human rights norms.

---

[1] Readers should know that I represented the American Civil Liberties Union as an arguing *amicus* in *Solorio*, as discussed below.

[2] See United States *ex rel. Toth v. Quarles*, 350 U.S. 11, 23 (1955) [quoting *Anderson v. Dunn*, 19 U.S. (6 Wheat.) 204, 230 (1821)].

Subject Matter Jurisdiction in the Uniform Code and the *Manual*

The starting points for this essay are the Uniform Code of Military Justice (UCMJ) and the *Manual for Courts-Martial*, an executive order that implements it and has the force of law. To be triable by court-martial, 'the offense must be subject to court-martial jurisdiction.' The Code's 'punitive articles' criminalize a host of familiar crimes such as murder, manslaughter, assault, larceny, and arson. Nothing in it requires that these civilian or 'common law' offenses need to be connected with the military or military duty; it is sufficient on the face of the statute that the accused be a person 'subject to' the Code.

The *Manual* could have imposed a service-connection or nexus requirement as a predicate to subject matter jurisdiction, but it did not do so. Before *Solorio*, Rule for Courts-Martial 203 (RCM 203 – 'Jurisdiction over the offense') provided:

> To the extent permitted by the Constitution, courts-martial may try any offense under the Code and, in the case of general courts-martial, the law of war.

The 1984 edition of the *Manual* included a reference to the service-connection limitation only in the 'Discussion'. The version of RCM 203 in the 2019 edition is the same, except that it refers to the UCMJ rather than the Code, and the 'Discussion' now recites:

> Courts-martial have power to try any offense under the UCMJ except when prohibited from so doing by the Constitution. The rule enunciated in *Solorio v. United States*, 483U.S. 435 (1987), is that jurisdiction of courts-martial depends solely on the accused's status as a person subject to the Uniform Code of Military Justice, and not on the 'service-connection' of the offense charged.

O'Callahan

So much has been written about the *O'Callahan* decision that there is little need to go into it in depth here. In a nutshell, the case involved the off-base rape of a 14-year-old girl in Honolulu. The then Court of Military

Appeals had twice upheld the conviction,[3] but on habeas corpus review, the Supreme Court held, by a 6-3 vote, that the Constitution required that an offense be service-connected[4] to sustain court-martial jurisdiction. In an opinion by Justice Douglas, the Court delivered a blistering attack on the military justice system, calling 'courts-martial as an institution . . . singularly inept in dealing with the nice subtleties of constitutional law.' The majority referred to the problem of unlawful command influence and asserted that '[a] court-martial is not yet an independent instrument of justice...'. '[H]istory,' Justice Douglas wrote, 'teaches that expansion of military discipline beyond its proper domain carries with it a threat to liberty.' Significantly, the Court took no account of the important changes that Congress had made in the system in the Military Justice Act of 1968. Justice Harlan's dissent quarreled powerfully with the majority's use of the historical materials, as well as the lack of clarity as to what might or might not be service-connected. Sergeant O'Callahan went free, and the service-connection era, which lasted 18 years, began with a bang.

The reaction was immediate and vociferous. One of the pivotal critical commentaries[5] came from Robinson O Everett, a professor at Duke Law School who had clerked at the Court of Military Appeals and was an Air Force reserve judge advocate (retiring as a colonel). He had written an early treatise on military justice under the Code[6] and had worked closely with Senator Sam Ervin, a fellow North Carolinian, on military personnel legislation. The ink was barely dry on the decision when Professor Everett's article, *O'Callahan v. Parker – Milestone or Millstone in Military Justice?*,[7] hit the street. After reviewing the history of the litigation and the uncertainty he thought it produced, he concluded:

---

[3] *United States v. O'Callahan*, 16 C.M.A. 568, 37 C.M.R. 188 (1967) (on petition for writ of error coram nobis); *United States v. O'Callahan*, CM 393590 (A.B.R. 1956), *pet. for review denied*, 7 C.M.A. 800 (1957).

[4] That the offense must have some nexus or connection with service in the military.

[5] The decision drew support as well as criticism. *See* Joshua E. Kastenberg, *Cause and Effect: The Origins and Impact of Justice William O. Douglas's Anti-Military Ideology from World War II to O'Callahan v. Parker*, 26 T.M. COOLEY L. REV. 163, 264 n.554 (2009). Prof. Kastenberg's article includes a fascinating account of the Court's internal deliberations. Justice Douglas originally was in the minority. *Id.* at 259-63.

[6] Robinson O. Everett, Military Justice in the Armed Forces of the United States (1956).

[7] 1969 DUKE L.J. 853.

> There are many devices available for limiting materially the effect of *O'Callahan*. However, in preference to a gradual erosion of its strength, the Supreme Court should take the earliest opportunity to overrule the case.

In the end, he got his wish, but it took 18 years. No mere 'Zelig'-like bystander was he;[8] to discuss service-connection in American military justice without mentioning him would truly be playing *Hamlet* without Hamlet.

It is difficult at this juncture to fully appreciate the electric effect of the decision on judge advocates in the field and handling appeals. There was a war on, the court-martial caseload was sky-high, and cases with *O'Callahan* issues were everywhere. If the Court of Military Appeals had had its hands full painting in the canvas in the 1950s, when both it and the UCMJ were new, it had plenty of work to do filling in the blanks that the Supreme Court had left. Some issues were easily and quickly resolved. For example, since the loss of grand jury and jury trial rights did not figure when an offense was minor, the court quickly created a 'petty offense exception'.[9] Similarly, it promptly recognized an 'overseas exception' for offenses committed outside the country, where those rights would not be available in local courts.[10] Significantly, it had no difficulty finding that service-connection was not established simply because the victim was a military dependent.[11] Drug cases proved to be an area of shifting doctrinal sands, but even there, the jurisprudence had settled down.[12]

O'Callahan's imprecision led only a few years later to *Relford*, where the Court provided additional guidance. The resulting twelve *Relford* 'factors' and nine 'considerations' were sufficiently straightforward that they

---

[8] See Woody Allen, *Zelig* (Orion Pictures 1983).

[9] *United States v. Sharkey*, 19 C.M.R. 26, 41 C.M.R. 26 (1969).

[10] *United States v. Keaton*, 19 C.M.A. 64, 41 C.M.R. 64 (1969).

[11] *United States v. McGonigal*, 19 C.M.A. 94 ,41 C.M.R. 94 (1969); *United States v. Shockley*, 18 C.M.A. 610, 40 C.M.R. 322 (1969); *United States v. Henderson*, 18 C.M.A. 601, 40 C.M.R. 313 (1969).

[12] See *United States v. Trottier*, 9 M.J. 337, 352 (C.M.A. 1980) (Everett, C.J.) ("We are now entirely persuaded that exercising 'the least possible power adequate to the end proposed,' it is necessary and proper in today's world that court-martial jurisdiction over most drug offenses be invoked as a proper exercise of the war powers. Nothing short of such exercise, we believe, will permit our nation's war machine to perform its constitutional duty to fight and to be fully prepared to fight to protect this country's national interests. In fact, anything short of such exercise would critically detract from this capability.") (Footnotes omitted).

could be summarized in the 1984 *Manual* in little more than a single page.[13] It is true, as the *Manual* observed, that the facts of the case might have to be examined, but the path was well charted. Before long, the flood of litigation had turned into a trickle, if that.

Despite this, critics of *O'Callahan* remained unfazed, and when the opportunity presented itself, they struck. *Solorio* was that opportunity.

Solorio

At issue in *Solorio* was whether the fact that the victim was the dependent of another member of the armed forces constituted service-connection within the meaning of *O'Callahan* and *Relford*. By the time the case reached the Court of Military Appeals, Professor Everett had become Chief Judge of that court. Enter *United States v. Solorio*.[14]

The case came up at a strange moment in the court's history. Judge Albert B Fletcher Jr had retired on disability (following a state conviction on sex charges) the year before, and it would be several more months before his place would be taken by Judge Eugene R Sullivan III. So, the court consisted of only two judges from the Carolinas: Chief Judge Everett and Judge Walter T Cox III.

Acknowledging its prior dependent-victim cases, the court concluded that they should be reconsidered in light of the increasing attention being paid to the interests of victims. The opinion sought to distinguish dependent-victim cases where, for example, the offense was mere larceny, from sex offenses such as those in *Solorio*:

> sex offenses against young children – offenses like those alleged in the charges against Solorio – have a continuing effect on the victims and their families and ultimately on the morale of any military unit or organization to which the family member is assigned. This continuing effect tends to establish service-connection.[15]

The problem with this is that the record was devoid of any evidence of adverse impact on morale.

---

[13] Manual for Courts-Martial, United States (1984 ed.), pp. II-14 to -15.
[14] 21 M.J. 251 (C.M.A. 1986).
[15] *Id.* at 256.

Granting certiorari for the first time in a case from the Court of Military Appeals, Chief Justice Rehnquist made quick work of the matter, overturning *O'Callahan* because of its 'doubtful foundations' and the confusion it allegedly generated. Justice Stevens concurred only in the judgment because he thought the facts made Petty Officer Solorio's offenses service-connected, rather than because *O'Callahan* itself was mistaken. Justice Marshall, joined by Justices Brennan and Blackmun, dissented. In their view, *O'Callahan* remained 'correct and workable'. *Solorio* is one of only 233 cases in which the Supreme Court has overruled one of its own precedents.[16]

On a personal note, the opportunity to participate in the oral argument remains vivid in memory for several reasons. First, it is rare for a non-governmental *amicus curiae* to be permitted to argue before the Supreme Court. I later learned how close I came to not be permitted to argue: when my wife was writing her book about Justice Blackmun,[17] she came across his notes from the conference at which the Justices considered my motion for leave. The vote was 5-4. To make matters worse, the opposing counsel was the Solicitor General himself, Charles Fried, who had been my Torts professor when I was a first-year law student (1L) at Harvard Law School.

I might as well also mention the dream I had the night before the argument. I dreamt I was in the Supreme Court chamber and was in the row of seats reserved for attorneys in the next case to be called. A young lawyer from the case before us was at the lectern. He began, 'Mr Chief Justice and may it please the Court' – and fainted. In my dream, the marshals came up to him, grabbed him under his armpits, and dragged him away from the lectern. It was a vivid dream; I even noticed the scuff marks his heels made on the plush carpet. When he had been pulled aside, the Chief Justice – again, in my dream – banged the gavel and said, 'The Clerk will call the next case.' Whereupon I woke up.

The argument went fairly well, although it was clear that Lieutenant Commander Robert W Bruce Jr (Solorio's counsel) and I had an uphill battle. The Justices seemed fixated on the government's claim that ser-

---

[16] See U.S. Congress, U.S. Const. Annotated, Table of Supreme Court Decisions Overruled by Subsequent Decisions. https://constitution.congress.gov/resources/decisions-overruled/
[17] Linda Greenhouse, Becoming Justice Blackmun (2005).

vice-connection was oh-so-uncertain and would lead to threshold litigation – even though threshold litigation over jurisdiction is hardly a novelty in federal cases. When my turn came at the lectern, I quickly sensed that Justice Scalia would soak up much of my limited time talking about drug cases even though *Solorio* had nothing to do with drugs. But the colloquy was not without its lighter moments:

> *Me:* It's not a confusing area. It was pretty much established by 1970, particularly as regards the specific narrow issue in this case, which is, is it enough that the victim happened to be a dependent.
>
> *Him:* Well, you could restate the law of torts in, you know, a couple of lines. [Laughter] That doesn't make it clear, does it?
>
> *Me:* I'd need more time. [Laughter]
>
> *Him:* . . . anything that a reasonable man wouldn't do. [Laughter]
>
> *Me:* But the problem...the problem, Justice Scalia, it might be my last clear chance. [Laughter][18]

In retrospect, I have grave doubts about the correctness of the Court's decision on several levels. As for the history, I've become increasingly skeptical about our ability to get a firm handle on the state of the law in the 18th century. But if the majority's evaluation of the history is that it is simply a wash or too uncertain, one would think that *stare decisis* would play a significant role. It didn't. Second, I thought and still think that Justice Stevens had a good point in observing that there was no need to reach the constitutional issue since, by his lights, the offenses at issue would have survived *O'Callahan/Relford* scrutiny. Third, I thought at the time – and still think – the Court was mistaken to reject Solorio's contention that the Court of Military Appeals had violated *Bouie v. City of Columbia*[19] when it altered its dependent-victim jurisprudence to his detriment after the fact. The fact that he had not raised a *Bouie* concern before that court cannot plausibly be deemed a waiver; any other rule would require every litigant to insert in every appellate brief an anticipatory *Bouie* objection, which would, of course, be ridiculous.

---

[18] Transcript of Oral Argument, *Solorio v. United States*, https://www.oyez.org/cases/1986/85-1581

[19] 378 U.S. 347 (1964).

O'Callahan's *Ghost*

A third of a century has elapsed since the Supreme Court overruled *O'Callahan*[20] in *Solorio*[21] and restored the status test for subject matter jurisdiction. Did it kill off the service-connection test? If it did, should we care? After all, if the military cannot bring a case – there's always the US Attorney or local DA 'downtown'.

In some respects, the service-connection test may have survived *Solorio* in part. For example, it remains an open question whether, as four Justices noted in *Loving v. United States*,[22] *O'Callahan* still governs capital cases. Should it?

Additionally, the *Manual for Courts-Martial* continues to cite factors that resemble the *O'Callahan* and *Relford*[23] test in guiding the exercise of convening authority discretion for adultery.[24] The provision is not binding, any more than the 'non-binding disposition guidance' factors set forth in Appendix 2.1 of the *Manual* are binding or enforceable. Service regulations that call for 'extraordinary circumstances', when determining whether to exercise court-martial jurisdiction over retirees may also contemplate something like service-connection.[25] Interestingly, some state codes of military justice limit state court-martial subject matter to offenses that are service-connected.[26] Legislators in these jurisdictions have

---

[20] *O'Callahan v. Parker*, 395 U.S. 258 (1969).

[21] *Solorio v. United States*, 483 U.S. 435 (1987).

[22] 517 U.S. 748, 774-75 (1996) (Stevens, J., concurring). Of the four Justices who signed Justice Stevens' opinion, only Justice Breyer remains on the Court.

[23] *Relford v. Commandant*, U.S. Disciplinary Barracks, 401 U.S. 355 (1971).

[24] Manual for Courts-Martial, United States 99c. (1) (2019 ed.).

[25] Army Regulation 27-10, Legal Services: Military Justice 5-4*c* (20 Nov 2020).

[26] E.g., Idaho Code of Military Justice art. 2(b), Idaho Stat. § 46-1102 ("Subject matter jurisdiction is established if a nexus exists between an offense, either military or nonmilitary, and the state military force, regardless of duty status."); Md. Code of Military Justice, Md. Code, Pub. Safety § 13A-102(b)(1) (2020) ("Subject matter jurisdiction is established if a nexus exists between an offense, either military or nonmilitary, and the State military force."); Mass. Code of Military Justice art. 2(b) (2018) ("Subject matter jurisdiction shall be established if a nexus exists between an offense, either military or nonmilitary, and the state military force."); N.M. Code of Military Justice, N.M. Code § 20-12-3 ("The code has applicability at all times, provided that either the member is in a duty status or, if not in a duty status, that there is a connection between the act or omission constituting the offense and the efficient functioning of the military forces..."); Okla. Uniform Code of Military Justice art. 2.B. ("Subject matter jurisdiction is established if more likely than not a nexus exists between an offense, either military or nonmilitary, and the state

concluded that a service-connection requirement is not inimical to military effectiveness, even though the federal government continues to treat it as a nonstarter. Given these state laws, it is difficult to see how the national armed forces' wide-open court-martial subject matter jurisdiction meets *Toth v. Quarles*'s 'least possible power' test.

I will speculate, in addition, that at least some convening authorities, even now, decline to refer cases for trial where there is no service-connection or where that connection is tenuous. They may do this on their own initiative or based on advice from their staff judge advocate. There are financial incentives for military commanders not to exercise their authority over cases that have no service connection: running a court-martial may cost quite a bit of money and other command resources that would otherwise be borne, depending on the offense, by a United States Attorney or a local prosecutor.

Nonetheless, from time to time, non-service-connected offenses do find their way into the military justice system, either alone or in combination with offenses that do have a nexus beyond the accused's status.[27] How many there are can only be a matter for speculation since the necessary information may not be recited in an appellate decision, and if there is an acquittal, there will not even be a meaningful record of trial. The services do not, to my knowledge, maintain data on the number of non-service-connected cases that enter the system.

Whatever the frequency, should we care? The answer here should be 'Yes' for two reasons. First, in some cases, the availability of a military forum may lead to abuses. For example, in a recent case from Massachusetts, a member of the US Marine Corps was charged in connection with

---

military forces."); W. Va. Code of Military Justice § 15-1E-2(b) ("Subject matter jurisdiction is established if a nexus exists between an offense, either military or nonmilitary, and the state military force."). *See also* Model State Code of Military Justice art. 2 (annotation) (2010). Some states limit courts-martial subject matter jurisdiction to specified military-type offenses. *E.g.*, Ill. Code of Military Justice art. 2(b), 20 Ill. L. Comp. Stat. 1807. *See also* 20 Vt. Stat. Ch. 39, § 941 ("An offense committed by a member of the national guard shall be tried in civil courts and prosecuted by civil authorities except offenses of a purely military nature.").

[27] E.g., Eugene R. Fidell, *Why Is This Case Being Tried by Court-Martial?*, Global Military Justice Reform, 21 April 2014.

a homicide that occurred off-base and where the victim had no connection to the armed forces.[28] The Marine Corps only became involved because the local grand jury refused to indict. The decedent's family appears to have lobbied the Marine Corps to exercise court-martial jurisdiction, as permitted after *Solorio*. I can think of another case some years ago where an Army officer was acquitted in the state court of a charge of a first-degree assault on his wife. The Army turned around and successfully prosecuted him for, among other things, attempted premeditated murder and perjury in his testimony in the state trial.[29] Indeed, in *United States v. Hennis,*[30] the Army obtained a capital sentence from a general court-martial after Master Sergeant Hennis had fought the state to a draw and DNA technology had improved. To be sure, *Schneider* and *Hennis* both involved military victims, and hence, would have been service-connected under the Court of Military Appeals' decision in *Solorio*, but even so, these, and cases like them, are an abuse of the military justice system. That system was not intended to serve as a fallback for cases in which victims or others feel a state defendant has cheated the hangman.

The use of the military justice system to prosecute non-service-connected offenses is undesirable because it tends to buttress the unfortunate notion that the military is a separate society. That notion – repeatedly advanced by the Supreme Court of the United States[31] – has been carried too far. Certainly, there are aspects of military life that justify a different standard from what we are accustomed to seeing in a democratic society. For example, expectations of privacy will be different in the military, and it is not hard to see why certain limits might properly be placed on freedom of speech that would never be tolerated in a civilian setting.[32]

Given the hazardous activities in which military personnel are called upon to engage, a case can be made for treating negligent conduct as criminal or criminalizing some breaches of the custom of the service. How-

---

[28] WHDH, Marine Charged With Murder in Death of 19-Year-Old Emerson Student in Brighton, noted in Eugene R. Fidell, *Why Is This Case In the Military Justice System?*, Global Military Justice Reform, 17 November 2020.

[29] *United States v. Schneider*, 38 M.J. 387 (C.M.A. 1993).

[30] 79 M.J. 370 (C.A.A.F. 2020).

[31] E.g., Parker *v. Levy*, 417 U.S. 733, 743 (1974).

[32] E.g., art. 88, UCMJ, 10 U.S.C. § 888 (criminalizing contemptuous speech about the President, Congress and certain other officials).

ever, where the exercise of court-martial jurisdiction has the effect of diluting constitutional rights relating to the trial of criminal cases, the separate society theory loses its analytical force and simply becomes a conclusion. The United States has not had the occasion to fear a military takeover, but doctrines that have the effect of permitting the military to drift ever further from the society as a whole are not desirable. It may be added that the increasing willingness of Americans to treat military service as a credential for elective office and the willingness of Congress to waive the cooling-off period that prevents retired personnel from holding certain senior civilian offices for a prolonged period (such as in the case of general-turned-secretary-of-defense James N Mattis as also Lloyd J Austin III) is difficult to reconcile with the notion that the military is a separate society.

A few other democratic countries have followed in the United States' footsteps either by explicitly embracing a status test for military jurisdiction or by applying a nexus test that is so credulous that any claim of impact on military effectiveness or morale, however, gossamer, will suffice. Canada's *Stillman*[33] and *Moriarity*[34] decisions and Australia's *Private R*[35] case are examples.

The human rights jurisprudence is to the contrary. Principle No 3 (Functional Authority of Military Courts) of The Yale Draft, a 2018 revision of the 2006 UN Draft Principles Governing the Administration of Justice Through Military Tribunals, states:

> The purpose of military courts is to contribute to the maintenance of military discipline inside the rule of law through the fair administration of justice. Military courts should only try cases that have a direct and substantial connection with that purpose, unless the accused is deployed overseas, and it would not be appropriate to subject him or her to the jurisdiction of the ordinary courts of the sending or receiving States.

Paragraph 24 explains:

> In determining whether there is a 'direct and substantial connection' between an alleged offense and the purpose of military justice systems,

[33] *Stillman v. H.M. The Queen*, 2019 SCC 40. Read more about it by Pascal Lévesque in this book.
[34] *R. v. Moriarity*, 2015 SCC 55.
[35] *Private R v. Brigadier Cowen*, [2020] HCA 31.

the following principles should be applied:

> (a) If the alleged offense is of a type which is prevalent in civil life and which is alleged to have been committed by a member of the armed forces in his or her capacity as an individual citizen, or if the alleged offense is likely to have affected the community at large in the same degree whether it was committed by a member of the armed forces or a civilian, then the allegation should be investigated and tried in the civilian criminal justice system.
>
> (b) If the alleged offense is of a type which is of particular concern to the discipline or efficiency of the armed forces (e.g., an offense by one member of the armed forces against another) or is alleged to have been committed in a defense establishment or in relation to military property, the allegation should be investigated and tried in the military justice system.[36]

Sadly, the view of the Defense Department (at least as articulated during the Trump administration) seems to be that human rights concerns have nothing to do with American military justice. A report submitted to Congress by the armed forces' Joint Service Committee on Military Justice in 2020 observed, shockingly, that 'ensuring the military justice system complies with human rights obligations is undoubtedly not a US concern.'[37]

What should be done? Since it is unlikely that the Supreme Court will reverse engines a second time, and since the United States has not ratified the First Optional Protocol to the International Covenant on Civil and Political Rights[38] (and thus is not subject to the Human Rights Committee's complaint procedure), any remedy for the current unfortunate state of the law in the United States must come from one of the political branches of the government. Under current law, the President could reimpose a service-connection requirement through the *Manual for Courts-Martial* since he has the power to withdraw types of cases from

---

[36] Draft Principles Governing the Administration of Justice Through Military Tribunals (2018), reproduced in Eugene R. Fidell, Elizabeth L. Hillman, Joshua E. Kastenberg, Franklin D. Rosenblatt, Dwight H. Sullivan & Rachel E. VanLandingham, Military Justice: Cases and Materials 887, 896-97 (3d ed. 2020).

[37] Dept of Defense, Joint Service Subcomm. on Prosecutorial Authority Study (JSS-PAS) Report 58 (2 September 2020).

[38] 999 U.N.T.S. 171 (1966).

other convening authorities.[39] Additionally, Congress could reimpose that requirement by legislation. A bill to that effect died in the committee in 1988,[40] but there is no reason such a bill might not be introduced again. The mere fact that service-connection is not required by the Constitution does not preclude – and should not discourage – Congress or the President from going the extra mile and setting the bar higher.

At times, the United States has been a leader in military justice reform. Its creation of a civilian Court of Military Appeals in 1950 was such a time. Another was when it created a proper trial bench in 1968. A third was when it applied the civilian Federal Rules of Evidence nearly lock, stock and barrel to courts-martial. Also, its grant of potential access to direct appellate review by the Supreme Court in 1983, imperfect as it was,[41] is a further landmark. Nonetheless, the country continues to assert and occasionally exercise an excessive claim to court-martial subject matter jurisdiction. An enlightened administration or Congress would do well to revisit this regrettable policy, reassert the country's leadership, and put its weight squarely behind contemporary human rights jurisprudence.

---

[39] "A superior competent authority may withhold the authority of a subordinate to dispose of charges in individual cases, types of cases, or generally." R.C.M. 401(a). "A superior commander may withhold the authority to dispose of offenses in individual cases, types of cases, or generally." R.C.M. 306(a).

[40] H.R. 4282, 100th Cong., 2d sess. (1988), noted in FIDELL et al., *supra* note 35, at 318.

[41] See art. 67a(a), UCMJ, 10 U.S.C. § 867a(a); 28 U.S.C. § 1259; see generally Eugene R. Fidell & Stephen I. Vladeck, Memorandum on the Servicemembers Equality Act of 2019, 18 March 2019, in FIDELL et al., *supra* note 36, at 731; Eugene R. Fidell & Stephen I. Vladeck, *Second-Class Justice in the Military*, N.Y. TIMES, 20 March 2019.

Eugene R Fidell is an Adjunct Professor at NYU Law School, a Senior Research Scholar at Yale Law School, and counsel at the Washington, DC firm Feldesman Tucker Leifer Fidell LLP. He graduated from Queens College and Harvard Law School and served as a judge advocate in the US Coast Guard. In addition, he graduated with honor from the Naval Justice School and has represented personnel in every branch of the Armed Forces as well as the Commissioned Corps of the US Public Health Service and National Oceanic and Atmospheric Administration.

He is a life member of the American Law Institute, president emeritus of the National Institute of Military Justice, and former chair of the Committee on Military Justice of the International Society for Military Law and the Law of War. Since 2014 he has edited the Global Military Justice Reform blog globalmjreform.blogspot.com. His books include *COVID-19: The Legal Challenges* (2020) (co-editor), *Military Justice: Cases and Materials* (3d ed. 2020) (co-author), *Guide to the Rules of Practice and Procedure for the United States Court of Appeals for the Armed Forces* (20th ed. 2021) (co-author), and *Military Justice: A Very Short Introduction* (2016).

Findlay: The Propeller of Independence and Impartiality of the Service Justice System

Judge Jeff Blackett

Findlay, The United Kingdom

Discipline and its enforcement are fundamental elements of command and essential for the operational effectiveness of any military formation. Since the earliest times, military personnel have been governed by strict disciplinary codes, breaches of which would be punished swiftly and often harshly. These codes include disciplinary offences and criminal conduct, and punishments for the latter are often different from those that might apply in a civilian setting. For example, a minor drug offence that might not even be prosecuted in the civilian courts might lead to a custodial sentence and dismissal in the service context. A system of justice that is separate from the civilian system enables the military to maintain control over its personnel in peace and war, and it has been guarded zealously by the chain of command, which, in the past, has brooked no interference from external agencies. Any challenges to the court-martial system were fiercely resisted because any loss of control of the system would undermine morale and operational efficiency.

In the UK, it was clear that the Parliament accepted this position and historically afforded the Armed Forces considerable deference about their disciplinary systems. However, by the early 1990s, civilian defence lawyers operating in the court-martial system increasingly questioned, and then challenged, the fairness of the trial process, suggesting that the court-martial deprived accused service personnel of their rights to a fair trial under Article 6 of the European Convention on Human Rights.[1] The then Judge Advocate General, His Honour Judge James Rant CB, QC, had been a Senior Circuit Judge of the Old Bailey before the appointment. He predicted that there would be challenges to the system and urged the Ministry of Defence to modernise Service justice before the system was forced to change, but his words of warning fell on deaf ears. Not long afterwards, the first successful challenge, which led to significant and all-encompassing changes to the UK court-martial system, came in the case of *Findlay v. UK.*[2]

This landmark judgment was the first in a succession of successful challenges to various aspects of the British court-martial between 1995 and 2003. It did not resolve all of the issues, but it caused significant changes which were streamlined and improved upon following further challenges. The last case of significance was *Cooper v. UK,*[3] which effectively gave the post-Findlay reformed system in the UK a clean bill of health by determining that the new courts-martial procedure was not unfair. The court concluded that there was nothing in the provisions of Article 6 which would, in principle, exclude the determination by service tribunals of criminal charges against service personnel. The court stated:

> The prosecuting authority being answerable to the Attorney General was free of any chain of command or service connection to the higher authority, and it could not, therefore, be said that the former was likely to be influenced by the latter. It followed that there was a proper separation of the prosecuting, convening and adjudicating roles in the court martial. As regards the conduct of the court martial itself, the presence of the judge advocate constituted an important safeguard and significant guarantee of the independence of the court martial.

This was not the case in the 1990s when the Service Discipline Acts[4] governed the court-martial system. Those statutes had themselves followed significant reform to the court-martial system after the Second World War, and little of real substance had changed in the intervening

---

[1] In the determination of his civil rights and obligations or of any criminal charge against him, everyone is entitled to a fair and public hearing within a reasonable time by an independent and impartial tribunal established by law...

[2] [1997] 24 EHRR 221, can be accessed at http://www.hrcr.org/safrica/administrative_justice/findlay_uk.html

[3] [2003] ECHR 48843/99.

[4] Naval Discipline Act 1957, Army Act 1955, Air Force Act 1955.

period, but they provided a system that was essentially internal with no external scrutiny. Even the external scrutiny of the Courts-Martial Appeal Court, a court composed entirely of civilian judges, was limited. That court could quash a conviction, but it could not interfere in any sentence passed (unless all convictions were quashed as well).

In November 1991, Lance Sergeant Findlay pleaded guilty at a general court-martial to three charges of common assault, two charges of prejudicial conduct and two charges of threatening to kill. These charges arose out of an incident in 1990 where he held members of his unit at pistol point and threatened to kill himself and some of his colleagues. He was sentenced to two years imprisonment, dismissal from the Army and reduction to the ranks. He appealed not only on the merits of the case but also by way of challenge to the fairness of his trial. His appeal was dismissed by the Courts-Martial Appeal Court and the House of Lords before he appealed to the European Court of Human Rights.

Before it reached the European Court, the case was first considered by the European Commission of Human Rights. In his application, Findlay made several complaints to the effect that he had been denied a fair hearing at his court-martial, which he argued was neither independent nor impartial, thereby violating his rights under Article 6(1). The Commission declared the applications admissible on 23 February 1995. In its subsequent report, the Commission expressed the unanimous opinion that there had been a violation of Article 6(1) in that the applicant was not given a fair hearing by an independent and impartial tribunal and referred the case to the European Court of Human Rights on 8 December 1995.

The UK Ministry of Defence realised that this application would succeed. Well before the court heard the case, work started to identify weaknesses in the system and propose legislative solutions through the Armed Forces Act 1996. By the time the final judgment in Findlay was handed down in 1997, many of the points of criticism had already been addressed, although the Ministry of Defence policy was to change as little as possible and only to change those areas which were criticised directly.

Some pertinent observations of the Court in the judgment are as below:

> ... The Commission found that although the convening officer played a central role in the prosecution of the case, all of the members of the

court martial board were subordinate in rank to him and under his overall command. He also acted as confirming officer, and the court martial's findings had no effect until confirmed by him. These circumstances gave serious cause to doubt the independence of the tribunal from the prosecuting authority. The judge advocate's involvement was not sufficient to dispel this doubt, since he was not a member of the court martial, did not take part in its deliberations and gave his advice on sentencing in private. In addition, it noted that Mr Findlay's court martial board contained no judicial members, no legally qualified members and no civilians, that it was set up on an ad hoc basis and that the convening officer had the power to dissolve it either before or during the trial. The requirement to take an oath was not a sufficient guarantee of independence. Accordingly, it considered that the applicant's fears about the independence of the court martial could be regarded as objectively justified, particularly in view of the nature and extent of the convening officer's roles, the composition of the court martial and its ad hoc nature. This defect was not, moreover, remedied by any subsequent review by a judicial body affording all the guarantees required by Article 6, Para. 1 (Art. 6-1), since the confirming officer was the same person as the convening officer, and the reviewing authorities were army officers, the second of whom was superior in rank to the first. The ineffectiveness of the post-hearing reviews was further underlined by the secrecy surrounding them and the lack of opportunity for Mr Findlay to participate in a meaningful way.... The question, therefore, arises whether the members of the court martial were sufficiently independent of the convening officer and whether the organisation of the trial offered adequate guarantees of impartiality.... In this respect also the Court shares the concerns of the Commission. It is noteworthy that all the members of the court martial, appointed by the convening officer, were subordinate in rank to him. Many of them, including the president, were directly, or ultimately, under his command (see paragraph 16 above). Furthermore, the convening officer had the power, albeit in prescribed circumstances, to dissolve the court martial either before or during the trial (see paragraph 40 above) .... In order to maintain confidence in the independence and impartiality of the court, appearances may be of importance. Since all the members of the court martial which decided Mr Findlay's case were subordinate in rank to the convening officer and fell within his chain of command, Mr Findlay's doubts about the tribunal's independence and impartiality could be objectively justified (see, mutatis mutandis, the *Sramek v. Austria* judgment of 22 October 1984, Series A no. 84, p. 20, para. 42) ....

> In addition, the Court finds it significant that the convening officer also acted as a 'confirming officer'. Thus, the decision of the court martial was not effective until ratified by him, and he had the power to vary the sentence imposed as he saw fit (see paragraph 48 above). This is contrary to the well-established principle that the power to give a binding decision which may not be altered by a non-judicial authority is inherent in the very notion of 'tribunal' and can also be seen as a component of the 'independence' required by Article 6, Para. 1 (Art. 6-1) ...

Stating the above reasons, the Court concluded that the concerns of the applicant regarding the central role played by the convening officer in the court-martial and the independence and impartiality of the tribunal were 'objectively justified'.

The most important change to make the court-martial objectively fair was the abolition of the convening authority. This was the superior officer within the chain of command who held sole responsibility for carrying out many functions in the disciplinary process. The convening authority decided whether charges would be brought against accused persons; decided the venue and time of trial; convened the court martial; appointed the president who presided over the trial, and members of the court-martial board; appointed the prosecutor; and in the case of the Army and Royal Air Force, confirmed or varied the court-martial's finding and sentence post-trial. This enabled the chain of command to maintain control over disciplinary matters, but it was that control that was so objectionable.

The 1996 Act established independent agencies to take over the functions of the old convening authority. Each service established an independent prosecuting authority under the superintendence of the Attorney General, which effectively decided whether an accused person should be prosecuted and what charges they would face. The heads of the prosecuting authorities were all in their last appointments before retirement and were of sufficient rank to be able to resist influence from the chain of command and take prosecuting decisions without fear or favour.

For each trial, the president and board members were selected by a court administrative officer, a civil servant with certain guarantees to their independence. They determined the venue and time of trial under the guidance of a judge advocate.

Further changes to the system – such as the establishment of the court-martial as a standing court, a single tri-service prosecuting authority, a single court administrative officer, the abolition of uniformed judge advocates, the independence from the chain of command of the service police and better case management by the judiciary were to come later in response to further challenges. However, the catalyst for change was provided by *Findlay*.

Changes to the Service Justice System during the decade following *Findlay* were incorporated into the Armed Forces Act 2006. The crowning glory of this legislation was to create a standing court-martial (as opposed to every trial being ad hoc whereby each court-martial had to be convened and dissolved). That is the bedrock of the modern, Article 6-compliant Service Justice System. Much has been written about the changes to the individual parts of the system, but the most significant change was that the whole process became independent of the Armed Forces and the Ministry of Defence. That independence is provided by civilians who are in key positions and who are not under military command and control. Additionally, those military personnel within the system have safeguards to protect their ability and confidence to make independent decisions.

At first, this imposition of independence created tension. The military viewed civilianisation with suspicion. There was a perception that civilians do not properly understand the ethos and culture of the Armed Forces and their personnel, the comradeship developed through training and operations, and their acceptance that they have fewer freedoms and more restrictions than civilians. Whilst to the European Court of Human Rights, and indeed the outside world, civilians generally provide the necessary independence and impartiality, which might not otherwise be apparent to the Armed Forces, there was a perception that civilians lacked empathy and their different priorities would adversely affect operational effectiveness and morale.

A quarter of a century has passed since the UK Armed Forces introduced the first changes following *Findlay's* case. Those who mounted the challenge to the system were first met with outrage and hostility, but the Ministry of Defence gradually accepted the criticisms and accommodated inevitable changes. There were many teething problems as the Service Justice System moved from a totally military-led-and-run system, which they said had served so well for so long, to the independent and impartial judicial-led system of today. Time and experience have alleviated many of the fears expressed initially by the Ministry of Defence and the Armed Forces. Of course, it was painful for them to come to terms with the fact that they no longer controlled their disciplinary system; the administration of the court-martial, the decision to investigate and prosecute all came under independent control. In court, the military president no longer presided, and quite correctly, the judge advocate became a proper judge rather than a legal clerk to the military board. Over time the military recognised that this modernised system did deliver justice fairly, and it has become accepted and acceptable. There has been no adverse effect on discipline and morale; the process is now objectively and subjectively fair and just; Service personnel and legal practitioners have confidence in the system, and there have been no recent Article 6-type challenges. In short, the Service Justice System is fit for the UK Armed Forces of the twenty-first century, in large part thanks to *Findlay*.

Many states have faced similar challenges to their systems of military justice over the last thirty or so years, and some are still wrestling with the tension between military control and the requirement for independence. Nevertheless, the central tenet remains true: no military justice system can be objectively fair without strong guarantees of independence and impartiality. Invariably the military does not wish to relinquish control and fear that a truly independent system will undermine discipline and thus operational effectiveness. The UK experience, starting with the *Findlay* reforms, is the opposite: there now exists a system which is fair, and seen to be fair, generates confidence internally and externally, and that assists rather than hinders the efficiency and effectiveness of the Armed Forces.

Judge **Jeff Blackett** joined the Royal Navy as a Logistics Officer in 1973. He graduated from University College London (Laws) in 1976 and was called to the bar of England and Wales in 1983. He obtained a Master of Studies from Oxford University (St Antony's College) in 2000. Judge Blackett remained Director of Naval Legal Services from 2000 to 2004 and the Judge Advocate General of the United Kingdom from 2004 to 2020. He also served as Senior Circuit Judge and Deputy High Court Judge. Bencher Gray's Inn and Honorary Professor of Law, Nottingham University, he is also the author of *Rant on the Court Martial and Service Law* (2009) and co-author of *The Manual of the Law of Armed Conflict* (2004).

The Engel Case – A Principled Approach to Military Justice

Jan Peter Spijk

Engel, The Netherlands

Introduction

This commentary provides a brief analysis of the far-reaching judgment of the European Court of Human Rights (hereinafter 'the ECHR' or 'the Court') in the case of *Engel and Others v. The Netherlands* of 8 June 1976.[1] The judgment eventually led to major changes in the system of military justice in the Netherlands' Armed Forces and provides a framework, still valid today, with enables us to judge systems of military justice and limitations of the rights of military personnel. It has a continuing and direct effect in all countries signatory to the European Convention for the Protection of Human Rights and Fundamental Freedoms (hereinafter 'the European Convention on Human Rights', or 'the Convention').[2] In addition, the judgment has provided the so-called 'Engel criteria', which are the starting point for the general assessment of the

---

[1] See for the text of the judgment in English: https://hudoc.echr.coe.int/tur#{%22itemid%22:[%22001-57479%22]} In subsequent footnotes referred to as 'Judgment'. Other languages are available.

[2] See, for example, the important case relevant for the development of military justice in the United Kingdom, *Findlay V. The United Kingdom*, 25 February 1997, 22107/93. See for the text of the Convention in English: https://www.echr.coe.int/documents/convention_eng.pdf Other languages are available.

criminal applicability of the criminal aspect of Article 6 of the Convention, which covers the 'Right to a Fair Trial'.[3] Also, given the status of the ECHR, the different standards developed in this judgment are relevant outside Europe[4] as well.

This commentary addresses the following topics:

A brief introduction to the Convention and the ECHR

The relevant issues before the Court

Does the European Convention also apply to military personnel?

Is the difference in treatment, based on rank, allowed?

How to appreciate 'deprivation of liberty' in the context of military service?

Disciplinary confinement in various ways

Can charges in military disciplinary procedures be considered 'criminal charges'?

Do military disciplinary proceedings have to offer the same guarantees as criminal proceedings?

Freedom of expression for military personnel

Freedom of association for military personnel

Conclusion

A Brief Introduction to the European Convention and the European Court of Human Rights

The European Convention on Human Rights is an international treaty under which the member states of the Council of Europe promise to secure fundamental civil and political rights, not only to their own citizens but also to everyone within their jurisdiction. The Convention,

---

[3] See para 20 below; see also https://www.echr.coe.int/documents/guide_art_6_criminal_eng.pdf last accessed on 13 July 2021.

[4] See, for example, the 2019 *Yale Draft Principles for Summary Proceedings*, https:// drive.google.com /file/d/16T2kbTDGdVKXCjkrazns-aOLjdHoYex4/view last accessed 13 July 2021.

which was signed on 4 November 1950 in Rome, entered into force in 1953. Currently, the 47 member states of the Council of Europe and the European Union, as an institution, have ratified the Convention.

The Convention secures in particular:

The right to life

The right to a fair hearing

The right to respect for private and family life

Freedom of expression

Freedom of thought, conscience and religion

The protection of property

The Convention prohibits in particular:

Torture and inhuman or degrading treatment or punishment

Slavery and forced labour

Death penalty

Arbitrary and unlawful detention

Discrimination in the enjoyment of the rights and freedoms set out in the Convention

The ECHR is an international court set up in 1959. It rules on individual or state applications alleging violations of the civil and political rights set out in the European Convention on Human Rights. Since 1998, it has sat as a full-time court with 47 judges, appointed by the Parliamentary Assembly of the Council of Europe. Judges are elected for a non-renewable term of nine years. An individual can apply directly to the Court if he[5] considers having been personally and directly the victim of a violation of the rights and guarantees set out in the Convention or its protocols. The alleged violation must have been committed by one of the states bound by the Convention. The individual must have used all the remedies in the state concerned that could provide redress for the situation he is complaining about. Usually, this will mean an application

[5] Where 'he' is mentioned, 'she' is included.

to the appropriate Court, followed by an appeal, where applicable, and even a further appeal to a higher court such as the supreme court or constitutional court, if there is one.

The Court has examined hundreds of thousands of applications since it was set up. Its judgments are binding on the countries concerned and have led governments to alter their legislation and administrative practice in a wide range of areas. The Court's case-law makes the Convention a modern and powerful living instrument for meeting new challenges and consolidating the rule of law and democracy in Europe. Based in Strasbourg, France, the Court monitors respect for the human rights of 830 million Europeans.[6]

The Relevant Issues Before the Court

The case of *Engel and Others v. The Netherlands* is considered a benchmark case. Given the importance of the different issues addressed, the judgment was rendered by the so-called Grand Chamber in the plenary session. The case is based on five applications by five Dutch individuals. At the time of their application to the Court, all were serving as conscript soldiers in different non-commissioned ranks. All applicants were members of and held relevant positions in the Conscript Servicemen's Association (Vereniging van Dienstplichtige Militairen – VVDM) which was created in 1966 and aimed at safeguarding the interests of conscripts. It was recognised by the Government for taking part in negotiations in this field, and its membership included about two-thirds of all conscripts.[7] The VVDM differed from most other unions of military personnel in that it was known for its 'vocal' posture. On separate occasions, various penalties had been passed on the applicants by their respective commanding officers for offences against military discipline, differing from various forms of 'arrest', limiting the freedom of movement, to posting in a disciplinary barrack for three months, which more or less resembled a prison facility. The applicants had first appealed

---

[6] See for information on the Court: https://www.echr.coe.int/Pages/home.aspx?p=court&c= and related pages.

[7] Although conscription in the Netherlands still formally exists and conscripts are still being formally registered as such – since 2020, not only men but also women – in practice, conscripts have not been called up for military training since 1996.

their sentences to the complaints officer and finally to the Netherlands' Supreme Military Court, which in substance confirmed the decisions challenged but reduced the punishment imposed in two cases. The factual background and legal issues are described in more detail below.

The Convention also Applies to Military Personnel

In an important opening consideration, the Court stated that the Convention applies in principle (also) to members of the armed forces and not only to civilians, since 'everyone within (the) jurisdiction' of the contracting states is to enjoy 'without discrimination' the rights and freedoms, mentioned in section I of the Convention. It notes that military service is exempted from the prohibition against forced or compulsory labour and that the Convention permits the states to introduce special restrictions on the exercise of the freedoms of assembly and association by members of the armed forces. As a preliminary point, the Court stated that it, when interpreting and applying the rules of the Convention in the present case, 'must bear in mind the particular characteristics of military life and its effects on the situation of individual members of the armed forces.'[8] This general applicability of the Convention to military personnel was repeated in a judgment in 2012:

> [T]he Convention does not stop at the gates of army barracks ... [M]ilitary personnel, like all other persons within the jurisdiction of the contracting States, are entitled to Convention protection. It is, therefore, not open to the national authorities to rely on the special status of the armed forces for the purpose of frustrating the rights of military personnel. Any restrictions on their Convention rights, to be justified, must satisfy the test of necessity in a democratic society.[9]

Is Difference in Treatment Based on Rank Allowed?

All five applicants had had disciplinary penalties and measures imposed on them, varying from confinement to quarters in their normal barracks

[8] Judgment, para 54.
[9] ECHR, Case of *Konstantin Markin v. Russia*, 22 March 2012, 30078/06, para 136.

to being held for more than 30 days in a cell in a specific disciplinary barrack unit – in essence, a prison-like facility where they were locked up during the night. Three of the five applicants complained in the first place of 'distinctions in treatment' between servicemen of different ranks since in the Dutch regulations at the time, a difference was made between officers on the one hand and non-commissioned officers (NCOs) and other servicemen on the other. This difference applied, for example, to the punishment of 'strict arrest', which entailed solitary confinement and exclusion of the performance of normal duties, with a maximum of 14 days. Officers were to serve this punishment in their dwellings, tent or quarters, whereas NCOs and servicemen were locked in a cell. Such distinction, based on rank, may run counter to Article 14 of the Convention, the Court observed. It noted, however, that the hierarchical structure inherent in armies entails differentiation in rank. 'Corresponding to the various ranks are differing responsibilities which in their turn justify certain inequalities of treatment in the disciplinary sphere'. In addition, the Court noted that such inequalities are traditionally encountered in the contracting states and are tolerated by international humanitarian law, with reference to Article 88 of the Geneva Convention of 12 August 1949, relative to the 'Treatment of Prisoners of War', which also allows a 'differentiated' treatment, based on state practice. 'In this respect, the European Convention allows the competent national authorities a considerable margin of appreciation'.[10]

In addition, the Court noted that the distinctions attacked by the three applicants had their equivalent in the internal (military) legal system of practically all the contracting states. Based on an element objective in itself, i.e., rank, these distinctions could have been dictated by a legitimate aim, namely the preservation of discipline by methods suited to each category of servicemen. While only privates risked committal to a disciplinary unit, they clearly were not subject to a serious penalty threatening the other members of the armed forces, namely reduction in rank. As for confinement in a cell during strict arrest, the Netherlands' legislator[11] could have had sufficient reason for not applying this to officers. Overall, the Court judged that the Dutch legislator, in the circumstances of the case, did not seem to have abused the latitude left

---

[10] Judgment, para 72.

[11] The term 'legislator' here is the classic Latin term for 'he who makes laws'.

to him by the Convention. Furthermore, the Court did consider the principle of proportionality, defined as the 'reasonable relationship of proportionality between the means employed and the aim sought', not to be offended.[12]

The Court also rejected the applicants' claim of inequalities of treatment between servicemen and civilians, based on the argument that civilians, subject by reason of their occupation to a particular disciplinary system, could not incur penalties analogous to the disputed deprivations of liberty. The Court's reply is brief:

> [T]his does not result in any discrimination incompatible with the Convention, the conditions and demands of military life being by nature different from those of civil life.[13]

How to Appreciate 'Deprivation of Liberty' in the Context of Military Service

The Court notes that a system of military discipline implies by its very nature the possibility of placing limitations on certain of the rights and freedoms of the members of these forces, which are incapable of being imposed on civilians. The existence of such a system does not in itself run counter to the obligations of the contracting states. Military discipline, however, does not fall outside the scope of Article 5, para 1 (5-1), of the Convention, which describes the situations in which a person can be lawfully deprived of his liberty. Therefore, a disciplinary penalty or measure may constitute a breach of this article.[14]

In order to determine whether someone has been deprived of his liberty, in the sense of Article 5, the starting point must be his concrete situation. Military service does not, on its own in any way, constitute a deprivation of liberty under the Convention since it is expressly sanctioned in Article 4, para 3-b of the Convention. In addition, rather wide

---

[12] Judgment, para 72. See also ECHR 23 July 1968, *Relating to Certain Aspects of the Laws on the Use of Languages in Education in Belgium v. Belgium*. P. 31, second subparagraph, in fine. This distinction was abolished in 1974 before the Court issued its verdict.

[13] Judgment, para 73.

[14] Judgment, para 57.

limitations upon the freedom of movement of the members of the armed forces is entailed by reason of the specific demands of military service so that the normal restrictions accompanying it do not come within the ambit of Article 5 either.[15]

The Court formulates the following interesting criteria for judging 'deprivation of liberty' in the context of military service:

> Each state is competent to organise its own system of military discipline and enjoys in the matter a certain margin of appreciation. The bounds that Article 5 requires the state not to exceed are not identical for servicemen and civilians. A disciplinary penalty or measure which on analysis would unquestionably be deemed a deprivation of liberty were it to be applied to a civilian may not possess this characteristic when imposed upon a serviceman. Nevertheless, such penalty or measure does not escape the terms of Article 5 when it takes the form of restrictions that clearly deviate from the normal conditions of life within the armed forces of the contracting states. In order to establish whether this is so, account should be taken of a whole range of factors such as the nature, duration, effects and manner of execution of the penalty or measure in question.[16]

Therefore, the 'clear deviation' from the normal conditions of life within the armed service of the specific state is the determining factor.

Disciplinary Confinement in Various Ways

In its analysis, the Court generally did not consider penalties or measures with the effect of confining servicemen to their barracks or base, or even in a specific building, as a 'deprivation of liberty'. The determining factor is – as stated in the previous paragraph – whether the individual was excluded from the performance of normal duties, as is the case when a person is locked in a cell – as was the situation when the measures of 'strict arrest' or 'provisional strict arrest' were imposed, in conformity with the then valid Dutch disciplinary legal regime.[17] In the

---

[15] Judgment, paras 57 – 59.

[16] Judgment, para 59.

[17] Judgment, para 26 and 63. The regulations at the time provided that any superior who had sufficient indication to suppose that a subordinate has committed a severe offence against military discipline was entitled, if necessary, to give notice of the subordinate's provisional arrest

specific circumstances of the case, the two days of 'provisional strict arrest' imposed on Mr Engel were considered a 'deprivation of liberty'. In addition, the measure was too long in duration and therefore unlawful since it exceeded the 24-hour maximum as prescribed by law. In addition, the 'provisional strict arrest' was judged not to be 'in order to secure the fulfilment of any obligation prescribed by law' as regulated in Article 5, para 1-b, and as the Government had argued, but as 'a preparatory stage of military disciplinary proceedings and thus situated in a punitive context'. Since no regular court had been involved before the 'provisional strict arrest' was effectuated, the Court, therefore, found that the measure was not in agreement with Article 5, para 1 of the Convention.[18]

Two other applicants, Messrs Dona and Schul, had been placed in the disciplinary barracks unit, Fort Nieuwersluis, by way of disciplinary measure. They had not been allowed to leave that unit for a month, were locked in a cell during the nights, and had to fulfil this disciplinary punishment in the same conditions as other servicemen who had been posted to the same unit by way of a supplementary punishment under military criminal law. For these various reasons in combination, the Court considered the posting to the disciplinary barracks a 'deprivation of liberty'. However, since this measure had only been effectuated after the Supreme Military Court had ruled on an appeal by Messrs Dona and Schul, which had included this disciplinary measure, the Court judged that the penalty was imposed and subsequently executed 'lawfully' and 'in accordance with a procedure prescribed by law' and did thus not contravene Article 5, para 1.[19]

The Court also considered whether the Supreme Military Court could be considered a 'competent court', in the sense of Article 5, para 1-a of the Convention. The Netherlands' Supreme Military Court, at the time, consisted of 2 civilian jurists, appointed for life, one of whom was the President, and four military members, with general officer rank.

(voorlopig arrest). The subordinate was obliged to comply immediately with that notification. Provisional arrest was usually served in the same way as light arrest (i.e., solitary confinement, but not 'behind bars') but, if required either in the interest of the investigation or to prevent disorder, it was served in a similar way to aggravated or strict arrest. The Netherlands' Ministry of Defence decided to abolish the punishment and measure of (provisional) strict arrest in 1974, even before the Court had issued its verdict.

[18] Judgment, paras 34, 63 and 69.

[19] Judgment, paras 64 and 68. The posting of military personnel to the disciplinary barracks by way of disciplinary 'penalty' was also abolished in 1974.

The Court noted that the four military members were not irremovable by law, but like the two civilian members, enjoyed the independence inherent in the Convention's notion of a 'court', since the appointments to the Supreme Military Court were normally the last in their service career. In addition, the military judges were not, in their function as judges, under the command of any higher authority and not under a duty to account for their acts to the service establishment.[20] The Court also considered that adequate judicial guarantees had been in place for the two applicants.

Can Charges in Military Disciplinary Procedures be Considered 'Criminal Charges'?

All five applicants alleged a violation of Article 6 of the Convention, which guarantees the 'Right to a Fair Trial'. Since Article 6, para 1, presupposes a determination of a 'criminal charge' as an essential element, the Court first had to investigate whether the disciplinary proceedings to which the five applicants had been subjected had to be qualified as 'any criminal charge' in the sense of Article 6, para 1, since these proceedings – although 'disciplinary' according to Netherlands law – had the aim of repressing through penalties offences alleged against the applicants, an objective analogous to the general goal of the criminal law.[21]

The Court recognised that all contracting States make a distinction, although in different forms and degrees, between disciplinary proceedings and criminal proceedings. Generally speaking, disciplinary sanctions are less severe than criminal sanctions and often do not appear in the criminal record of an individual. On the other hand, disciplinary proceedings often have fewer procedural guarantees for a defendant than criminal proceedings. Therefore, the relevant question is whether a national decision to classify a proceeding as 'disciplinary' therefore makes Article 6 of the Convention non-applicable. This issue gains relevance when an act or omission can be treated as a 'mixed offence', that is both criminal and disciplinary, with the option of opting between, or

---

[20] Judgment, paras 68 and 30. See also ECHR, Case of *Morris v. The United Kingdom*, 26 February 2002, application 38784/97, para 59 ff.

[21] Judgment, para 79.

even cumulating, criminal and disciplinary proceedings.[22]

In developing a standard, later also referred to as the Engel criteria, the Court notes first that states, as guardians of the public interest, indeed do have the discretionary power to make a distinction between criminal law and disciplinary law and thus draw a 'dividing line', but only subject to certain conditions. This discretionary power cannot imply that a state, in its freedom to classify an act or omission as disciplinary or to prosecute an individual in a disciplinary rather than a criminal proceeding, may thus subordinate the operation of the fundamental clauses of Articles 6 (The Right to a Fair Trial) and 7 (No Punishment Without Law) to the sovereign will since this could lead to results incompatible with the purpose and object of the Convention. Therefore, the Court has jurisdiction to satisfy itself that 'the disciplinary does not improperly encroach upon the criminal'.[23]

Specifically, in the context of 'military service', the Court puts forward the following questions:

> As a starting point: does the provision defining the offence charged belong to criminal law, disciplinary law or both concurrently, according to the legal system of the state concerned?
>
> More importantly: what is the very nature of the act of omission? Does it contravene a legal rule governing the operation of the armed forces? In the latter case, the state may employ in principle disciplinary law, rather than criminal law.
>
> What is the degree of severity of the penalty the person concerned risks incurring? In this respect, the Court notes that certain deprivations of liberty imposed by way of punishment belong to the 'criminal sphere'. The duration of the deprivation of liberty is an important indicative factor in this respect.[24]

In the circumstances of this specific case, the Court found that the disciplinary charges which (de facto ultimately did not but) could have led to a posting to the disciplinary barracks, as mentioned in para 14 above, did indeed come within the 'criminal sphere', since their initial

---

[22] Judgment, para 80.

[23] *Ibid.*

[24] Judgment paras 81 and 85. A deprivation of liberty in terms of a few days is too short to belong to the 'criminal' sphere.

aim was the imposition of serious punishments, involving 'deprivation of liberty'. These charges, therefore, had to be considered a 'criminal charge'. Subsequently, these defendants had to be afforded guarantees of Article 6, namely:

> A fair and public hearing,
>
> Within a reasonable time,
>
> By an independent and impartial tribunal, established by law,
>
> Leading to publicly announced judgment.

While, in addition, the defendants had the right:

> To be informed promptly, in a language which they understood and in detail, of the nature and cause of the accusation against them;
>
> To have adequate time and facilities for the preparation of their defence;
>
> To defend themselves in person or through legal assistance of their own choosing;
>
> To examine or have examined witnesses against them and to obtain the attendance and examination of witnesses on their behalf under the same conditions as witnesses against them.

Since the applicants had appealed their sentences by the military superior to the Military Supreme Court, and since this Court had completely investigated the case, the ECHR found that all requirements had been met, except that of a 'public hearing', since at that time the appeal in a disciplinary procedure before the Supreme Military Court was held in camera. This resulted in a violation of Article 6, para 1.[25]

Do Military Disciplinary Proceedings Have to Offer the Same Guarantees as Criminal Proceedings?

The brief answer to the above question is, 'No'. The Court notes that a

---

[25] Judgment, paras 89–90.

military disciplinary procedure is not attended by the same guarantees as criminal proceedings brought against civilians, but on the other hand, offers substantial advantages to military personnel, e.g., in the sense of the severity of the sentences passed. Disciplinary sentences, in general, are less severe, do not appear in the person's criminal record and entail more limited consequences. The distinctions between the two proceedings are explicable by the differences between the conditions of military and of civil life and cannot be taken as entailing discrimination against members of the armed forces, the Court notes.[26]

Freedom of Expression for Military Personnel

Two of the five applicants had been sentenced to three months committal to the disciplinary barracks because of an article written in the VVDM's journal *Alarm*, of which both applicants were editors. This article, titled The Law of the Strongest, contained the following paragraphs, which referred to a VVDM-demonstration in the General Spoor barracks at Ermelo on 13 August 1971. The demonstration had been quickly terminated by the protesting soldiers, following a promise by General Smits, the commanding officer of the barracks, that no disciplinary sanctions would ensue if all protesters would immediately return to their quarters. Nevertheless, two of the protesters (two soldiers named Daalhuisen and Duppen) were later allegedly transferred for having participated in the incident. The article contained the following paragraph:

> (a) There happens to be a General Smits who writes to his 'inferiors': 'I will do everything to keep you from violating the LAW!' But this very General is responsible for the transfers of Daalhuisen and Duppen. Yet, as you know, measures are never allowed to be in the nature of a disguised punishment. How devoted to the law the General is – as long as it suits him;
>
> (b) ... in addition to ordinary punishments, the army bosses have at their disposal a complete series of other measures – of which transfer is only one – to suppress the soldiers. That does not come to an end by questions in Parliament – that makes them at most more careful.

---

[26] Judgment, para 80 and 92.

> That only comes to an end when these people, who can only prove their authority by punishment and intimidation, have to look for a normal job.[27]

At the time of these proceedings, the Dutch Military Discipline Act of 27 April 1903 allowed for 'criminal acts', as described in the Common Penal Code or Military Penal Code, to be judged and punished by the competent military superior in a disciplinary procedure, provided the act or omission was inconsistent with military discipline and order 'but at the same time of such trivial nature that the matter can be dealt with in proceedings other than criminal proceedings'.[28]

On this legal basis, the two applicants had been sentenced by their military superior for having taken part in the publication and distribution of a writing 'tending to undermine discipline', as defined in article 147 of the Military Penal Code:

> Any person who, by means of a signal, sign, dumb show, speech, song, writing or picture, endeavours to undermine discipline in the armed forces or who, knowing the tenor of the writing or the picture, disseminates or exhibits it, posts it up or holds stocks of it for dissemination, shall be liable to a term of imprisonment not exceeding three years.

Article 10 of the Convention reads:

> Everyone has the right to freedom of expression. This right shall include the freedom to hold opinions and to receive and impart information and ideas without interference by public authority and regardless of frontiers. This Article shall not prevent states from requiring the licensing of broadcasting, television or cinema enterprises.
>
> The exercise of these freedoms, since it carries with it duties and responsibilities, may be subject to such formalities, conditions, restrictions or penalties as are prescribed by law and are necessary in a democratic society, in the interests of national security, territorial integrity or public safety, for the prevention of disorder or crime, for the protection of health or morals, for the protection of the reputation or rights of others, for preventing the disclosure of information

---

[27] Judgment, para 40–50.

[28] Judgment, para 15.

received in confidence, or for maintaining the authority and impartiality of the judiciary.

The Court notes that the penalty of committal to the disciplinary barracks and the consequent deprivation of liberty unquestionably represented an 'interference' with the exercise of the freedom of expression, as mentioned in Article 10, para 1. The Netherlands' Government had pleaded before the Court that the measures taken were 'necessary in a democratic society for the prevention of disorder' as stipulated in Article 10, para 2.

The Court subsequently emphasises that the concept of 'order', as envisaged in Article 10, not only refers to 'public order', but also covers the order that must prevail within the confines of a specific social group. This is so, for example, when, as in the case of the armed forces, a disorder in that group can have repercussions on order in society as a whole. It follows that the disputed penalties met this condition if and to the extent that their purpose was the prevention of disorder within the Netherlands Armed Forces.[29]

The Court stresses that the freedom of expression 'applies to servicemen just as it does to other persons within the jurisdiction of the contracting states'. However, the proper functioning of an army is hardly imaginable without legal rules designed to prevent servicemen from undermining military discipline, for example, by writings. The Court finds that Article 147 of the Netherlands Military Penal Code, as quoted above, is based on this legitimate requirement and does not in itself run counter to Article 10 of the Convention.

The Court continues to confirm that it has jurisdiction to supervise, under the Convention, the manner in which the domestic law of the Netherlands has been applied in the present case, but that in doing so it must not disregard either the 'particular characteristics of military life' (paragraph 54 in fine above), the specific 'duties' and 'responsibilities' incumbent on members of the armed forces, or the margin of appreciation that Article 10, para 2 and 8, para 2 leave the contracting States.

In applying these standards, the Court notes that the atmosphere in the barracks at Ermelo was already 'somewhat strained' and that Su-

[29] Judgment, para 98.

preme Military Court may have had well-founded reasons for considering that the two applicants had attempted to undermine military discipline and that it was necessary for the prevention of disorder to impose the penalty inflicted. There was, thus, no question of depriving them of their freedom of expression but only of punishing the abusive exercise of that freedom on their part. Consequently, the Court concludes, it does not appear that its decision infringed Article 10, para 2 of the Convention. In response to the claim of the applicants that civilians in comparable situations do not at all risk penalties like the ones imposed here, the Court reiterates its position that the distinction at issue is explicable by the differences between the conditions of military and civil life and, more specifically, by the 'duties' and 'responsibilities' peculiar to members of the armed forces in the field of freedom of expression.[30]

Freedom of Association for Military personnel

The same two applicants who had been punished for the publication of the article argued that the Netherlands military employed 'systemic measures' aimed at impeding the functioning of the VVDM, thereby infringing Article 11 of the Convention. Article 11, para 1, reads:

> Everyone has the right to freedom of peaceful assembly and to freedom of association with others, including the right to form and to join trade unions for the protection of his interests.

Limiting its judgment to the situation of the two applicants, the Court found that the two had not been punished by reason either of their membership of the VVDM or their participation in its activities, including the preparations and publication of the journal *Alarm*, but because of the way they had used their freedom of expression with a view to undermining military discipline.[31]

The Court addressed the freedom of association for military personnel in a later judgment, in which it ruled that although even significant restrictions could lawfully apply in the context of Article 11 of the Convention to an association of military personnel and its members and

---

[30] Judgment, paras 99–103.

[31] Judgment, paras 105–108.

its activities and expressions, these restrictions could not result in denying military personnel and their unions the right of freedom of association, aimed at defending their professional and moral interests.[32]

Concluding Observations

The case of *Engel v. The Netherlands* had a tremendous impact on the system of military justice in the Netherlands' Armed Forces. Already when the procedure was underway towards 'Strasbourg', the Minister of Defence abolished both the measure of 'strict arrest' and the posting to a disciplinary barrack by way of disciplinary measure. The judgment subsequently triggered a complete overhaul of the entire structure of military disciplinary law and military penal law, as well as the organisation of military courts. The new system, fully compliant with the Convention, entered into force in 1991.

Engel v. The Netherlands remains a 'benchmark' decision for the judgment on the restrictions on fundamental rights in the context of military service. This judgment assures on the one hand that the fundamental rights of the European Convention do indeed apply to military personnel, with on the other hand a keen eye for the 'particular characteristics of military life and its effects on the situation of individual members of the armed forces and also on the necessary restrictions of these rights, as are prescribed by law and are necessary for a democratic society.

---

[32] ECHR, *Affaire Matelly V. France*, 2 October 2014, Requête no 10609/10, para 71.

A Netherlands' Royal Military Academy graduate, Brigadier General **Jan Peter Spijk** read Constitutional Law at Leiden University and graduated *cum laude* in 1990. Having gained experience in the fields of operational law and personnel policy, he was promoted to brigadier general in 2004 and appointed the Director Personnel Policy at the Ministry of Defence in the Hague. In 2006, General Spijk was posted to Kabul, Afghanistan, as Netherlands' Contingent Commander. In 2007, he completed the Royal College for Defence Studies and read International Studies at King's College, London, UK. Subsequently, he was appointed the Director Personnel Policy at NATO's Allied Command Operations. In 2010, he was appointed TJAG of the Netherlands' Armed Forces and Senior Military Judge in the Military Chamber of the Court of Appeals. From 2012 until 2018, he was the President of the International Society for Military Law and the Law of War. He was elected Honorary President in 2018. Currently, he is a member of the Society's board of directors, of the Council of the International Institute for Humanitarian Law, San Remo, Italy, and chair of the Netherlands' Military Law Review Editorial Board. He is married to Dr Wendy Broesder Spijk.

General Spijk gratefully acknowledges the comments on an earlier version of his essay by Lieutenant Colonel RNLAF JJM van Hoek LLM, senior military legal advisor and attached to the University of Amsterdam, where he teaches Military Criminal Law and Military Disciplinary Law.

An Equal Fate

Aditya S Puar

Lt Col Prithi Pal Singh Bedi, India

In August 1982, a bench of three judges of the Supreme Court of India considered a series of writ petitions filed by military officers aggrieved by orders of courts-martial delivered against them. The peripheral commentary of the Supreme Court would have far-reaching consequences for the Indian military justice system on the options for judicial review available to those who were so affected.

At the time of the framing of the Constitution of India, the Constituent Assembly had considered whether or not the wide-ranging freedoms and rights that they were about to confer upon their fellow citizens should apply equally to members of the armed services.

After some consideration, it was decided that the freedoms of members of the armed forces must necessarily be curtailed to an extent, to accommodate the oft necessarily stern precepts of service discipline. Accordingly, among other provisions, Article 33 of the Constitution was inserted, which essentially allowed the Parliament the discretion to legislate curbs upon general freedoms available to the citizenry, insofar their application to members of the armed forces was concerned.[1]

It is pertinent to note that at the time of the passage of the Army and Air Force Acts in 1950, no appellate or review procedure by judicial process was enshrined in the legislation. Whereas a number of suggestions were mooted at the time, none of them fructified. The net result of such

[1] The Constitution of India, 1950, Art. 33; can be accessed at https://indiankanoon.org/doc/829916/

a situation was that service members who were subjected to courts-martial were deprived of any appellate judicial procedure whatsoever, in effect being left with only departmental and statutory remedies lying with superior officials of the self-same service. While judicial review by constitutional courts was possible, the scope for the same was extremely limited and did not include examination of evidence or a strict merits review.

The Indian Navy, perhaps being a much smaller service, took a modestly different view on the question of appeals for service members subjected to punitive measures. When the Navy Act, 1957, was enacted, while many provisions were *in pari materia* to those of the legislations enacted to regulate the functioning of the two larger services, one provision, in particular, stood out—section 160 of the Navy Act, 1957. It made the following allowances:[2]

> Judicial review by the Judge Advocate General of the Navy
>
> (1) All proceedings of trials by court-martial or by disciplinary courts shall be reviewed by the Judge Advocate General of the Navy either on his own motion or on application made to him within the prescribed time by any person aggrieved by any sentence or finding, and the Judge Advocate General of the Navy shall transmit the report of such review together with such recommendations as may appear just and proper to the Chief of the Naval Staff for his consideration and for such action as the Chief of the Naval Staff may think fit.
>
> (2) Where any person aggrieved has made an application under sub-section (1), the Judge Advocate General of the Navy may, if the circumstances of the case so require, give him an opportunity of being heard either in person or through a legal practitioner or an officer of the Indian Navy.

The above provision provided the first tenuous semblance of judicial review within the Indian military justice system. While in theory, it was not very different from the provisions of the Army and Air Force Acts, which provided for departmental review, given that the Judge Advocate General of the Navy was, of course, a naval officer, sub-section (2) of section 160 *supra* provided for the first time, the all-important benefit of representation through a legal practitioner.

---

[2] Accessible at https://www.indiacode.nic.in/show-data?actid=AC_CEN_28_38_00006_195762_1517807321397&sectionId=29370&sectionno=160&orderno=164

It is in this legislative backdrop that the question of what precisely must be the remedy for India's soldiers, sailors and airmen, should they run afoul of the law as laid down by the Parliament to regulate their services, came to be considered by the Supreme Court of India, in a judgement arising out of Civil Writ Petitions No 4903 of 1981, 1513 of 1979 and 5930 of 1980 *Lt Col Prithi Pal Singh Bedi etc v. Union of India & Others, 1983 SCR (1) 393* as decided on 25 August 1982.[3]

The captioned case was heard by a bench of three judges of the Supreme Court, and while the actual sins of omission or commission of the officers and men who fought this long legal battle are relatively immaterial for the purposes of this write-up, each of the cases that were decided *en bloc* vide this judgement came to the court under Article 32 of the Constitution of India, which guarantees enforcement and protection of fundamental rights as promised to every citizen of the Republic of India.

Amongst other things, the Supreme Court had occasion to consider the following broad points in the course of deciding the said case:

> The role of the so-called 'command influence' in the process of courts-martial and its repercussions insofar as the constitution of the quorum of courts-martial under Army Rule 40 is concerned.
>
> The interplay of Army Rules 22–24, which deal with the procedure for taking of evidence, and Article 21 of the Constitution of India, which protects the right to life and personal liberty and their constitutionality. More specifically, the right of the accused to confront his accuser(s), and to cross-examine them, per the principles of natural justice.

While answering the said questions, the Court concluded that it had limited scope for interference in the above-mentioned matters, and ultimately was compelled to dismiss the petitioners' cases. However, of special note is the pertinent observations that the Court saw fit to record, while nevertheless dismissing the cases of the Petitioners:

> ... Reluctance of the apex court more concerned with civil law to interfere with the internal affairs of the Army is likely to create a distorted picture in the minds of the military personnel that persons subject

[3] Supreme Court of India: *Lt Col Prithi Pal Singh Bedi Etc v. Union of India & Others* decided on 25 August 1982; can be accessed at https://indiankanoon.org/doc/278740/

to Army Act are not citizens of India. It is one of the cardinal features of our Constitution that a person by enlisting in or entering armed forces does not cease to be a citizen so as to wholly deprive him of his rights under the Constitution. More so when this Court held in *Sunil Batra v. Delhi Administration and ors* that even prisoners deprived of personal liberty are not wholly denuded of their fundamental rights. In the larger interest of national security and military discipline, Parliament in its wisdom may restrict or abrogate such rights in their application to the armed forces but this process should not be carried so far as to create a class of citizens not entitled to the benefits of the liberal spirit of the Constitution. Persons subject to Army Act are gritty and wholly unbiased. A marked difference in the procedure for trial of an offence by the criminal court and the courts-martial is apt to generate dissatisfaction arising out of this differential treatment...

...Absence of even one appeal with power to review evidence, legal formulation, conclusion and adequacy or otherwise of punishment is a glaring lacuna in a country where a counterpart civilian convict can prefer appeal after appeal to a hierarchy of courts. A submission that full review of finding and/or sentence in confirmation proceedings under section 153 is provided for is poor solace. A hierarchy of courts with appellate powers, each having its own power of judicial review, has, of course, been found to be counterproductive, but the converse is equally distressing in that there is not even a single judicial review...

...With the expanding horizons of fair play in action even in an administrative decision, the universal declaration of human rights and retributive justice being relegated to the uncivilised days, a time has come when a step is required to be taken for at least one review, and it must truly be a judicial review as and by way of appeal to a body composed of non-military personnel or civil personnel. The Army is always on alert for repelling external aggression and suppressing internal disorder so that the peace-loving citizens enjoy a social order based on the rule of law; the same cannot be denied to the protectors of this order. And it must be realised that an appeal from Caesar to Caesar's wife – confirmation proceeding under section 153 has been condemned as injudicious and merely a lip sympathy to form. The core question is whether at least there should be one appeal to a body composed of non-military personnel and who would enjoy the right of judicial review both on law and facts as also determine the adequacy of punishment being commensurate with the gravity of the offence charged. Judicial

> approach by people well-versed in objective analysis of evidence trained by experience to look at facts and law objectively, fair play and justice cannot always be sacrificed at the altar of military discipline. An unjust decision would be subversive of discipline. There must be a judicious admixture of both. And nothing revolutionary is being suggested. Our Army Act was more or less modelled on the UK Act. Three decades of its working with the winds of change blowing over the world necessitate a second look so as to bring it in conformity with a liberty-oriented constitution and the rule of law which is the uniting and integrating force in our political society. Even the UK has taken a step of far-reaching importance for rehabilitating the confidence of the Royal Forces in respect of judicial review of decisions of court-martial...
>
> ...The wind of change blowing over the country has not permeated the close and sacrosanct precincts of the Army. If in civil courts the universally accepted dictum is that justice must not only be done but it must seem to be done, the same holds good with all the greater vigour in case of court-martial where the judge and the accused don the same dress, have the same mental discipline, have a strong hierarchical subjugation, and a feeling of bias in such circumstances is irremovable. We, therefore, hope and believe that the changes all over the English-speaking democracies will awaken our Parliament to the changed value system. On this behalf, we would like to draw pointed attention of the Government to the glaring anomaly that courts-martial do not even write a brief reasoned order in support of their conclusion, even in cases in which they impose the death sentence. This must be remedied in order to ensure that a disciplined and dedicated Indian Army may not nurse a grievance that the substance of justice and fair play is denied to it. ...

This scathing and wide-ranging criticism of the system of appeals (or lack of the same) inherent in the Indian system of military justice by the highest court of the land could not but shake the collective conscience of the Indian republic. While it ultimately took years for changes to fructify, the ripples of this judgement have been felt for long. In Parliamentary debates in 2004, the then Union Minister for Defence of India, Mr George Fernandes, stated in answer to queries raised by his fellow parliamentarians that:

> ...
>
> (c) The Supreme Court in the case of *Lieutenant Colonel PPS Bedi v. Union of India* (AIR 1982 SC 1413) suggested setting up of a judicial

> forum to act as an appellate body against the courts-martial verdict. The apex court reiterated their suggestion in this context in the case of *Union of India v. Major CS Gill.*
>
> ...
>
> (e) A proposal for setting up of an Armed Forces Tribunal to adjudicate the appeals arising out of the verdicts of court-martial cases and service matters of Armed Forces personnel is under active consideration of the Government.[4]

Clearly then, the echoes of the Court's judgement in *Bedi's* case were resonating even 22 years later, in the corridors of power, and it was rapidly becoming the consensus that something must be done to ensure justice to service members.

On 15 June 2008, the Union Cabinet notified the Armed Forces Tribunal Act, 2007, thereby fulfilling the long-standing cry for reform, the first spark of which was perhaps lit by the Court in its hard-hitting judgement in *Bedi*. The Tribunal now hears appeals arising out of courts-martial and also hears 'service matters', which includes matters related to employment such as promotions, pay, pensions, benefits, allowances etc. – an aspect not actually envisaged in *Bedi*. Though from the military justice point of view, this has gone a long way in alleviating the shortcomings which were highlighted by the Supreme Court, institutional resistance to change, and organisational inertia continue to dog the process of transition. The system of military justice still remains mired in outdated concepts that do not meet the test of impartiality and independence. Of particular note is another development in this light. In the mid-2010s, the then Union Minister for Defence, Mr Manohar Parrikar, had constituted a high-level committee of experts, to consider, amongst other things, ways and means to reduce the litigation involving the Ministry of Defence through amelioration of its root causes. The committee submitted its report in 2015. It had a full chapter devoted to military justice reform, which went into the nuts and bolts of very pertinent issues. The committee, while considering the said matter before it, inter-alia made detailed observations on the topic,[5] a part of which is the following, and which

---

[4] See http://loksabhaph.nic.in/Questions/QResult15.aspx?qref=70472&lsno=13

[5] Raksha Mantri's Committee of Experts: Review of Service and Pension Matters Including Potential Disputes, Minimizing Litigation and Strengthening Institutional Mechanisms Related to

conveys the essence of the shortcomings of the existing system:

> ...Interestingly, while some nations have willingly embraced the march towards the reconfiguration of military justice with modern democratic principles, we have lagged behind, nay, lost the race. Since Mr Fidell talks about it in the citation above, we would amplify that there has been enlightenment in this area even in smaller nations like Nepal, and we are tempted to gainfully reproduce here some passages from the decision of the Supreme Court of Nepal in *Writ 65-WS-0010 In re: Order of Mandamus be issued declaring null and void provisions of the Army Act, 2006* decided on 30-06-2011:
>
>> Maintaining the chain of command of the military organisation and ensuring discipline and honour of the armed force is not the only subject matter that should be incorporated in the military justice system; providing military personnel with the opportunity to express their grievances in a proper manner and obtaining judicial remedy is also one of the goals. Therefore, while reviewing the structure and jurisdiction of courts-martial, such types of judicial mechanisms also should be kept in mind. This matter is also crucial from the perspective of creating an environment of trust and allegiance among military force towards the military justice system...It is not enough just to talk about the independence and fairness of a tribunal, the investigations and prosecutions must similarly also be independent, fair and effective. If an institution does not possess expertise in its own field, then it is not possible for it to accomplish the expected task. In the context of military justice, investigation, prosecution and defence in relation to an offence falling within the jurisdiction of courts-martial have to be effective, along with an effective court-martial. There should not be any possibility of direct interference by army officers in these processes. If the terms and conditions of service, and the regulation of human resources serving in such a mechanism, are the same as that of other military personnel, it is not possible for the mechanisms to perform their tasks in a fair and independent manner...The act of empowering the same authority or mechanism with the power to be involved in the investigation, prosecution, defence and adjudication of a case undermines the military justice system itself. Such a judicial system cannot be imagined in a civilised and democratic country that is committed to the rule of

---

Redressal of Grievances, 2015, pp 161-65, accessible at https://www.mod.gov.in/others/measures-reducing-litigation-and-public-grievances

> law...Further, the provisions that subject decisions or orders rendered by a General Court Martial or a Summary Court Martial to approval by military authority ultimately show that decisions or orders rendered by a General Court Martial, Summary General Court Martial, Summary Court Martial and District Court Martial, with the exception of the Special Court Martial, all fall under the control of the army administrative organisation. A judgment delivered by a judicial body can only be reviewed through a judicial procedure, and no other institution or authority may exercise a power to confirm or nullify such decision. This is what we call the universal character of the judicial decision...A system that authorises military officers to confirm or nullify judgments or orders rendered by trial-level courts-martial cannot be justified by any argument...In the absence of subject-wise expertise of law and justice, it is not possible to impart justice...The trend that has been emerging is to constitute tribunals with a majority of civilian judicial authorities who are able to impart justice in an independent and impartial manner rather than with a majority of military and administrative officers.

Suffice it to say that whatever may be put up in defence of the existing dispensation, to the eye of even a layperson, the current system of military justice does not meet the basic norms of independence or separation of powers guaranteed by the Constitution of India. Swiftness or quickness of trial or a high rate of conviction may reflect procedural efficiency but not judicial soundness of the system. Most of the democracies have moved on, but we are clinging to a system long aborted by others. For example, though the US has a jury system, it also has proper military judges. In the United Kingdom, the Judge Advocate General (JAG) is a proper judge functioning under the Ministry of Law and Justice and is a civilian (though he can be a former Member of the Military). Service in the JAG branch in India is judicial service theoretically (see paragraph 82(f)(i) of Regulations for the Army, 1987), but in practice, the officers are merely functioning as advisers without any judicial or executive role. Independent directorates of prosecution have been established in many nations, and forays have been made to ensure that there is no conflict of interest in the dispensation of justice in the military. Regrettably, introspection in this regard is lacks in our country, and we seem unwilling to exert and work hard towards betterment and robustness of military justice, which would boost not only confidence but also reduce litigation within and outside the military. One strikingly disorienting feature of courts-martial is also that of the 'judgement' (reasons in support) that is to be rendered in support of a conviction or acquittal. Many questions arise. We wonder as to how the Judge Advocate has been authorised to do so by the rules? (For example, see Rule 62(1) of Army Rules, 1954.) Does this not affect their independence or neutrality? What if the Judge Advocate renders advice of acquittal to the jury, but the jury decides on conviction? Would it be proper then for the Judge Advocate to write the reasons for conviction against their very own thought process? How can the Presiding Officer of the court-martial be expected to record reasons when they are not legally trained? Why is there a provision that the court-martial, if unable to reach the conclusion of 'guilt', could refer the issue to the 'confirming authority' for an opinion? (See Rule 62(3).) When the confirming authority remains so intimately involved in the evidence, the prosecution, the jury and the process of court-martial, how could separation of powers be expected and what then would remain of the pre-confirmation and post-confirmation provisions or petitions? Isn't it correct that members of courts-martial and even the Judge Advocate keep in touch with and keep seeking clarifications on various subjects from the formation which is responsible for convening the court-martial or even from other officers of the JAG branch? Members of the court-martial and even the judge advocates are expected to operate as a self-contained institution, like judges on the civil side, without being influenced by actions, thoughts or ideas outside the four corners of the courtroom. Whatever inputs that are required are to be provided from the two sides – prosecution and defence within the courtroom and not from external (official) entities. The practical ground reality clearly reflects a judicial overreach of another kind, where the members of the court themselves are neither trained nor legally educated nor confident and depend upon extraneous influences. Sadly, this situation is also supported by statutory rules. For example, to take the case of the Army Rules 49, 51, and 53 of the Army Rules, 1954, provide for objections and pleas by the accused but in all these rules, the matter can be reported/referred by the court-martial to the convening/confirming authority which again reflects a conflict of interest. As also stated above, the court-martial, rather than being a standalone, independent, self-contained confident institution, acts more as a wing or an extension of the convening authority, thus resulting in an overreliance of the entire system of military justice on the official side rather than maintaining a balance by being independent, dispassionate and impartial. So much so that the Judge Advocate General, who is (and whose officers are) supposed to independently advise the system of military justice, is also the Adviser to the Chief of the Army Staff and is even supposed to assist the Adjutant General in matters related to discipline (See Regulation 33 of the Regulations for the Army, DSR). So, on the one hand, the JAG branch is supposed to assist in the maintenance of discipline; on the other hand, the same branch is supposed to render independent legal/quasi-judicial advice when disciplinary proceedings are initiated. Though we are not for a minute suggesting that the JAG branch or even other cogs of the official machinery are unfair towards their responsibility, but then, we are again tempted to reproduce the oft-repeated phrase from *R v. Sussex Justices, ex-parte McCarthy (1923) All England Reporter 233*, wherein Lord Chief Justice Hewart of the King's Bench recorded that:

> Justice should not only be done but should manifestly and undoubtedly be seen to be done.

It is not for the establishment to feel satisfied by fairness but for the persons facing the process of law.

Rationalising by way of justifying that 'all is well', or shutting the eyes to the hazards of ad hocism, or brushing aside the entire range of issues referred above, is hardly the solution, and it is high time we take the bull by the horns and get down to the brass-tacks by discarding our respective comfort zones and challenging the status quo. The final result of such an exercise may decrease the intensity of clout concentrated in some power-centres but would be in the overall fitness of things, and the balance would shift towards objectivity, fairness and judiciousness, even when observed from the ringside. Every limb of military justice, therefore, needs to be weighed purposefully against the backdrop of constitutional principles, international standards, best practices and democratic norms. ...

The above observations (albeit long, but their significance makes their reproduction unavoidable), along with a roadmap for further action, were made by the Committee of Experts and submitted to the Government in 2015, but the implementation of the recommendations has been patchy and slow, if at all. It is understood that the Defence Minister had approved many parts of the recommendations and had directed action on their implementation within a period of 45 days, but many years later, nothing seems to have moved in the direction of reform.

In the ultimate analysis, despite challenges, Indian military law has come far since the case of *Bedi* was decided in the 1980s. Today, service personnel who have been subjected to courts-martial, or for that matter, other disciplinary proceedings by departmental procedure, have a codified process of appeal or challenge, guaranteed by law available to them in the form of the Armed Forces Tribunal, staffed by retired judges of the high courts, and superannuated generals, admirals, or air marshals. Perhaps even this innovation is far removed from a perfect solution, as the report of the Committee of Experts (*supra*) has brought out, but equally, it is a long way from the unequal justice which was excoriated by the Supreme Court of India on 25 August 1982.

Aditya S Puar is a lawyer based in New Delhi, India, who works in the fields of military, media, commercial and civil laws. He holds a Bachelor's degree in Economics from the University of the Pacific, California. He is also a Master of Science in Management from the University of Reading, England and a First in Law from the Faculty of Law, University of Delhi. Before becoming a lawyer, Aditya worked for several years in the publishing industry with the Scholastic Corporation.

The Fork in the Road and the Path Not Taken

Rory Fowler and Afton Brooke David

Généreux, Canada

Introduction

In the three decades following the judgment in *R v. Généreux*,[1] the Judge Advocate General of the Canadian Forces (JAG) and the Director of Military Prosecutions (DMP) have consistently relied upon this decision as the binding basis for the constitutionality of concurrent jurisdiction of the Code of Service Discipline[2] with the civilian criminal justice system, and the resulting derogation therefrom.[3] The JAG typically adopts the position that the Supreme Court of Canada (SCC) considered the independence and impartiality of courts-martial and that the majority endorsed that a separate system of military justice, where members of the military are tried by military officers performing judicial roles, complies with the *Canadian Charter of Rights and Freedoms*.[4]

This same argument has been advanced recently in the multiple appeals brought principally by DMP (on behalf of the Minister of National

[1] *R v. Généreux*, [1992] 1 SCR 259 [Généreux], online: https://www.canlii.org/en/ca/scc/doc/1992/1992canlii117/1992canlii117.html?autocompleteStr=R%20v%20genereux&autocompletePos=1

[2] National Defence Act, RSC 1985, c N-5, Part III [NDA].

[3] *Généreux*, note 1, 293.

[4] *Ibid*, 295. *Canadian Charter of Rights and Freedoms*, Part I of the Constitution Act, 1982, being Schedule B to the Canada Act 1982 (UK), 1982, c11 [Charter].

Defence) before the Court Martial Appeal Court of Canada (CMAC) arising from applications by the accused relating to the independence and impartiality of the military judiciary.[5] These appeals were brought after different military judges stayed the prosecutions of several accused when the judges concluded that orders issued by the Chief of the Defence Staff (CDS) gave rise to a reasonable apprehension that their independence as military judges was impaired.

The justification for a parallel military disciplinary code, functioning as a derogation from the civilian criminal justice system, has been further reinforced by the SCC in judgments subsequent to *Généreux*.[6] However, this 'received wisdom' runs the risk of overstating the impact of *Généreux* and overlooking what the judgment did not address (or did not address adequately).

The appellant in *Généreux* was charged with three counts of possession of narcotics for the purpose of trafficking contrary to section 4 of what was then the Narcotic Control Act.[7] Normally, such offences would have been prosecuted before a civilian court of criminal jurisdiction. However, by virtue of what was section 120(1) [now subsection 130(1)] of the National Defence Act (NDA), a prosecution proceeded under the Code of Service Discipline. The appellant initially attempted, unsuccessfully, to bar the prosecution by seeking a writ of prohibition (a form of permanent injunctive relief) before the Federal Court.

The appellant was convicted of three charges under the Narcotic Control Act as well as one charge of being Absent Without Leave under section 90 of the NDA. The appellant was sentenced to 15 months imprisonment and was released from the Canadian Forces. The appellant raised several issues at law before the Judge Advocate who presided over the trial, including the admissibility of evidence obtained in breach of his right under section 8 of the *Charter* to be free from unreasonable search and seizure, his equality rights under section 15 of the *Charter*, and the independence of the general court-martial under section 11(d) of the *Charter*. The Judge Advocate rejected all three applications.

---

[5] *R v. Edwards*, et. al., 2021 CMAC 2 [Edwards]; *R v. Proulx*, 2021 CMAC 3.

[6] *R v. Moriarity*, 2015 SCC 55, [2015] 3 SCR 485 [*Moriarity*]; *R v. Stillman*, 2019 SCC 40 [*Stillman*].

[7] RSC 1985, c N-1. This statute was subsequently superseded by the Controlled Drugs and Substances Act, SC 1996, c 19.

The appellant appealed to the CMAC, the initial appellate court under the NDA, raising six principal issues, including the aforementioned *Charter* rights. The central issue on appeal concerned section 11(d) of the *Charter*:

> 11. Any person charged with an offence has the right ... (d) to be presumed innocent until proven guilty according to law in a fair and public hearing by an independent and impartial tribunal.

Two of the three judges held, for different reasons, that, notwithstanding courts-martial may differ from civil courts and, more specifically, that judge advocates differed from civilian judges, the requirement for independence was satisfied. Justice Décary dissented, concluding that, although the *Charter* permits the existence of a separate system of military law and military tribunals, the distinct system failed to comply with section 11(d) of the *Charter*.

As a result of the dissent, the accused had a right of appeal to the SCC, Canada's apex court. Although the issues on appeal included equality of rights under section 15 of the *Charter* as well as the exclusion of evidence obtained in breach of a *Charter* right, the determinative issue was whether trial by general court-martial restricted the accused's right to a fair and public hearing by an independent and impartial tribunal guaranteed by sections 7 and 11(d) of the *Charter*.

Summary of the Judgment

A significant majority of the SCC held that, although a separate and parallel military disciplinary process was justified under the Canadian constitution, the configuration of courts-martial, at that time, infringed the right of an accused to trial before an independent and impartial tribunal as guaranteed under paragraph 11(d) of the *Charter*.

Généreux was expressed in three separate judgments[8]: a majority

[8] In Canada, the written reasons of an appellate judge are described as a judgment, even if it does not represent the majority view. Thus, there can be unanimous judgments, majority judgments, concurring judgments (by one or more judges who are not part of the majority, but who concur with the final disposition), plurality judgments (by two or more judges who form the largest group of judges subscribing to a judgment, but do not comprise a majority) or a dissent.

judgment (per Lamer CJ and Sopinka, Gonthier, Cory and Iacobucci JJ) authored by Chief Justice Lamer; a concurring judgement (per La Forest, McLachlin and Stevenson JJ) authored by Justice Stevenson; and a lone dissent from Justice L'Heureux-Dubé.

Eight of the nine judges held that the judge advocates who presided over courts-martial lacked security of tenure and financial security. They also lacked sufficient institutional independence generally, and particularly regarding their selection. At that time, the JAG maintained a list of potential judge advocates, from which the JAG would select a specific judge advocate for each court-martial. Thus, representatives of the executive would convene courts-martial, select the prosecutor, and select the presiding judge advocate. This process undermined the institutional independence of general courts-martial, and the selection of personnel to serve on the panel of a general court-martial (analogous to a civilian jury) was not sufficiently free from the influence of the executive.

The judgment in *Généreux* represented not only the merit of the existence of a parallel military disciplinary code but also highlighted the frailties of such systems and identified safeguards that would be necessary for such a system to function fairly in a constitutional democracy governed by the rule of law and constitutionally entrenched legal rights.

With the benefit of hindsight, we know that *Généreux* had an important impact on the Canadian military justice system and precipitated significant reforms. However, not all of these reforms withstood subsequent judicial scrutiny, and not all of the judicial scrutiny was entirely consistent with the potential reforms suggested by the majority in *Généreux*. In particular, although *Généreux* hinted at an examination of whether courts-martial are properly placed within the executive branch or the judicial branch, none of the judgments offered a definitive answer to that issue. Elements of this lacuna have resurfaced in the recent appeals regarding the independence of the military judiciary. Had the majority (or any of the judges) in *Généreux* examined this issue more definitively, the conclusions arising from that examination could have dramatically changed the trajectory of the military justice system in Canada.

The Fork in the Road and the Path Not Taken

Majority

The same span of three pages in the 80-page judgment in *Généreux* is cited consistently in support of the constitutionality and viability of Canada's military justice system.[9] Chief Justice Lamer, writing for the majority, began his analysis by describing the history of the Code of Service Discipline as a derogation from the norm.[10] In his examination of section 11 of the *Charter* in the context of the 'military justice system', he relied upon *Wigglesworth*[11] to include offences of a public nature which '... promote public order and welfare within a public sphere ...', and offences that involve '... true penal consequences ...'. He then reviewed the purpose of military tribunals and referred to the military justice system and Code of Service Discipline as part of the military's internal[12] disciplinary system with special needs for which 'ordinary courts' are inadequate.[13]

Lamer CJ relied on a pre-*Charter* case, *MacKay v. Rippon,*[14] regarding a conclusion that merits greater attention:

> All members embark upon rigorous training to fit themselves physically and mentally for the fulfilment of the role they have chosen and paramount in that there must be rigid adherence to discipline.[15]

In *MacKay v. Rippon,* Cattanach J observed that training is important in the maintenance of discipline; we suggest it is as important as the Code of Service Discipline in the furtherance of the habit of obedience. However, the judgments in *Généreux* leave the impression that the Code of Service Discipline is the main factor for ensuring discipline, efficiency, and morale in the armed forces – potentially to the exclusion of

[9] *Généreux,* note 1, 293-296.

[10] *Ibid,* 280.

[11] *R v. Wigglesworth,* [1987] 2 SCR 541.

[12] On the term 'internal', which can sometimes be overused, see Rory Fowler, 'What is an "internal process"?', Law Office of Rory G. Fowler, online: http://roryfowlerlaw.com/in-the-administration-of-the-affairs-of-the-canadian-forces-what-is-an-internal-process/

[13] *Généreux,* note 1, 281.

[14] *MacKay v. Rippon,* [1978] 1 FC 233, per Cattanach J.

[15] *Ibid,* 235-236. Also see *Généreux,* note 1, 293-294.

other effective mechanisms.

The majority cited James B Fay's 1975 study of military justice, which asserted that the Canadian Forces (CF) could never truly have an independent judiciary because a '... military officer must be involved in the administration of discipline at all levels ...' and that the strength of the system lies in officers with judicial roles with military knowledge. According to Fay, independence could only be achieved by severing that connection; however, if that were to happen '... the advantage of independence of the judge that might thereby be achieved would be more than offset by the disadvantage of the eventual loss by the judge of the military knowledge and experience ...'.[16]

Although the majority in *Généreux* concludes that courts-martial must be presided over by an independent and impartial tribunal,[17] the Court's reliance on Fay's analysis raises potential ambiguity. Fay's principal conclusion was that courts-martial fall under the authority of the executive and not the judiciary and that the decision maker's independence is guaranteed by their status as a legal officer. Although the majority relied upon Fay's analysis and conclusions, they discussed neither the full history of the Code of Service Discipline nor how the application of the same evolved over time. The eventual implied conclusion that courts-martial fall within the judicial branch arises with no analysis distinguishing their conclusion from Fay's analysis, nor substantive discussion regarding why courts-martial are not an extension of the executive.

Nor did the majority examine how other federal common law countries characterize their military courts.[18] The reason for the absence of

---

[16] *Généreux*, note 1, 295-296. Also, see James B. Fay, *Canadian Military Criminal Law: An Examination of Military Justice* (1975) 23 Chitty's L J 120, 228. This was one of four articles that, together, comprised a larger LLM thesis completed by James B. Fay, a legal officer and occasional judge advocate. It represented one of the very few examples of peer-reviewed scholarship on Canadian military justice at the time.

[17] Both the presiding judge advocate and, for a general court-martial, a panel selected by an independent administrator.

[18] In *Re Nolan; Ex parte Young* (1991) 172 CLR 460, the High Court of Australia (HCA) focused on whether courts-martial were distinct from what were characterized as 'Chapter III courts' – i.e., courts established under Chapter III of the Australian Constitution., which vests the judicial power of the Commonwealth exclusively in courts created under that Chapter. Relying, in part, upon *Re Tracey; Ex parte Ryan,* [1989] HCA 12, 166 CLR 518, the majority of the HCA held that courts-martial stand outside the operation of Chapter III. Much of the analysis focused on the division of powers between the Commonwealth (which exercised legislative authority over the armed forces) and the states (which exercise legislative authority over criminal or penal law). This

any explicit discussion could be that neither the appellant nor the respondent raised this issue, just as neither party seemed to challenge the derogation of the Code of Service Discipline from the civilian system.[19]

The majority of the SCC did examine why there ought to be a separate system of military justice,[20] resulting in a status quo conclusion. The majority began with an examination of *MacKay v. The Queen*,[21] a pre-*Charter* decision from the SCC. In *MacKay*, the majority of the SCC held that the extant provisions for courts-martial did not contravene an accused's right to '... equality before the law and the protection of the law ...' under subsection 1(b) of the Canadian Bill of Rights.[22] The Court held that differences between the treatment of service personnel and civilians were not inconsistent with the concept of equality before the law. The British North America Act (as it was then known)[23] permitted Parliament to enact laws for the governance of the armed forces and, for sound reasons of legislative policy, Parliament chose to apply a regime to one class of persons and not to another class. Similarly, the majority held that there was no evidence to suggest that the president of the court-martial, an officer of the Canadian Forces, acted in a partial manner or that

---

characterization has been further refined more recently: *Private R v. Cowen* [2020] HCA 31, at para 60: "... there can be no doubt that the power exercised by service tribunals is not the judicial power of the Commonwealth". The United States has been more unequivocal that courts-martial represent federal tribunals, distinct from courts; courts-martial are 'Legislative' or Article I courts. Although it post-dates *Généreux*, the judgment of the Supreme Court of the United States (SCOTUS) in *Weiss v. United States*, 510 US 163, 178 (1994) upheld the appointment of military officers (i.e., representatives of the executive) as military judges as well as a lack of fixed terms or security of tenure for military judges, in recognition that the role of a military judge is one of several roles to which such officers may be assigned. More recently, in *Ortiz v. United States*, 138 S Ct 2165 (2018) [*Ortiz*], the Court held: "As this Court early held, Article I gives Congress the power – 'entirely independent' of Article III – 'to provide for the trial and punishment of military and naval offences in the manner then and now practiced by civilized nations.'", 2178 [quoting *Dynes v. Hoover*, 61 US 65, 79 (1858)].

[19] *Généreux*, note 1, 287: "The appellant concedes that a separate system of military law, along with a distinct regime of service tribunals to apply this law, is consistent with section 11*(d)* of the *Charter*."

[20] *Ibid*, 290.

[21] *MacKay v. The Queen*, [1980] 2 SCR 370 [*MacKay*]: an appeal of a court-martial, related to, but distinct from, *MacKay v. Rippon*, note 13. *MacKay v. Rippon* represented an earlier attempt to seek a writ of prohibition barring the application of the *Code of Service Discipline* – specifically, the convening of a court martial. It was unsuccessful.

[22] Canadian Bill of Rights SC 1960, c 44.

[23] Now called The Constitution Act, 1867 (UK), 30 & 31 Victoria, c 3.

his appointment deprived the accused of an independent and impartial tribunal.[24]

In light of the judgment in *MacKay*, the Crown likely anticipated a successful outcome in *Généreux*. Certainly, the constitutionality of general courts-martial had been upheld by the Judge Advocate, at first instance, and by the CMAC. Both levels of court relied heavily on *MacKay*, which held that a court-martial was an independent and impartial tribunal due to the narrow language of the Canadian Bill of Rights. Arguably, the impugned Code of Service Discipline provisions were upheld in *MacKay* because the application of the Canadian Bill of Rights was more narrowly construed than the *Charter*.[25] Section 2 of the Canadian Bill of Rights, which contains language similar to the 'notwithstanding clause' of the *Charter*,[26] called for legislation to be interpreted and applied so as to not abridge the enumerated rights. The *Charter*, on the other hand, provides the courts with more robust power to declare legislative provisions of no force or effect. Consequently, the Court in *Généreux* derogated from the conclusions in *MacKay*. As we have witnessed in subsequent decisions,[27] reform of the Code of Service Discipline typically arises because of successful applications and appeals by the accused.

Objectively, the majority judgment in *Généreux* might have appeared to signal the same outcome as in *MacKay*. However, in applying the three-part test for judicial independence from *Valente v. The Queen*,[28] which, itself, derogated from *MacKay*, the majority (and the concurring justices) held that the procedures for convening general courts-martial were insufficient to guarantee institutional independence.

While DMP has consistently relied upon this judgment as the justification for the merit of a concurrent and separate military justice system, the focus of *Généreux* was, ostensibly, judicial independence. While the justification for a separate and parallel system of military justice formed the contextual backdrop for the *Charter* analysis, that principle was not at issue in the appeal. Nor did any of the judgments in *Généreux* expressly

---

[24] *MacKay*, note 21, 395.

[25] The Constitution Act, 1867, note 23, ss 1 & 2. Also, *MacKay*, note 21, 382, 389 & 390.

[26] *Charter*, note 4, s 33.

[27] *R v. Trépanier*, 2008 CMAC 3 [*Trépanier*]; *R v. Leblanc*, 2011 CMAC 2 [*Leblanc*].

[28] *Valente v. The Queen*, [1985] 2 SCR 673 [*Valente*].

examine whether the status of a judge advocate (now a military judge), as an officer of the CF, would either undermine the judge advocate's independence or, more broadly, signal that courts-martial are actually an extension of the executive rather than the judiciary. That issue has now been raised, nearly 30 years later, in relation to the independence of the military judiciary.[29]

Concurring Reasons

In concurring reasons, Justice Stevenson compares courts-martial to disciplinary bodies of self-governing professions.[30] Using the example of the Law Society of Ontario as a self-governing profession, this comparison appears inapt. First, the powers attributable to disciplinary tribunals of self-governing professions are markedly narrower: lawyers can be disbarred (i.e., have their licence revoked); their practice can be subjected to supervision for a period of time, or they can be fined.[31] However, they cannot be imprisoned (or detained) for breaching their Rules of Professional Conduct, nor can they be subjected to lesser forms of punishment. Professional regulation results in remedial measures or termination of membership in the profession. Professional regulation does not involve penal consequences.

Second, the governing body of Benchers of the Law Society is selected from among the members of the Law Society (i.e., licensed lawyers and, more recently, paralegals who have asymmetric standing).[32] All member-lawyers are eligible to stand for such positions and to vote for candidates. The Benchers are responsible for both creating and enforcing the Rules of Professional Conduct.[33] To put it simply, the Law Society creates and enforces its own disciplinary code.[34] The same is not true of the Code of Service Discipline, which is a product of the legislative processes of Parliament and the Governor in Council. Although the Code of

---

[29] See note 5.

[30] *Généreux*, note 1, 316: "The Court Martial is not dissimilar from the disciplinary body of a self-governing profession which is often, ultimately, the executive board of the profession".

[31] Law Society Act, RSO 1990, c L-8, at s. 33 & 35.

[32] *Ibid*, s 10ss.

[33] See the Law Society of Ontario *By-Law* 3, available at https://lso.ca/about-lso/legislation-rules/by-laws/by-law-3

[34] Law Society Act, note 31, s 4.1.

Service Discipline is administered by senior members of the CF, it is not a product of exclusive enfranchisement of members of the CF.[35]

The concurring justices also declined to pursue the 'path not taken'. At the time that *Généreux* was decided, Canadian military law was at a fork in the road: courts-martial could have been characterized expressly as falling under either the executive or the judiciary. Stevenson J came close to suggesting this very outcome: '... if the executive is defined to include the entire hierarchy, military tribunals will always be subject to the executive'.[36] In hindsight, addressing the issue of whether courts-martial are properly characterized as falling within the executive branch may well have identified problems that arose after Bill C-25 was enacted in 1998.[37]

In comparing Canada's military justice system with federal common law comparator nations like Australia and the United States, it appears that we depart from our allies in that neither *Généreux* nor subsequent decisions[38] touch on the distinction between powers granted to the federal Parliament on militia, military and defence under section 91(7), and provincial jurisdiction over the administration of justice under section 92(14), of the Constitution Act, 1867.[39] Neither is a distinction drawn between superior courts of justice with inherent jurisdiction[40] and federal statutory tribunals, which have consistently been characterized as extensions of the executive.[41]

---

[35] Members of the Regular Force component of the Canadian Forces are prohibited from taking "... an active part in the affairs of a political organization or party ..." and shall not "...make a political speech to electors, or announce himself or allow himself to be announced as a candidate, or prospective candidate, for election to the Parliament of Canada or a provincial legislature ...": Queen's Regulations and Orders for the Canadian Forces [QR&O], art 19.44(7), available at https://www.canada.ca/en/department-national-defence/corporate/policies-standards/queens-regulations-orders.html

[36] *Généreux*, note 1, 318.

[37] An Act to amend the National Defence Act and to make consequential amendments to other Acts, SC 1998, c 35 [Bill C-25].

[38] See *Moriarity* and *Stillman*, note 6.

[39] The Constitution Act, 1867, note 23.

[40] There is a compelling argument that a Superior Court of Justice, with inherent jurisdiction, could have the capacity to preside over *Code of Service Discipline* offences. See *Ontario v. Criminal Lawyers' Association of Ontario*, [2013] 3 SCR 3, paras 18 to 26.

[41] This principle has been a consistent factor from *Nicholson v. Haldimand-Norfolk Regional Police Commissioners*, [1979] 1 SCR 311 [Nicholson] to *Baker v. Canada* (Minister of Citizenship and Immigration), [1999] 2 SCR 817 [Baker] to *R v. Conway*, 2010 SCC 22, [2010] 1 SCR 765

Administrative tribunals, as extensions of the executive, apply statutory disciplinary codes.[42] Administrative tribunals perform adjudicative functions that can significantly affect the rights, interests and privileges of the person subject to the tribunal's decisions.[43] Administrative tribunals may consider, adjudicate, and even remedy *Charter* issues,[44] and the review of the decisions by administrative tribunals is not limited to the prerogative of courts for judicial review; administrative tribunals can be subject to statutory appeal processes.[45]

Instead, the majority and concurring judgments in *Généreux* implicitly concluded that courts-martial fall within the judicial branch, notwithstanding the absence of express analysis that distinguishes courts-martial from other federal tribunals and reliance upon scholarship that tended to suggest that courts-martial are tribunals drawn from the executive rather than representative of the judiciary. This distinguishes Canadian courts-martial from American and Australian jurisprudence, which characterize their military tribunals as arising within their executive as non-judicial federal tribunals.[46] In *Généreux* and thereafter, the SCC has not examined this potential distinction. The difference in the division of powers in those comparator states may be one reason.

Dissent

Justice L'Heureux-Dubé was the sole dissent. Her examination of section 11 of the *Charter* stressed the importance of context,[47] and she concluded that the existence of true penal consequences in courts-martial requires judicial independence comparable to courts of criminal jurisdiction. She appeared to mirror the judgments of Lamer CJ and Stevenson J; however, her dissent also suggests that courts-martial represent a different type of court. She does not go as far as suggesting that courts-martial are federal tribunals drawn from the executive or that we need not

[Conway] to *Canada (Minister of Citizenship and Immigration) v. Vavilov*, 2019 SCC 65 [Vavilov].

[42] Nicholson, *ibid*.

[43] *Baker*, note 41.

[44] *Conway*, note 41.

[45] *Vavilov*, note 41.

[46] See *Private R v. Cowen*, note 16, from the HCA and *Ortiz*, note 18, from the SCOTUS.

[47] *Généreux*, note 1, 320.

focus on the separation of the executive and judiciary because of the same.[48] As with the majority and concurring judgments, that is a path that L'Heureux-Dubé J chose not to take.[49]

Although she drew a different conclusion than the majority, Justice L'Heureux-Dubé relied on the same excerpts from *MacKay*.[50] She, too, relied on Fay's conclusion that disciplinary decision-making is best left to officers rather than to civilian courts,[51] as well as his comparison of the CF to a self-regulated professional organization.[52] This comparison with 'self-regulated professions' resurfaced recently in Bill C-77.[53] Among a variety of provisions, including many which have not yet come into force, Bill C-77 establishes a new disciplinary regime within the Code of Service Discipline: Summary Hearings. Although these provisions have not yet come into force, prosecution of 'service infractions' (a new term introduced in Bill C-77), which will be defined in the Queen's Regulations and Orders for the Canadian Forces, will be based upon the civil burden of proof (balance of probabilities) similar to the disciplinary regimes of self-regulated professions. As noted above, analogic comparison with regulated professions may be problematic.

L'Heureux-Dubé J did not focus on the nature of courts-martial as ad hoc tribunals, distinguishable from permanent courts. However, she did rely on *Valente* in characterizing them as a 'specific adjudicative task';[54] thus, her dissent came closest to the American and Australian approach to military tribunals. Considering how administrative law has

---

[48] *Ibid*, 324, where L'Heureux-Dubé J affirms Justice McIntyre's statement: "From the earliest of times, officers of the armed forces in this [country] had this judicial function".

[49] *Ibid*, 329, "[...] I feel that there may well be occasions when it simply does not make sense to evaluate a given tribunal according to the standards established [in] *Valente*". In saying we do not need to subject certain tribunals like courts-martial to the *Valente* test, L'Heureux-Dubé J appears to imply that drawing a distinction between the judiciary and executive is not necessary.

[50] *Ibid*, 323 & 324.

[51] *Ibid*, 325.

[52] Fay also compared the *Code of Service Discipline* to the RCMP disciplinary process extant at that time. This, too, can be a potentially inapt comparison, as RCMP members cannot be jailed for breaching their code. However, the principal issue arising from this comparison is that RCMP disciplinary tribunals are clearly 'administrative tribunals', representative of the executive. Yet, as with the majority and concurring judgments, L'Heureux-Dubé J does not examine that distinction.

[53] An Act to amend the National Defence Act and to make related and consequential amendments to other Acts, SC 2019, c 15 [Bill C-77].

[54] *Généreux*, note 1, 330.

evolved more recently in Canada,[55] this set the tone for a modern interpretation of administrative tribunals without altering their place within the executive. Yet, in Canada, courts-martial have only rarely been subject to this examination.[56]

L'Heureux-Dubé J came closest to choosing 'the path not taken' when she discussed institutional independence. She lay the groundwork for a persuasive argument categorizing courts-martial as falling under the exercise of CF leadership in maintaining discipline, which would translate into a specific executive function.[57] Instead, she relied on *Mackeigan v. Hickman*[58] to conclude that courts-martial are a special kind of judiciary not remote from the executive.[59]

A generation after *Généreux*, the unresolved characterization that judge advocates (now military judges) are representative of the judiciary has now culminated in argument before the CMAC regarding the independence of military judges.[60] The conclusions in *Généreux* were drawn absent a determinative examination of whether courts-martial are, as federal tribunals, extensions of the executive rather than the judiciary. *Généreux* never resolved whether military judges, as commissioned officers and, therefore, members of the executive, truly exhibit or require the judicial independence of their civilian counterparts.[61] Nor did it resolve

---

[55] See *Conway*, note 41, in which Justice Abella, for a unanimous court, held that administrative tribunals could grant remedies under the *Charter*. The distinction between tribunals is no longer between 'judicial' and 'administrative' decisions. Nor must a tribunal fall within the judicial branch to grant *Charter* remedy.

[56] *R v. Rutherford*, [1983] 4 CMAR 262 1 represents a rare circumstance in which such examination has been conducted.

[57] *Généreux*, note 1, 336: "[I]n the context of the Armed Forces, these characteristics may well be a necessary part of the chain of command which, when followed link by link, ultimately leads to the same destination no matter where one begins. Hence, in my opinion, the *Charter* permits a sufficient degree of connection between the executive and the participants of a General Court-martial such that the third criterion of institutional independence was satisfied at the time of the appellant's trial."

[58] *Mackeigan v. Hickman*, [1989] 2 SCR 796.

[59] *Généreux*, note 1, 334 & 335.

[60] *Supra* note 5.

[61] Note that *Généreux* also led to the creation of the position of Chief Military Judge under Bill C-25, note 37. Thereafter, the Office of the Chief Military Judge was established by the Minister of National Defence, which replaced the short-lived Office of the Chief Military Trial Judge (Ministerial Organization Order, Office of the Chief Military Trial Judge, dated 27 September 1997). However, could this be said to place military judges, who preside at courts-martial, within

whether this was necessary.

The failure to do so can be seen to resonate in the recent CMAC judgment in *Edwards*. A unanimous 3-judge panel overturned prior judgments of three different military judges and held that military judges remain subject to the Code of Service Discipline and that their roles as officers of the Canadian Forces are not incompatible with their roles as military judges.[62] Consistent with the SCC reasoning in *Généreux*, the CMAC did not expressly identify courts-martial (and military judges) as part of the judiciary. Instead, it appeared to perpetuate *Généreux*' ambiguity:

> There is a common thread throughout the decisions of the military judges in the cases under appeal, that one cannot be a military officer and part of the executive and still perform the role of a judge. According to them, having executive responsibilities is inconsistent with the judicial role. To put it another way, one is "transferred" from the executive branch to the judicial branch upon appointment as a judge (*supra*, para. 25). With respect, such an approach does not reflect the reality of our Westminster system of government.[63]

Reinforcing the conclusion that military judges are representative of both the executive and judicial branches of government, the CMAC offered examples of circumstances[64] in which '... members of the judicial branch perform executive functions without compromising institutional independence or giving rise to a concern about impartiality. '[65] However lacklustre the analysis, this rationale seems to be consistent with the ambiguity arising in *Généreux*.

Unexplored Factors

The focus of received wisdom arising from the judgment in *Généreux* is the importance of the Code of Service Discipline as a mechanism – impliedly, *the* mechanism – for the maintenance of discipline, efficiency,

---

the judicial branch, notwithstanding that the judges themselves, as commissioned officers, were clearly members of the executive?

62 *Edwards*, note 5, paras 67 to 75.

63 *Ibid*, para 68.

64 *Ibid*, paras 69 and 70.

65 *Ibid*, para 73.

and morale of the armed forces of Canada and for promoting the 'habit of obedience'. Notwithstanding that portions of the judgment hint at other factors or mechanisms that support these outcomes, when *Généreux* is cited in support of the continued viability of the Code of Service Discipline, there can be a seemingly disproportionate emphasis on its role in achieving these outcomes. In addition to a variety of administrative and remedial mechanisms that complement the Code of Service Discipline,[66] training (particularly initial training), culturalization, and effective leadership all contribute to efficiency, positive morale, and a culture of discipline and obedience. Although the importance of training is mentioned at several points in the judgment, there is little examination of its impact on the central issues.[67] *Généreux* is consistently cited in support of the justification for the Code of Service Discipline, operating in parallel to the civilian criminal justice system, to maintain discipline, efficiency and morale. However, this myopia can be a disservice to other equally relevant factors in achieving the same end state.

---

[66] For example: the statutory grievance process pursuant to s 29 of the *NDA*, note 2, Chapter 7 of the QR&O, and Defence Administrative Order and Directive (DAOD) 2017-0/-1, available at https://www.canada.ca/en/department-national-defence/corporate/policies-standards/defence-administrative-orders-directives/2000-series/2017/2017-0-military-grievances.html; Summary Investigations and Boards of Inquiry pursuant to s 45 of the *NDA*, note 2, Chapter 21 of the QR&O, and DAOD 7002, available at https://www.canada.ca/en/department-national-defence/corporate/policies-standards/defence-administrative-orders-directives/7000-series/7002/7002-0-boards-of-inquiry-and-summary-investigations.html; Administrative Review pursuant to DAOD 5019-2, available at https://www.canada.ca/en/department-national-defence/corporate/policies-standards/defence-administrative-orders-directives/5000-series/5019/5019-2-administrative-review.html, and Remedial Measures pursuant to DAOD 5019-4, available at https://www.canada.ca/en/department-national-defence/corporate/policies-standards/defence-administrative-orders-directives/5000-series/5019/5019-4-remedial-measures.html

[67] *Généreux*, note 1. See 294 & 295, citing *MacKay v. Rippon*: "All members embark upon rigorous training to fit themselves physically and mentally for the fulfilment of the role they have chosen and paramount in that there must be rigid adherence to discipline" [...] "Their training is designed to ensure that they are sensitive to the need for discipline, obedience and duty on the part of the members of the military and also to the requirement for military efficiency". Also see 324: "I am unable to say that service officers, trained in the ways of service life and concerned to maintain the required standards of efficiency and discipline [...]", and 325, "Discipline can be defined as an attitude of respect [...] leadership, percept and training".

Changes Arising in the wake of *Généreux*

In the years following *Généreux*, legislative changes have altered the landscape of the Code of Service Discipline. Many of the significant changes have been prompted by appellate judgments arising from applications and motions brought by the accused. Following the enactment of Bill C-25, it was the military prosecutor who exercised discretion in selecting the type of courts-martial.[68] The seed of change was planted in *R v. Nystrom*[69] in 2005 but did not bloom until *R v. Trepanier*[70] in 2008; now, the accused has the right to select the mode of court-martial in certain circumstances.[71]

Similarly, the security of tenure for military judges was strengthened as a consequence of the CMAC judgment in *Leblanc* in 2011.[72] The majority's conclusion in *Généreux* regarding the security of tenure[73] was likely the impetus for the creation of the Office of Chief Trial Judge, which evolved into the Office of the Chief Military Judge following the enactment of Bill C-25. Conceptually, there was an expectation that legal officers appointed as military judges would not necessarily serve in that capacity until retirement. This rationale, presumably based, in part, upon the judgment of Chief Justice Lamer,[74] was the basis for appointing judges for five years with a possibility for reappointment[75] if they did not wish to return to the duties of a legal officer. The legislative regime envisioned appointment as a temporary or limited status. Such status is not unlike members of tribunals drawn from the executive. However, in the 13 years

---

[68] Bill C-25, note 37, s 42. Prior to the enactment of Bill C-60, *infra*, note 67, which came into force 18 July 2008, section 165.14 of the NDA, note 2, stated: "When the Director of Military Prosecutions prefers a charge, the Director of Military Prosecutions shall also determine the type of court-martial that is to try the accused person and inform the Court Martial Administrator of that determination."

[69] *R v. Nystrom*, 2005 CMAC 7.

[70] *Trépanier*, note 27.

[71] An Act to amend the National Defence Act (courts-martial) and to make a consequential amendment to another Act, SC 2008, c 29 [Bill C-60].

[72] *Leblanc*, note 27; An Act to amend the National Defence Act (military judges) [Bill C-16], enacting the Security of Tenure of Military Judges Act, SC 2011, c 22.

[73] *Généreux*, note 1, 302.

[74] *Ibid*, 304.

[75] NDA, note 2, section 165.21, as amended by Bill C-25, note 37, s 42.

between the enactment of Bill C-25 and the judgment in *Leblanc*, the perspective regarding the tenure of military judges changed markedly into a gradual civilianization,[76] but the path has not been direct.

The failure of the SCC to expressly distinguish whether courts-martial represent a function of the judiciary or a function of the executive gave rise to the ambiguity illustrated in *Généreux* and Bill C-25, both of which envisioned military judges who serve a fixed term. Arguably, *Généreux* represented only a partial examination of the issue, which was revised in subsequent judgments.[77] Military judges serving on fixed terms would have been consistent with a characterization of courts-martial as federal tribunals and extensions of the executive. Despite the ambiguous hybrid arising from *Généreux* and Bill C-25, it is not surprising that the weight of appellate judgments pulled definitively toward the judicial branch. However, that ambiguity continues to resonate.[78]

The reform of the military justice system has followed a clear trend of piecemeal amendment following successful applications or appeals by the accused, which highlight frailties. The legislative reforms precipitated by *Généreux* did not correct all deficiencies in the system, nor did they prevent subsequent successful applications under para 11(d) of the *Charter*.[79] In *Généreux*, the SCC examined a general proposition of the merit

[76] Chief Justice Lamer appeared to change his opinion during his review of Bill C-25 in 2003: Rt Hon Antonio Lamer, "The First Independent Review by the Right Honourable Antonio Lamer P.C., C.C., C.D. of the provisions and operation of Bill C-25, *An Act to amend the National Defence Act and to make consequential amendments to other Acts*, as required under section 96 of Statutes of Canada 1998, c.35", 3 September 2003 [Lamer Report], 19 to 21. See also, *Leblanc*, note 27, para 52, per Letourneau JA: "The late Chief Justice Lamer recognized ... [that] ... [h]aving further reflected on the matter since the position he had taken in *Généreux* [,] he recommended that military judges hold office during good behaviour in order to provide them with guarantees of institutional independence against a reasonable apprehension of bias". Also see para 47: "It seems inconceivable to me, and I say this with all due respect for the contrary view, that military judges, who exercise the same functions and have essentially the same powers as superior and provincial courts of criminal jurisdiction, should be subject to the whims, the unknowns, the uncertainty and anxiety of having their positions come up for renewal every five years. In fact, they are the only judges with such jurisdiction to be subject to short, renewable terms of employment." Also see paras 34, 35, 38 & 42.

[77] *Trépanier* and *Leblanc*, note 27. See also *Moriarity* and *Stillman*, note 6.

[78] *Edwards*, note 5.

[79] The precursor to the Office of the Chief Military Judge – the Office of the Chief Trial Judge – pre-dates the legislative reforms of Bill C-25. Other legislative changes enacted in 1998, which were clearly influenced by *Généreux*, involve the creation of the Court Martial Administrator (CMA) as a convening authority separate from the chain of command. The CMA also randomly

and constitutionality of a military disciplinary system that paralleled the civilian criminal justice system. Since then, the Crown has consistently cited this judgment for that same conclusion. However, the judgment is less informative regarding specific vulnerabilities of the military judiciary to unreasonable influence by the executive.

Conclusion

The focus of the appeal in *Généreux* was the independence and impartiality of a military tribunal – specifically, a general court-martial. However, it is most consistently cited for a principle that was not contested before the SCC and which was included in the judgment principally as background for the issues that were examined by the court. Notwithstanding that the judgments focused on judicial independence, the SCC did not definitively resolve whether courts-martial represent an extension of the executive or the judiciary. Instead, the majority, the concurring judgment, and even the dissent appeared to conclude, implicitly, that courts-martial are a special kind of judiciary notwithstanding that the judge advocates who presided over them, as commissioned officers, were clearly representatives of the executive.

The significance of the judgment in *Généreux* is two-fold in terms of what it did and what it did not do. First, the majority of the Court held that the process of convening and conducting general courts-martial did not ensure that the tribunal was sufficiently independent. The judge advocates presiding over the courts-martial lacked the security of tenure, security of remuneration and sufficient institutional independence. The means of empanelling general court-martial also lacked safeguards for institutional independence. These conclusions laid the framework for significant reform six years later with the enactment of Bill C-25.

However, none of the judgments in *Généreux* appears to address, explicitly and definitively, what ought to have been a central theme in the judgment: whether courts-martial arise within the executive or the judiciary. Nor did the Court determine whether military judges may simul-

---

selects the panel for a General Court Martial. The Chief Military Judge, as opposed to the Judge Advocate General, appoints the presiding Military Judge (formerly, Judge Advocate).

taneously occupy positions in both the executive (as commissioned officers) and the judiciary. That lacuna has now manifested in a series of appeals nearly 30 years later. Despite relying on both jurisprudence and scholarship that appeared to suggest that courts-martial are an extension of executive authority, none of the judgments in *Généreux* addresses that issue. All three arrived at a 'fork in the road', yet none of them opted to venture down that path.

All three appeared to agree that the responsibility for maintaining the discipline, efficiency, and morale of Canada's Armed Forces lies with the chain of command and is a function of the executive branch of government. Each judgment concluded that a separate military justice system, distinct from the parallel civilian justice system, was justified as an exercise of executive power and consistent with the *Charter*. Yet, notwithstanding that distinction, all three judgments gravitated toward concluding, impliedly, that courts-martial fall, at least partially, within the judicial branch of government.

Ironically, the principle for which *Généreux* is consistently cited by the Crown – the justification for a separate military justice system – was the one factor that was not at issue in the appeal. Even the appellant acknowledged the need for a separate military justice system. It was Chief Justice Lamer who concluded that it needed to be examined. One cannot help but wonder what the Crown would be relying on presently had the majority not felt compelled to present this analysis.

Lieutenant Colonel **Rory Fowler** (Retired) served in the Canadian Forces for nearly 28 years, first as an infantry officer with Princess Patricia's Canadian Light Infantry and subsequently as a Legal Officer with the Office of the Judge Advocate General. In the latter role, he worked extensively in the area of Public and Administrative Law as both a legal advisor and educator. Throughout his service, he developed a keen interest in the nature of the Crown-soldier relationship, how it was distinguishable from more traditional employment paradigms, and how this unique constitutional and statutory relationship could be better explained and understood. His interest in this subject is driven by a desire to ensure that the governance of the Canadian Forces reflects a just and fair approach to decision-making and complies with the rule of law so that the discipline, efficiency and morale of the Canadian Forces support its overall operational effectiveness.

Despite the significant and far-reaching impact of statutory decision-making within the Canadian Forces, the legal theory of this unique relationship has been the subject of limited scholarship and is not well understood by the statutory actors who wield significant power within this governance regime. Colonel Fowler's intent is to improve this understanding through his research at Queen's.

Since embarking in private practice in 2017, national television, radio and print media often call upon him for commentary on legal issues pertaining to the Canadian Forces and military law generally.

Afton Brooke David (née Maisonneuve) is Legal Counsel & Manager at Thales Canada Defence & Security and a member of the Reserve Force in the infantry with the Cameron Highlanders of Ottawa. She is a former university and provincial-level athlete, and a graduate of the University of Ottawa's National Program, with a degree in Civil Law (LL.L) and Common Law (J.D.). She was called to the Ontario Bar in 2018. Her bachelor's degree is in International Development and Globalization from the University of Ottawa. She articled at the law office of Kelly Santini LLP, where she later became an associate practising in private and commercial law. Her main academic interests are military law, constitutional law and international humanitarian law. She is the winner of the 2017 Canadian Bar Association's Sword & Scale essay contest with her paper titled *Neither Charity nor Special Treatment: Amendments to Sustainably Modernize the Canadian Forces Members and Veterans Re-establishment and Compensation Act*, which she wrote during her articles. She is also published in the area of medical assistance in dying and is mentioned in the *Oxford Handbook of the Canadian Constitution* for her work on *Amending the Constitution of Canada.*

Military Justice in Canada – A Living Organic Entity

Pascal Lévesque

Stillman, Canada

Overview

In *R v. Stillman*,[1] the Supreme Court of Canada concluded that service members could be charged with any serious civil offence (i.e., for which the maximum sentence is imprisonment for five years or more) and tried by court-martial without negating their right to a jury trial enshrined in the *Canadian Charter of Rights and Freedoms* (*Charter*).[2] There is no need to establish a connection – a 'military nexus' – between the circumstances of the alleged offence and a potential impact on military discipline; the accused's military status suffices.

Background

In Canada, anyone charged with an offence for which 'the maximum punishment for the offence is imprisonment for five years or a more severe

[1] *R v. Stillman*, 2019 SCC 40 [*Stillman*], accessible at www.decisions.scc-csc.ca/scc-csc/scc-csc/en/item/17891/index.do

[2] Part I of the Constitution Act, 1982, being Schedule B to the Canada Act 1982 (UK), 1982, c 11 [*Charter*].

punishment' (a 'serious offence') has the constitutional right to a jury trial 'except in the case of an offence under military law tried before a military tribunal'.[3] This is called the 'military exception'. Section 130(1)(a) of the National Defence Act (NDA)[4] [hereinafter 'section 130(1)(a)'] transforms criminal and other federal offences into 'service offences' similar to offences that are established under the NDA. Parliament has thus made them 'offence(s) under military law', subject to the 'military exception'. If charged by military authorities with a serious offence that is established other than under the NDA but incorporated into the Code of Service Discipline, service members are precluded from a jury trial, although they are entitled to a panel of five military members before a general court-martial.

Analysis — Majority

Two judges writing for a majority of five[5] (of a seven-judge bench) began by stating that a *Charter* right has to be interpreted generously, but it does not mean the 'widest possible reading'. Exceptions in the *Charter* also have to be interpreted purposively.

Jury trials have evolved to correct the imbalance of power in protecting the accused and proceedings. Today, jury trials protect individuals by giving them the benefit to be judged by their peers. However, this right is not without limit as the *Charter* provides for an exception.

Evolution of Military Justice

Historically, the purpose of military justice has been to ensure that military leadership can maintain discipline, efficiency, and morale.[6] To be

---

[3] *Id*, s 11(*f*).

[4] National Defence Act, RSC 1985, c N-5, [NDA]. Section 2 defines a 'service offence' as 'an offence under this Act, the Criminal Code or any other Act of Parliament, committed by a person while subject to the Code of Service Discipline'.

[5] *Stillman*, note 1, Moldaver and Brown JJ (Wagner CJ and Abella and Côté JJ concurring).

[6] 'Morale' as the 'confidence and feeling of well-being of a person or group at a particular time'. Not to be mistaken with 'moral', which are 'standards of behaviour, or principles of right and wrong' (*Oxford Concise Dictionary*).

ready, forces must be able to maintain discipline 'efficiently and effectively' by dealing with breaches promptly and often with more severity than what would have occurred in civilian life.[7] The civilian justice system would be ill-suited to deal with those matters.[8] Although military justice has adapted to legal, military and societal changes, these goals have remained.

From its origins until after Second World War, military justice focused on decision-making by commanders, without the involvement of lawyers and without a right of appeal.

In 1950, Canada integrated features of the criminal courts with the NDA.[9] A unified Code of Service Discipline gave a right to appeal to a board, harmonised procedures and punishments with civilian counterparts, and imposed a judge to preside over general courts-martial. Yet, commanders continued to play a large role in that system.

In the 1990s, several changes were adopted. The regulations[10] were modified to make the main actors more independent. The Supreme Court of Canada rendered its decision in *Généreux*.[11] It was followed by two comprehensive studies, which made recommendations to improve the military justice system.[12]

Parliament adopted reforms in 1998,[13] which notably improved the independence of military judges; established new independents actors;[14] transferred the determination of sentence from panel members to presiding military judge; and modified the composition of court-martial panels.

It also included a recurrent independent review of the legislation. Two independent reviews have been conducted since (a third one was

---

[7] That is the essence of a famous quote made by former Chief Justice Antonio Lamer in *R v. Généreux*, 1992 CanLII 117 (SCC), [1992] 1 SCR 259, at 293 [*Généreux*] quoted here by Justices Brown and Moldaver.

[8] *Id.*

[9] SC 1950, c 43.

[10] Queen's Regulations and Orders for the Canadian Forces or QR&O.

[11] *Généreux*, note 7. See Rory Fowler & Afton Brooke David on *R v. Généreux* in this book.

[12] *Report of the Commission of Inquiry into the Deployment of Canadian Forces to Somalia, vol. 1, Dishonoured Legacy: The Lessons of the Somalia Affair* (1997); *Report of the Special Advisory Group on Military Justice and Military Police Investigation Services* (1997).

[13] Bill C-25, An Act to amend the National Defence Act and to make consequential amendments to other Acts, 1st Sess., 36th Parl, 1998 (assented to 10 December 1998).

[14] Director of Military Prosecutions (DMP); Director of Defence Counsel Services (DDCS), and the Court Martial Administrator (CMA).

concluded on 1 June 2021). Both found that the system generally works well. The first review concluded that military panels should have a unanimous verdict and that the accused, and not the military prosecutor, should choose, most of the time, between a judge and a military panel or a judge alone.[15] A few years later, in *R v. Trépanier*, the Court Martial Appeal Court held that the accused had to be given that option.[16] In reaction, the Parliament adopted legislation that made the choice of the type of court-martial analogous to the function before civilian courts.[17] On court-martial panels, the second independent review recommended that reservists be allowed to sit as panel members and that the selection process should follow a random methodology.[18]

However, the Court acknowledged there remained problems. They referred to the external review conducted by another former Supreme Court Justice, who concluded that 'there is an underlying sexualised culture in the (Canadian Armed Forces) that is hostile to women and LGTBQ members, and conducive to more serious incidents of sexual harassment and assault'.[19] The ten recommendations to address that 'serious problem' required a 'deep cultural change'.

In sum, the Court stated that military justice has continuously evolved over the past 30 years due to periodic independent reviews 'ensuring the system is rigorously scrutinised, analysed, and refined at regular intervals.' They believe the evolution would continue in the future.[20]

---

[15] Canada, Department of National Defence, The First Independent Review by the Right Honourable Antonio Lamer P.C., C.C., C.D. of the provisions and operation of Bill C-25, An Act to amend the National Defence Act and to make consequential amendments to other Acts, as required under section 96 of Statutes of Canada 1998, c 35 (2003).

[16] *R v. Trépanier*, 2008 CMAC 3 [Trépanier].

[17] Bill C-60, An Act to amend the National Defence Act (court martial) and to make a consequential amendment to another Act, 2nd Sess., 39th Parl, 2008 (assented to 18 June 2008, SC 2008, c 29).

[18] Canada, Department of National Defence, Report of the Second Independent Review Authority to The Honourable Peter G. Mackay, Minister of National Defence, by The Honourable Patrick J. LeSage (2011), at pp 44-45.

[19] Marie Deschamps, External Review into Sexual Misconduct and Sexual Harassment in the Canadian Armed Forces, 27 March 2015, at p. I.

[20] *Stillman*, note 1, para 53.

The Code of Service Discipline Today

The main features of military justice serve a dual purpose: maintaining discipline (specific to the CAF) and protecting public order (shared with civilian justice). The Code of Service Discipline (*CSD*) [21] applies to persons who are related to the military to various degrees, not only regular forces and reservists (while on active service) but others, such as any person accompanying the CAF. In that system, the 'service offences' are not only the 'unique military offences', but also ordinary civil offences incorporated under the *CSD*. This is not new. Since the nineteenth century, military legislation has transformed ordinary civil offences into service ones.[22]

Under the *CSD*, there are summary trials and courts-martial. The latter are intended for minor offences, presided over by non-legally trained officers, straightforward, and permitting only limited punishments. Courts-martial are more formal, presided over by military judges, allow the legal representation of the accused, and have procedures similar to civilian criminal court. There are two types of courts-martial: standing courts-martial (a military judge sitting alone) and general courts-martial (a military judge and a panel of five service members).

Here, the majority focused on the latter. Even though there has never been a jury in military law, there is a panel. A panel is akin to a jury; it is a trier of fact, leaving legal issues to the military judge. Like a civilian jury, its verdict must be unanimous,[23] and it is the judge who imposes the sentence.

Yet, a panel is different from a jury. There are 12 individuals in a jury as opposed to five in a panel. Jurors are drawn from the society at large; panel members are selected from the forces – a specific society. A jury has but one criterion: citizenship. In a panel, the rank of the panel members would vary depending on the rank of the accused. Lastly, panel members can rely on their general knowledge of the service (such as common mili-

---

[21] Part III of the NDA, note 4.

[22] Army Act, 1881 (UK) 44 & 45 Vict, c 5, s 41; Naval Discipline Act, 1866 (UK) 29 & 30 Vict, c 109, s 45.

[23] That this has only been the case since 2008 following *Bill* C-60, note 21, triggered by *Trépanier*, note 16.

tary terminology, traditions, operating procedures), while jurors are permitted to rely upon their general knowledge.[24]

The specific essence of the panel is mixed: a) to try a service member by someone who can understand the military context; b) to try anywhere the CAF is located in the world. It would be more difficult to achieve these objectives with a jury.

Meaning of 'An Offence Under Military Law'

Context of the Inclusion in the *Charter*

In 1950, Canadian military law was described by the Minister of National Defence as:

> The law which governs the members of the army and regulates the conduct of officers and soldiers as such, in peace and war, at home and abroad.[25]

From that time until today, it has defined 'service offences' as including civil offences. This broad definition has been (and is still) reflected in the Criminal Code.[26] In light of a previous Court's analysis,[27] ordinary civil offences are part of military law in the same way that mutiny or insubordination are service offences.

When the *Charter* was enacted, it was understood by the Minister of Justice that military law has never allowed for jury trials. For the Court, it is 'doubtful' that the military exception was created to change anything. But two interpretations have since developed.

Interpretation 1: 'Offence(s) Under Military Law' are 'Purely Military Offences'

Accused persons claim that only offences setting 'special standards of military discipline'[28] are covered by the military exception. They invoke

---

[24] Military Rules of Evidence, CRC, c 1049, s 16(2)(a).

[25] House of Commons, Minutes of Proceedings and Evidence of the Special Committee on Bill 133: An Act Respecting National Defence, No 1, 2nd Sess., 21st Parl., May 23, 1950, at pp. 11-12 (Brooke Claxton).

[26] *Criminal Code*, RSC 1985, c N-46, s 2: "military law includes all laws, regulations or orders relating to the Canadian Forces".

[27] *MacKay v. The Queen*, 1980 CanLII 217 (SCC), [1980] 2 SCR 370.

[28] NDA, note 4, ss. 73-129.

the Mutiny Act (1689)[29] to support their argument, as the right to a jury trial was allowed for service members in that, in a very limited situation.

The Court dismissed that interpretation for three reasons. First, it is clear that an ordinary civil offence is a service offence, like any 'purely' military offence. The fact that ordinary civil offences are made service offences by way of simply incorporating offences from the Criminal Code or any other act does not change that equal status. Secondly, if the intent was to limit the military exception to 'purely' military offences, the wording of the section of the *Charter* would have been different. Lastly, Mutiny Act (1689) is not useful here. Military law and the society in which it is set has changed a lot since.

Interpretation 2: 'Offence(s) Under Military Law' involve a 'Military Nexus'

Another interpretation is that the expression requires a link with the military. The accused's military status would not suffice in itself. This doctrine (called the 'military nexus' doctrine in Canada, or 'service connection' in other jurisdictions) has its origins in the 1969 United States case, *O'Callahan v. Parker*.[30] The US Supreme Court decided that to try an offence allegedly committed by a service member, the circumstances surrounding it must be connected to the service.[31] But that decision was later reversed in another US case, *Solorio v. United States*, where the doctrine was abandoned.[32]

In that window (1969-1987), the doctrine was imported to Canadian military law and had an evolution of its own,[33] but it was eliminated in the 2015 decision, *R v. Moriarity*, concluding that the only link required is the accused's military status.[34] Applying that analysis with nuances to

---

[29] An Act for punishing Officers or Soldiers who shall Mutiny or Desert Their Majestyes Service (Eng.) 1689, 1 Will. 3 & Mar. 2, c. 5.

[30] (1969), 395 US 258.

[31] *Id*, 272.

[32] (1987), 483 US 435.

[33] *MacKay*, note 29, 410; *R v. MacDonald* (1983), 1983 CanLII 3128 (CMAC), 4 CMAR 277; *Ionson v. The Queen* (1987), 4 CMAR 433; *Ryan v. The Queen* (1987), 4 CMAR 563; *R v. Brown* (1995), 5 C.M.A.R. 280; *R v. Moriarity*, 2014 CMAC 1, 455 NR 59; *R v. Larouche*, 2014 CMAC 6, 460 NR 248.

[34] *R v. Moriarity*, 2015 SCC 55, [2015] 3 SCR 485, paras 48-49; 51-54. See also Pascal Lévesque, *Moriarity: Military Justice Now Based on Status, Not Nexus: Wider Issues Remain*, (February 2016) 24(2) *Criminal Reports* (7th series) 377-84.

the present case, the majority sees no need to revive the matter. It would invite litigation; courts-martial would have to enquire each time if there were a sufficient link between the offence and the military.

Additionally, sending all serious civil offences to civilian authorities runs the risk of having civilian decisions that are lenient from a military perspective. Maintaining military discipline, efficiency, and morale sometimes requires a more severe punishment than what civilian justice would have imposed.[35] Although these distinct systems share some sentencing objectives, military justice is concerned with the promotion of operational effectiveness and promoting a habit of obedience to lawful commands and orders. If a matter is tried before a civil court of criminal jurisdiction, the civilian judge may not consider those objectives.

Furthermore, systematically sending serious civil offences into the ordinary criminal justice system, partially suffering from backlogs, could increase the delay. So, it would take longer to restore discipline, efficiency, and morale. Plus, it would send the message that military justice cannot deal with those matters, hence having a negative impact on morale. Thus, the majority sees no benefit from restoring the 'military nexus doctrine'.

'An Offence Under Military Law' is one that is validly enacted under Section 91(7) of the Constitution Act, 1867

For the majority, 'an offence under military law' is simply an offence created by the Parliament according to its power given by the Constitution.[36] The accused persons argued that when the Parliament defines what 'an offence under military law' is, it varies the military exception, hence defining the scope of a constitutional right through ordinary legislation. However, this argument failed, as the Parliament's power to define military offences is not without limits. The Court had already decided that section 130(1)(a) was within the Parliament's powers[37] and that it was not overbroad.[38] It is, therefore, not inconsistent with the *Charter*. It does not negate the trial by jury to someone who is entitled to it.

---

[35] This view of the majority is not shared by some critics who believe that, on sexual assault, military justice is not as effective as its civilian counterpart, see Elaine Craig, *An Examination of How the Canadian Military's Legal System Responds to Sexual Assault* (2020) 43:1 Dal LJ 63.

[36] Constitution Act, 1867 (UK), 30 & 31 Victoria, section 91(7).

[37] *Mackay*, note 27, 397.

[38] *Moriarity*, note 34, generally.

Analysis — Dissent

Justices Karakatsanis and Rowe disagreed. For them, the practical effect of section 130(1)(a) is to remove from civilian courts the trial of those offences where normally the accused would have the right to trial by jury. The right is to be interpreted together with the exception, not focusing on the exception in order to diminish the right. And that exception should be interpreted restrictively; generally speaking, the *Charter* guarantees the right to a jury trial to *any* accused.

Although acknowledging the ratio in *Moriarity*, the Dissent concluded it does not resolve the issue under section 11(f) of the *Charter*. The judgment was limited to determining if the provision was overbroad regarding the general protection of section 7 of the *Charter*[39], not necessarily to one of the nine more specific guarantees applicable to any accused.[40] The Court in *Moriarity* expressly stated that its conclusion left open the issue about the right to trial by jury.[41]

They also differed from their colleagues' analysis on three factors. Military panels differ significantly from juries, as the broader society is not eligible to serve on panels. Thus, jury trials should not be refused for service members in circumstances that have no direct link to the military.

It is for courts to define the scope of a *Charter* right. The Parliament cannot limit the exercise of the right through ordinary legislation, and the Courts must not renounce that role by giving too much deference to military justice.[42]

In addition, the minority interpreted the historical evolution of the Code of Service Discipline differently. In their view, military courts have always been limited in their capacity to deal with civil offences, from the beginning in 1689 until now. For example, when the NDA was first enacted in 1950, the Minister of National Defence stated that civil offences

---

[39] *Charter*, note 2, section 7. Everyone has the right to life, liberty and security of the person and the right not to be deprived thereof except in accordance with the principles of fundamental justice.

[40] *Charter*, note 2, section 11 (a) to (i).

[41] *Moriarity*, note 34, para 30.

[42] Justices Rowe and Karatkasanis cite P. T. Collins', *The Civil Courts' Challenge to Military Justice and its impact on the Civil Military Relationship*, in *Military Justice in the Modern Age*, by A. Duxbury and M. Groves, eds (2016), 57, 58.

were made service offences for military justice to deal with those cases 'where the civil court does not act or cannot act' adding that 'the civil authority is always supreme'.[43]

Later, the military connection or nexus test was developed to limit military courts' capacity to deal with 'offences that are military in nature or take place in military circumstances'. In other words, the exercise of jurisdiction by military tribunals over civil offences ought to be the exception, not the rule.

The Dissent agreed that the expression 'offences under military law' does not limit those offences to 'purely military' ones.[44] Yet, they concluded that considering the essence, wording and history of the right to trial by jury and its exception, section 130(1)(a) denies service members that right when facing a serious charge not connected with the military context. It, therefore, infringes the *Charter*. It cannot be justified as a 'reasonable limit' to a right in a 'free and democratic society' because it does not impair the right as little as possible.[45] Besides, removing rights from troops potentially decreases morale, as soldiers may see this as unfair.

To save section 130(1)(a), the Dissent suggests that a military connection test must be read into the provision.[46] It is a better solution than just striking it down. To assist military courts, they proposed the guidance:[47] Was the offence committed 'while the accused was on duty, on military property or using the military property'? If so, the direct link is implicit. But there may be other circumstances.

---

[43] *Stillman*, note 1, para 158 citing House of Commons, *Official Report of Debates of the House of Commons*, vol IV, 2nd Sess, 21st Parl, 1950, 3429.

[44] NDA, note 4, ss 73-129.

[45] *Charter*, note 2, section 1: "*The Canadian Charter of Rights and Freedoms* guarantees the rights and freedoms set out in it subject only to such reasonable limits prescribed by law as can be demonstrably justified in a free and democratic society."

[46] NDA, note 4, section 130 (1) An act or omission committed by a service member that is military in nature or is committed in circumstances directly connected to the military (a) that takes place in Canada and is punishable under Part VII, the *Criminal Code* or any other Act of Parliament, [...] is an offence under this Division and every person convicted thereof is liable to suffer punishment as provided in subsections (2). [Underlined in the text].

[47] *Stillman*, note 1, paras 177-182.

Conclusion

Stillman has arguably now become the principal landmark decision in Canadian military justice, displacing *Généreux*. Generally speaking, this decision is an affirmation of the incremental approach adopted in 1998 and continues thereafter regarding military justice reform. In short, unless significant changes are recommended by independent reviews or imposed by courts, military justice should mainly 'stay the course' and limit changes to what is required.[48]

As to the right to trial by jury, the majority of the Court did not intervene, essentially because they believe military justice now offers something quite similar, yet distinct, from ordinary criminal justice. However, it is no invitation for military justice to sit on its laurels. The Dissent from two judges is stark. Had no evolution been perceived from the Court, the result might have been different.

The legal consequence of *Stillman,* together with *Moriarity,* is that military justice can deal with all ordinary offences, including serious ones that would otherwise give rise to the right to a jury trial. This applies not only to Criminal Code offences but also to those of *any* other federal statute. If the accused is subject to the Code of Service Discipline at the time of the alleged offence, the jurisdiction can be exercised. It falls upon military prosecution – which voluntarily applies a service connection test in practice – to exercise discretion. *Stillman* does not appear to fetter that discretion. In dismissing one interpretation of 'Offence Under Military Law', the Court opened a door by stating that its analysis leaves open potential legal challenges.[49] The composition of military panels and their independence from the chain of command could be examined in light of the right of a fair trial.[50]

Would their status as service members impair the right of an accused to be tried by a fair and independent tribunal? As service members, panel members are subject to decision-making by the chain of command regarding performance evaluation and selection for advancement and pro-

[48] For example, when a change in ordinary criminal law would, by way of consequence, logically affect military law.

[49] *Stillman,* note 1, para 86.

[50] *Charter,* note 2, section 11(*d*).

motion. Does that factor undermine the impartiality of the panel members? Are current measures sufficient to protect the role and independence of panel members as triers of fact? Are five individuals sufficient to decide a verdict with a reasonable chance of avoiding errors? If the accused is a civilian contractor, DND employee or military spouse or dependant – who, as a 'result of accompanying the force', is subject to the Code of Service Discipline – does this distinction in status alter the application of the *Charter* and the *CSD?*

It would be interesting to see if any review, challenge, or change is initiated in Canada or elsewhere as a result of that door opened by the Court in *Stillman.*

Dr **Pascal Lévesque**, LL.B. (Laval), MA (Laval), LLM (Ottawa), PhD (Queen's), Post-Graduate Diploma in Education (Montreal), has practised mostly in criminal and military law. He served for 15 years in the Canadian Armed Forces as a legal officer. During his military career, he has successively served as unit legal advisor, defence counsel, military justice policy development advisor and teacher of the law of armed conflict at the Royal Military College of Canada. His master's degree thesis is on the celerity of the court-martial system. He's the author of *Frontline Justice: The Evolution and Reform of Summary Trials in the Canadian Armed Forces* (Montreal: McGill-Queen's University Press, 2020).

After his military career, he has been a prosecutor, an ombudsman, and a university legal advisor. He was the Chair of the Advisory Committee on Criminal Law of the Bar of Quebec (2017-2020). In that capacity, he reviewed numerous legislative initiatives and appeared before parliamentary committees a number of times. Dr Lévesque has also appeared before all levels of the judiciary, including the Court Martial Appeal Court and the Supreme Court of Canada. He currently works in parliamentary ethics. He is also a volunteer at Éducaloi, a charitable organization dedicated to explaining the law to the public.

The views expressed are his own.

Reinstating Rights and Curtailing Summary Courts Martial by the Supreme Court of India

K Parameshwar and A Sregurupriya

Vishav Priya Singh, India

Introduction

The Indian Army grew from an organisation of guards employed by the East India Company to a significant force of the British colonial government, consisting both of European and Indian troops, organised as three separate armies for each presidency and was finally amalgamated into one unified body in 1895.[1] However, this transition was riddled with resistance and revolts from within the forces due to the discriminatory treatment meted out by the higher-ranked British officers to the lower ranked 'Indians'.[2] The Revolt of 1857[3] is one of the more prominent incidents which sparked a slew of legislative changes to control and discipline the military forces and gave birth to the Indian military justice system. Pursuant to this, the colonial government introduced the Army Act

---

[1] 169th Report of the Law Commission of India on Amendment of Army, Navy and Air Force Acts, 1999.

[2] Persons belonging to various regions of the Indian subcontinent.

[3] This refers to the incident wherein *sepoys* in the military revolted against the British officers due to the introduction of Enfield rifles, cartridges of which were rumoured to have cow and pig fat which went against the religious sentiments of the sepoys, amongst other reasons. It has been called *Sepoy* Mutiny by British historians and the First War of Independence by Indian nationalist historians. It has now settled somewhat as The Revolt of 1857.

of 1911. This was subsequently replaced by the Army Act of 1950, a few months after the Constitution of India came into effect.

The framers of the Constitution chose to make special allowances to the existing body of military law. Article 33[4] of the Constitution places the citizens working in the Armed Forces on a different, and arguably more vulnerable, footing than that of civilian citizens. It is an exception to the universal applicability of fundamental rights to all citizens and confers upon the Parliament the power to abrogate their fundamental rights by way of any legislation for the purpose of 'proper discharge of duties' and for the 'maintenance of discipline'[5] which is seen as the force that binds the Armed Forces into a cohesive unit.[6]

Until the late 1980s, the Supreme Court, having recognised the additional aspect of national security,[7] largely adopted a deferential attitude to the wisdom of the Parliament in matters concerning the Armed Forces.[8] Although Article 33 by itself does not restrict any rights and requires the enactment of specific legislation to do so, the Court refrained from interfering in allegations of fundamental rights violations in the Armed Forces.[9] Instead, the Court interpreted Article 33 in an expansive

---

[4] Article 33: 'Power of Parliament to modify the rights conferred by this Part in their application to Forces, etc. Parliament may, by law, determine to what extent any of the rights conferred by this Part shall, in their application to, –
(a) the members of the Armed Forces; or
(b) the members of the Forces charged with the maintenance of public order; or
(c) persons employed in any bureau or other organisation established by the State for purposes of intelligence or counterintelligence; or
(d) persons employed in, or in connection with, the telecommunication systems set up for the purposes of any Force, bureau or organisation referred to in clauses (a) to (c), be restricted or abrogated so as to ensure the proper discharge of their duties and the maintenance of discipline among them.'
The Indian Navy Discipline Act (1934), and the Indian Air Force Act (1932) were also subsequently introduced but are beyond the scope of the present paper. For more information on the origin of Indian military law, see Manual of Military Law; 169th Report of the Law Commission of India on Amendment of Army, Navy and Air Force Acts, 1999.
This article was amended by the Constitution (Fiftieth Amendment) Act, 1984 to include persons working in forces charged with the maintenance of law and order and intelligence services. This amendment was upheld by the Supreme Court in the case of *Intelligence Bureau Employees' Association And Others v. Union Of India*, (1997) 11 SCC 348.

[5] Article 33, Constitution of India, 1950.

[6] Para 19, *Union of India v. Vishav Priya Singh*, (2016) 8 SCC 641.

[7] *Prithi Pal Singh Bedi v. Union of India*, (1982) 3 SCC 140 at Para 44.

[8] *Ram Sarup v. Union of India*, AIR 1965 SC 247.

[9] *Ibid.*

manner. It opined that the law abrogating the fundamental rights of those in the Armed Forces does not require any specific reference to Article 33.[10] Further, the Parliament need not specify the right sought to be abrogated, let alone detail the extent of curtailment.[11]

As per the Army Act of 1950, which was enacted by the Parliament, quasi-judicial tribunals known as courts-martial have been established to adjudicate upon offences committed by persons employed in the Armed Forces.[12] Until the establishment of the Armed Forces Tribunal in 2009,[13] no appeal was permissible against the decision of the court-martial.[14] The proceedings of courts-martial are still, to a great degree, excluded from the purview of judicial review so far as enforcement of fundamental rights is concerned.[15] However, writs for 'any other purpose' can still be issued by the High Court.[16] Courts-martial are considered to be proceedings that are *sui generis* in nature.[17] The procedure followed by them need not comply with the requirements of Article 21[18] so long as it is in accordance with the provisions of the Army Act. Courts-martial have even been arguably exempted from adhering to the principles of natural justice,[19] and this non-adherence is almost characteristic of one of the four types of courts-martial[20] – the summary court-martial (SCM).

Summary courts-martial (SCsM) were first introduced in 1869. They were intended to enable prompt and swift punishment against *sepoys* in the aftermath of the Revolt of 1857.[21] Consequently, they were

---

[10] *Ibid.*

[11] *R Viswam v. Union of India*, (1983) 3 SCC 401.

[12] Section 59, Army Act, 1950.

[13] Section 15, Armed Forced Tribunal Act, 2007.

[14] Article 136(2) and Article 227(4), Constitution of India, 1950.

[15] Article 33, Constitution of India, 1950.

[16] Article 226, Constitution of India, 1950.

[17] *M/S Kranti Associates Pvt. Ltd. & Anr v. Masood Ahmed Khan*, (2010) 9 SCC 496.

[18] Article 21 of the Constitution of India guarantees the right to life and personal liberty and has been expansively interpreted over the years to recognise several facets to this right and include several rights, including the right to counsel, fair representation and other criminal procedural rights, within its ambit.

[19] *S.N. Mukherjee v. Union of India*, 1990 (4) SCC 564. It was held that no speaking order was required to be pronounced by courts-martial.

[20] Section 108, Army Act, 1950. There are four kinds of courts-martial: (a) general courts-martial;(b) district courts-martial;(c) summary general courts-martial; and (d) summary courts-martial.

[21] Para 20, *Ex. LNk. Vishav Priya Singh v. Union of India*, 2008 SCCOnLine Del 95.

applicable only to the lower-ranked 'native army', and their discipline was seen to greatly depend upon the routine use of the SCM.[22] Unfortunately, this colonial reasoning continues to exist today,[23] as does the distinction between officers and 'persons below the rank of officers' for the purpose of maintenance of discipline. This arguably violates both Article 14, which guarantees the right to equality before the law, and Article 21 of the Constitution, which includes the facet of access to justice. As it stands today, an SCM cannot be convened against accused who are officers, junior commissioned officers or warrant officers.[24]

Unlike other courts-martial, where the composition consists of at least three officers,[25] it is the commanding officer (CO) alone who constitutes the court in an SCM.[26] Before constituting an SCM, the CO is required to hear the charges against the accused in his presence. The accused has the liberty to cross-examine witnesses and make statements in his defence.[27] Pursuant to this, the CO is required to dispose of the charges by imposing the statutorily prescribed penalties[28] or refer the case to a superior military authority or, depending on the rank of the accused, order trial within a reasonable time frame. Two other officers or junior commissioned officers are required to attend the proceedings of the SCM throughout, but they are not to be sworn or affirmed[29] and effectively have no part to play in the SCM.

In these proceedings of the SCM, which are not open to the public and often last for mere minutes, personnel, as per the interpretation of the military establishment, are not permitted any legal assistance, and no

---

[22] Rule 12, Indian Articles of War (1869): 'The discipline of the native army depends in great measure on the SCM. When a soldier amenable to the Indian Articles of War has committed an offence which is ordinarily tried by SCM, CO, when determining by what court the prisoner to be tried, are to bear in mind that the legislature, in conferring upon them the powers of SCM, intends that they shall exercise these powers.'

[23] Para 447, Regulations for the Army, 1987. The earlier rule has been retained verbatim save for making it applicable to people subject to the Army Act, 1950. Also see U.C. Jha, *Summary Courts Martial Scuttle Fair Trials for Armed Forces, Daily News and Analysis* (December 19, 2017).

[24] Section 120(3), Army Act, 1950.

[25] Sections 113-115, Army Act, 1950.

[26] Article 116, Army Act, 1950.

[27] Rule 22, Army Rules, 1954.

[28] Section 80, Army Act, 1950.

[29] Section 116(2), Army Act, 1950.

rules of evidence are applicable.[30] In other words, the CO performs the functions of both the judge and the prosecutor, the accused is not allowed representation or counsel by a lawyer, and there is no legally trained person to monitor the proceedings. This violates several facets of Article 21 of the Constitution, including the right to legal assistance, the right to a fair trial, and the principles of natural justice.[31] The position on the right to be represented by a counsel in an SCM somewhat stands altered by way of a decision of the Supreme Court in 2018.[32] The proceedings of the SCM need no confirmation but are forwarded to the appropriate authority for review after promulgation.[33] Unfortunately, this *post-facto* review is merely procedural. The appropriate authority may set aside the proceedings or reduce the sentence if the merits of the case warrant such action in their opinion,[34] after which the record of proceedings is preserved for a period of three years.[35] The procedure of SCsM, which do not allow for an independent trial, was intended as a wartime provision. Regular procedures of other forms of courts-martial were seen as hampering the quick dispensation of justice when there was a grave need for immediacy of action.[36]

As per the rules governing the constitution and conduct of a general court-martial (GCM) or a district court-martial (DCM),[37] there are adequate safeguards in place to ensure that no one is a judge in their own cause and that the proceedings are not vitiated by bias. The CO of the accused or a CO belonging to the same corps as that of the accused is specifically disqualified from serving on a GCM or DCM. With respect to a GCM, it is mandated that it be composed of officers of different

---

[30] Para IIIA (12-15), Report of the United Nations High Commissioner of Human Rights, "Summary of the discussions held during the expert consultation on the administration of justice through military tribunals and the role of the integral judicial system in combating human rights violations"(2015); U.C. Jha, *Military Justice in Difficult Circumstances: The South Asian Countries* (2015) 54(2) Military Law and Law of War Review 301.

[31] *Hussainara Khatoon & Ors. (IV) v. Home Secy., State of Bihar,* (1980) 1 SCC 98; *Maneka Gandhi v. Union of India,* 1978 SCC (1) 248.

[32] *Jaswant Singh v. Union of India* (2019) 2 SCC 360.

[33] Rule 133, Army Rules, 1954.

[34] Section 162, Army Act, 1950.

[35] Rule 146(2), Army Rules, 1954.

[36] MoD Report of Committee of Experts on Review of Service & Pension Matters Including Potential Disputes, Minimising Litigation and Strengthening Institutional Mechanisms ..., accessible at https://www.mod.gov.in/others/measures-reducing-litigation-and-public-grievances

[37] Rules 39-40, Army Rules, 1954.

corps or departments.[38] Additionally, the accused has the right to challenge his trial by the members of the GCM, DCM or summary general court-martial (SGCM).[39] It is also crucial to note that the validity of the finding and sentence prescribed by the GCM, DCM and SGCM is subject to confirmation by the appropriate authority.[40]

None of the aforementioned safeguards exists with respect to an SCM. In an SCM, the CO has been conferred drastically wide powers. He can adjudicate upon all offences arising from the Act[41] with certain limitations on the sentence that can be awarded.[42] A strictly textual reading of the Act reveals that there is no express statutory fetter on the powers of the CO to institute and conduct an SCM. The only requirement is a demonstration of grave reason for immediate action if no reference has been made to the appropriate authority in cases of more serious offences.[43] In several cases, COs have presided over cases where the alleged offence was committed against him or under his supervision. This routine denial of procedural rights and the excessive punishments prescribed by the SCM have severely infringed upon the fundamental rights of those in the Armed Forces and drawn much criticism.

Changing Role of Supreme Court in Military Law

Indeed, it has been long lamented by the Supreme Court that persons in the Armed Forces, too, are citizens who ought to be permitted to cherish their right to personal liberty and adequate procedural safeguards under the Constitution and that the Parliament ought to take effective steps towards that direction.[44] The Law Commission, too, concurred that there was a need to balance the need for discipline with the concepts of justice to, and dignity of, those serving the country.[45] However, there have been

---

[38] Rule 40, Army Rules, 1954.

[39] Section 130, Army Act, 1950.

[40] Section 153, Army Act, 1950.

[41] Section 120(1), Army Act, 1950.

[42] Section 120(4)(5), Army Act, 1950.

[43] Section 120(2), Army Act, 1950.

[44] *Prithi Pal Singh Bedi v. Union of India*, (1982) 3 SCC 140; *Union of India v. Charanjit S Gill*, (2000) 5 SCC 742.

[45] 169th Report of the Law Commission of India on Amendment of Army, Navy and Air Force Acts (1999).

no statutory changes effected with respect to SCsM and their conduct of proceedings. This has prompted the Court to step into its role as the protector of the fundamental rights of those in the Armed Forces and also sparked a significant shift in administrative law beyond the pale of military law.

The decision in the case of *Ranjit Thakur v. Union of India*[46] marks one of the earliest attempts of the Supreme Court to uphold the rights of the citizens in the Armed Forces. This was despite the restrictive contours of Article 33 which had arguably been tightened by the Court itself in the preceding years. The decision in the *Ranjit Thakur* case is remarkable for reasons more than one. In this case, the accused had not commended himself well to the CO of the regiment and had been subjected to a sentence of 28 days rigorous imprisonment for making representations to higher officers. While serving this sentence, he disobeyed the command to eat the food that was given. The CO convened an SCM the very next day, and, pursuant to the accused pleading guilty, a sentence of one year of rigorous imprisonment was imposed. This was challenged before the Court on several grounds, including the argument that the SCM was vitiated by bias.

Interestingly, the Court opined that given the wide powers and severity of the consequences of an SCM, the procedural safeguards contemplated in the Army Act ought to be liberally constructed.[47] Thus, the Court drew upon the scheme of the Army Act itself to go beyond a strict textualist approach and to expand the scope of fundamental rights that remained unabrogated by the Army Act, and hence, available to the accused persons. Following this line of reasoning, the Court held that Section 130, which conferred the right of the accused to challenge his trial by the members of the court-martial, extended to SCsM despite SCsM being expressly excluded from the provision. Consequently, non-compliance with Section 130 would vitiate proceedings of SCsM as well.[48] The Court also held that the award of the SCM would be a nullity if there is a reasonable apprehension of bias and minimal requirements of natural justice are not followed.[49] Crucially, the *Ranjit Thakur* case was the first

---

[46] *Ranjit Thakur v. Union of India* (1987) 4 SCC 611.

[47] Para 11, *ibid.*

[48] Para 14, *ibid.*

[49] Para 16, *ibid.*

case in which the doctrine of proportionality was articulated as a facet of judicial review in India. The Court held that the choice and quantum of punishment awarded by the SCM had to be proportionate to the offence and could not be 'shockingly disproportionate'[50] or an 'outrageous defiance of logic.'[51]

While the decision of the Supreme Court in *Ex-Havildar Ratan Singh v. Union of India*[52] did not contain any reference to the *Ranjit Thakur* case, it was contended that there was an implicit evaluation of proportionality to determine whether an SCM ought to have been conducted. In this case, the accused quit his place without orders from the superior officer when fired upon by a group of terrorist militants during an armed operation against them. An SCM was constituted, and he was convicted and sentenced to suffer rigorous imprisonment for a year. The accused, who had pleaded 'not-guilty', contended that the offence he was charged with was incorrect and that he ought to be charged with a more serious offence. The charge of a more serious offence required the CO to make a reference to the appropriate authority since the trial for the same was to ordinarily be conducted by a DCM or SGCM. In the absence of reference, the CO ought to have demonstrated a grave reason for immediate action. The Court opined that no grave reason for immediate action existed so as to justify trial by an SCM.[53] In other words, the urgency and gravity of the circumstances must be proportionate to the harm caused by the lack of procedural safeguards in an SCM. However, the Court refrained from extending this requirement of urgency and gravity to all offences. Instead, it restricted itself to the category of offences for which it was statutorily stipulated that such reason must be demonstrated.

Proportionality: A Military Law Import

This reference to proportionality as a part of judicial review in administrative law was expanded upon in the realm of service law by the Supreme Court in the cases of *Union of India v. G Ganayutham*[54] and *Om Kumar*

[50] Para 27, *ibid.*

[51] Para 25, *ibid.*

[52] *Ex-Havildar Ratan Singh v. Union of India* (1992) Supp (1) SCC 716.

[53] Para 7, *ibid.*

[54] *Union of India v. G. Ganayutham* (1997) 7 SCC 463.

v. Union of India.[55] The Court opined that when fundamental freedoms are affected, the freedom and need for restriction will have to be balanced so that the restriction is not excessive or disproportionate.[56] The Court stated that administrative actions and legislation affecting fundamental rights have always been tested on the 'anvil of proportionality' even if it were not articulated in such terms.[57] The Court further developed the doctrine of proportionality in the case of *Modern Dental College and Research Centre v. State of Madhya Pradesh.*[58] It went to the extent of stating that any limitation imposed on a constitutional right by way of law would be constitutional *only if* it is proportional.[59] In order to determine proportionality, the Court referred to the four-stage Barakian model,[60] wherein the law imposing restrictions must first be evaluated to see if it is meant to achieve a proper purpose and if the measures taken to achieve such a purpose are rationally connected to the purpose, and such measures are necessary. Thereafter, the competing principles involved[61] must be properly balanced, keeping in mind the relevant social values of each competing aspect in the appropriate context.[62] This is to ensure that the restriction on the rights does not disproportionately impact the citizen.

---

[55] *Om Kumar v. Union of India* (2001) 2 SCC 386.

[56] Para 31, *supra,* note 54.

[57] Para 54, *supra,* note 55.

[58] *Modern Dental College and Research Centre v. State of Madhya Pradesh* (2016) 7 SCC 353. Also endorsed by *KS Puttaswamy (Privacy-9J.) v. Union of India,* (2017) 10 SCC 1 at Para 638 (J. Kaul) and *KS Puttaswamy (Aadhaar-5J.) v. Union of India,* (2019) 1 SCC 1.

[59] Para 57-64, *ibid.*

[60] Aharon Barak, *Proportionality: Constitutional Rights and Their Limitation* (Cambridge University Press 2012). The four stages are:
(a) A measure restricting a right must have a legitimate goal (legitimate goal stage);
(b) It must be a suitable means of furthering this goal (suitability or rational connection stage);
(c) There must not be any less restrictive but equally effective alternative (necessity stage);
(d) The measure must not have a disproportionate impact on the right-holder (balancing stage).

[61] Para 62, *supra,* note 58. 'This phenomenon – of both the right and its limitation in the Constitution – exemplifies the inherent tension between democracy's two fundamental elements. On the one hand is the right's element, which constitutes a fundamental component of substantive democracy; on the other hand, is the people element, limiting those very rights through their representatives. These two constitute a fundamental component of the notion of democracy, though this time in its formal aspect.'

[62] *Supra,* note 58.

It is contended that this development of the doctrine of proportionality has, to a certain extent, reflected back positively with respect to judicial review of decisions rendered by courts-martial. In a marked shift from the *Ranjit Thakur* case, where the Court merely undertook a secondary review[63] of the punishment awarded, and the *Ratan Singh* case, where the Court strictly confined itself the text of the statute, the Courts can now undertake a primary review of both the statute and the decision of the courts-martial. This allows the Court to balance the countervailing values of military discipline and fundamental rights while interpreting the provisions of the Army Act itself. In other words, the scope of restrictions imposed by the Army Act on fundamental rights of the Armed Forces must be informed by proportionality, and this cannot be bypassed by virtue of Article 33.

A Positive Change: Proportionality and Constitution of SCsM

Arguably, these precedents paved the way for the much welcome decision of the Supreme Court in *Union of India v. Vishav Priya Singh*.[64] Although the Court did not adopt the four-pronged Barakian model, it implicitly applied the doctrine of proportionality and held that powers of CO to convene, constitute and complete SCM are to be exercised extremely rarely and only when it is absolutely imperative that immediate action is called for. This case involved a batch of matters arising out of decisions rendered by SCsM. One of the issues for consideration was the circumstances under which an SCM could be convened rather than the other forms of court-martial. The High Courts of Delhi and Rajasthan had rendered conflicting decisions on this issue, requiring the law to be settled by the Supreme Court.

The Supreme Court comprehensively considered the relevant provisions of the statute and the subordinate legislation. It undertook a comparative analysis of the different types of courts-martial and noted the relative lack of procedural safeguards in SCsM. The Court noted that

---

[63] Evaluation of administrative decisions on the grounds of perversity or irrationality.

[64] *Union of India v. Vishav Priya Singh* (2016) 8 SCC 641, can be accessed at https://indiankanoon.org/doc/69192244/

despite the restrictions in the Act and Rules thereunder, the power of the CO to constitute the SCM was excessive. It thus effectively conducted a proportionality analysis of the administrative decision to constitute an SCM at the initial stage of hearing the charge. In noting that the power conferred was 'quite drastic', the Court implicitly stated that the necessity for restriction of the fundamental rights of the accused by constituting an SCM did not exist except in the rarest of cases. In requiring the CO to establish that it is 'absolutely imperative that immediate action is called for', the Court conditioned the decision to constitute an SCM with the balancing test. This is a clear departure from the statute, which only requires urgency and gravity to be established when the SCM hears a specified category of serious offences, as noted in the *Ratan Singh* case.

The Supreme Court endorsed the ruling of the High Court of Delhi. The High Court had held that an SCM must be the exception. If the alleged offence or indiscipline was individual in character or had civil law dimensions or any delay was involved, an SCM ought not to be constituted.[65] An SCM is an emergent provision and is to be used only when there are no viable alternatives. Some instances where recourse to a regular procedure is not possible, and there is a need for constituting an SCM, could be when deployed in high altitude and isolated posts or in the frontline during war or travelling towards deployment, including by sea. The Supreme Court enunciated the requirement that the CO must record the reasons for constituting an SCM in writing, and that should be available on record in order to aid judicial forums in considering the merits of the matter on appeal. This was implemented from the date the judgment was rendered.[66]

The Court, in the *Vishav Priya Singh* case, interpreted the intent behind the requirement of reference to a superior authority,[67] provided both in the statute and the subordinate legislation, to be a salutary check on the exercise of the drastic powers conferred upon the CO. Thus, the Court imputed the intent of conditioning the decision to constitute an SCM with proportionality to the Parliament enacted statute itself. While this line of reasoning did help the Court arrive at the conclusion of the

---

[65] Para 25, Ex L Nk *Vishav Priya Singh v. Union of India*, 2008 SCCOnLine Del 95.

[66] Review Petition No 3927 of 2016 (Supreme Court of India).

[67] Provided in both Section 120(2), Army Act, 1950 and Rule 22(3) of the Army Rules, 1954.

exceptionality of SCsM, the balancing it sought to do between the competing principles of rights and military discipline would have been better served by the four-pronged tests of proportionality. According to this, the legitimate goal of constituting an SCM would be the urgent need for immediate discipline. The rational connection would be that an SCM allows the CO to dispense with the procedure that would delay the sanctions imposed, which in turn, would serve as a deterrent and bring back discipline within the unit. The necessity stage would make it clear that less restrictive measures of other court-martials would be equally effective in all but the most extraordinary circumstances. This would help circumscribe the limits within which the balancing test would need to apply where each case would need to be evaluated to see if the need for immediate discipline was so grave as to warrant the constitution of an SCM and hence, squarely settle the issue of when to constitute an SCM.

Proportionality, Principles of Natural Justice, and SCsM

Yet another issue for consideration in the *Vishav Priya Singh* case was whether an SCM could be constituted by a CO of a unit to which the accused did not belong. As noted by the Court in the *Ranjit Thakur* case, there are cases where the accused is tried for offences allegedly committed against the CO constituting the SCM. In such cases, the CO ends up being a judge in his own cause, and this gives rise to the perception of bias and goes against the principles of natural justice. According to the factual matrix of the lead matter in this case, the accused had made a complaint against the prejudicial treatment allegedly meted out to him by the CO of his unit. In order to circumvent the issue of bias, the CO of his unit allegedly manipulated the circumstances so that his close friend and CO of another unit constituted the SCM to investigate the charges against the accused.

It was contended by the accused that the CO of another unit could not constitute an SCM. Indeed, if the necessity of conferring such vast powers upon the CO is to maintain discipline amongst the soldiers of the unit which binds the unit, conferring powers upon the CO of another unit to constitute an SCM would not only be excessive but would not serve the purpose for doing so. Although the High Court of Delhi did not articulate this issue in terms of the rational connection test, it undertook a holistic reading of the Act and concluded that 'there was an abiding and umbilical connection between the CO and his regime'. The absence of this connection would not help achieve the legitimate goal of furthering military discipline. Thus, according to the High Court of Delhi, the conferral of power upon a CO of another unit to constitute an SCM failed at the second stage of proportionality analysis itself. Thus, this power could only be exercised by the CO of his unit, and, in cases where bias is an issue of concern, another form of court-martial ought to be constituted.

However, the Supreme Court adopted a different approach to this issue. It balanced the countervailing factors of the need for urgent resolution in exceptional cases versus the conferral of wide powers upon the CO of another unit, such that it reached the conclusion that the accused could be tried by the CO of another unit. The Court refers to the definition of CO in the subordinate legislation,[68] which, it concluded, is wide enough to include the CO of other units. Further, the Court notes that the expression 'to which the accused belongs' is not mentioned with respect to SCM. The Court does attempt to balance the rights of the accused by mandating that even in cases where the CO could 'be a judge in his own cause', reference to the appropriate authority is made. Further, the Court's holding about the exceptionality of the constitution of SCsM extends to situations where the CO belongs to another unit. This reasoning does not appear to tackle the point regarding the lack of rational connection raised by the High Court of Delhi. Instead, the Court directly jumped into the balancing stage. The four-pronged proportionality analysis could have helped justify the conferral of power upon COs of other units better and also given greater clarity about the situations that would warrant this conferral.

Conclusion

The decision in the *Vishav Priya Singh* case has enabled the Courts to exercise a two-fold judicial review of SCsM – with respect to their constitution and the choice and quantum of punishment awarded. While the doctrine of proportionality has been held to be applicable in all cases

[68] Regulation 9, Defence Service Regulations.

where rights and limitations upon them are involved by way of precedent, the Supreme Court has additionally sourced proportionality from the scheme of the Army Act itself in the *Vishav Priya Singh* case. This allows the Court to safeguard the rights of those in the Armed Forces because of Article 33 and not in spite of it since the restrictions imposed by the parliamentary enactment is itself conditioned by proportionality analysis. This has paved the way for greater intervention at the threshold level, as has been reiterated by the Court in the case of *Randhir Singh v. Union of India.*[69] In this case, the accused allegedly committed an offence in August 2007. However, the SCM took place in May 2008. The Court held that in light of the decision in the *Vishav Priya Singh* case, the ground of delay in the constitution of the SCM alone would suffice to invalidate the decision of constituting an SCM. This is because grave urgency is the only factor proportionate to harm caused by the deprival of procedural safeguards of an SCM.

The provision for SCsM in the Army Act is a colonial relic we have carried into the present day. Despite the fact that SCsM were devised to buttress colonial rule and to suppress the movement for independence, better conditions and more agency for Indians within the ranks of the colonial army, it remains a feature of the military system of independent India. As KG Kannabiran postulated, transformative constitutionalism requires the courts to recognise the political content of liberty while adjudicating upon the restraints imposed on rights, a necessary corollary of the transformation of the individual from a 'subject' to a 'citizen'.[70] The idea of transformative constitutionalism, which has now been judicially endorsed,[71] requires a rethink as to the constitutionality of the continued existence of such blatantly colonial provisions and the extent to which rights can be scuttled or abridged. In fact, it would not be a stretch to say that an express application of the four-pronged proportionality framework, as informed by the concept of transformative constitutionalism, could have led to far-reaching positive conclusions in the *Vishav Priya*

---

[69] *Randhir Singh v. Union of India* (2020) 14 SCC 513.

[70] KG Kannabiran, *The Wages of Impunity: Power, Justice and Human Rights*, 66-68 (2004).

[71] *KS Puttaswamy (Privacy-9J.) v. Union of India*, (2017) 10 SCC 1; *Kalpana Mehta v. Union of India*, (2018) 7 SCC 1; *Navtej Singh Johar v. Union of India*, (2018) 10 SCC 1; *BK Pavitra (II) v. Union of India*, (2019) 16 SCC 129; *Indian Young Lawyers Association v. State of Kerala*, (2019) 11 SCC 1.

Singh case. Perhaps, military law would have once again been the source of a step forward in judicial review by extending proportionality analysis to the circumscription of administrative discretion and pursuit of procedural remedies. Hopefully, the Courts will build upon this and make great strides in checking the unbridled powers of the Parliament under Article 33 in the pursuit of military discipline.

K Parameshwar is an Advocate-on-Record at the Supreme Court of India. He has been appointed as *amicus curiae* to assist the Supreme Court of India in several landmark cases. These include *Indian Young Lawyers Assn. v. State of Kerala* (entry of women into the inner sanctum of the Sabarimala temple), *Mukesh v. State* (Nirbhaya gang-rape case), *TN Godawarman Thirumulpad v. Union of India* (Forest Bench for environmental matters), *All India Judges Association v. Union of India* (pay and emoluments of the subordinate judiciary), *In Re: Deficiencies in Criminal Trials, In Re: Expeditious Trial of Cases Under Section 138 N.I. Act* (cheque bounce cases), to name a few. He was conferred the Mukesh Goswami Memorial Prize for exceptional performance in the Advocate-on-Record examination. He holds a BA, LLB (Hons) degree from the NALSAR (National Academy of Legal Studies and Research) University of Law where he was awarded nine gold medals for overall excellence and outstanding performance in several subjects, including constitutional law.

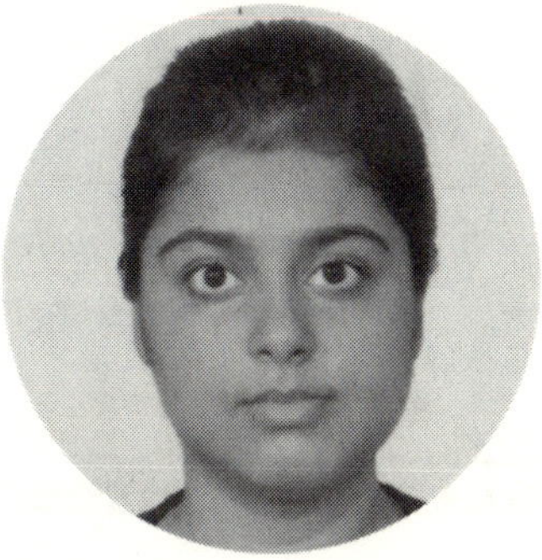

A Sregurupriya is an advocate currently working in the Chambers of K Parameshwar, Advocate-on-Record, Supreme Court of India. She has formerly worked in the Chambers of (Late) Justice MM Shantanagoudar, Supreme Court of India. She holds a BA, LLB (Hons) degree from the National Law School of India University, where she was awarded two gold medals by the Chief Justice of India for exceptional academic excellence. She was selected to represent the Government of India as the Indian Delegate at the International Youth Educational and Cultural Festival held at Siem Reap, Kingdom of Cambodia, which resulted in the Joint Statement on Youth Development. She was also awarded a grant by the Anil Divan Foundation in association with LAWASIA (The Law Association for Asia and the Pacific) for her research on transnational environmental crimes in Asia. She was conferred a scholarship by the Australian Government under the Endeavour Leadership Program for short-term professional development in the field of alternative disputes resolution. She has also served as Deputy Editor-in-Chief and Editor on the Socio-Legal Review and the National Law School of India Review, both of which have been cited by the Supreme Court of India.

Inherently Suspect

Katherine K Stich

Frontiero, United States of America

(Disclaimer: The views presented in this article are those of the author and do not necessarily represent the views of the Department of Defense, the Department of the Army, and the US Army Judge Advocate General's Corps)

In 1970, a newly married young Air Force officer applied for the standard medical, dental, and housing allowance for their spouse as provided by the military. The problem? This airman was a woman.[1]

Regardless of gender, service in the armed forces can be challenging work not only for those in uniform but also for a service member's family. Even in today's telework era, frequent moves still make it difficult for military spouses to secure employment at each duty station readily. Recognizing the challenges servicemembers with families faced, Congress authorized basic allowance for housing in 1949[2] and later medical and dental for service members and their families.[3] Nevertheless, these benefits were not applied, or even equally available, to male and female service members.

Air Force Lieutenant Sharron Frontiero learned this the hard way,

---

[1] Ruth Bader Ginsburg with Mary Hartnett and Wendy W. Williams, *My Own Words* (Simon and Schuster, 2016) 131.

[2] Career Compensation Act of 1949, Pub L NO 81 351, 63 STAT 802, 841 1949.

[3] US Armed Forces, 10 USC 1071. "The purpose of this chapter is to create and maintain high morale in the uniformed services by providing an improved and uniform program of medical and dental care for members and certain former members of those services, and for their dependents."

but fortunately her plight and subsequent fight brought this disparity to the nation's attention and ultimately enabled real change.[4]

Sharron married her husband, Joseph, in 1969 and entered military service after becoming a physical therapist. Like many young families, the allowances available through the Air Force, in addition to her standard pay, would make their new life together much easier. So, Sharron applied for the benefits they believed they were entitled to.

At the time, male servicemembers with dependents automatically received benefits for their spouses and children. This determination was made based on the definition of who was deemed a dependent under the Career Compensation Act of 1949. Female servicemembers, on the other hand, were required to show proof that they contributed 50 percent or more support towards livelihood of their spouses or children in order to receive the benefits. Specifically, the rule explained that 'in the case of female members of the uniformed services, the term 'dependent' shall include a husband, in addition to those persons otherwise defined as dependents in this subsection, but only when such husband, or children, as defined above, are dependent upon the said female member for over half of his or her support.'[5]

Joseph was enrolled in college, but having been in the Navy, he received approximately $205 a month in benefits from his service, and his living expenses were approximately $350.[6] In other words, earning more than three times than he did,[7] Sharron helped support her husband, but her contributions to his livelihood did not exceed 50 percent. She was, therefore, denied.

No rationale was provided as to the reasoning behind the disparity. Perhaps it was assumed that it would be too time-consuming to have men prove their support to their spouse in an era of a nearly all-male force?

---

[4] Ginsburg, Harnet and Williams, *supra* note 1.

[5] Career Compensation Act of 1949, Pub L No 81-351, 63 STAT. 802-841 1949 The term 'dependent' shall include at all times and in all places the lawful wife and unmarried legitimate children, under twenty-one years of age, of any member of the uniformed services, except as hereinafter limited in this subsection....That in the case of female members of the uniformed services, the term 'dependent' shall include a husband in addition to those persons otherwise defined as dependents in this subsection, but only when such husband, or children, as defined above, are in fact dependent upon said female member for over half of his or her support.

[6] *Frontiero v. Laird*, 341 F. Supp. 201 (M.D. Ala. 1972).

[7] *Frontiero v. Richardson* 411 U.S. 677 (1973) (Oral Argument Transcript).

Maybe this was coupled with the belief that most men, even when married to service-women, would find it unlikely to be so dependent on their spouse to meet the definition of a 'dependent?' Regardless, the result was that men could effectively provide little or no support to their spouse and still be entitled to receive the benefit, but female service members would have to prove that they provided half of their husband's support to receive any additional pay.

Lieutenant Frontiero would not accept the Air Force's answer and sought help in fighting this injustice from Attorney Joe Levin, a former US Army Military Intelligence officer and co-founder of the Southern Poverty Law Center.[8] In the spring of 1972, Mr Levin filed suit. He ultimately tried the case alongside his partner, Morris Dees, in the Federal District Court. They argued that the statutes that provided for the benefits but also the disparity[9] were unconstitutional. In short, they explained that these rules resulted in discrimination based on sex, and therefore, violated the Fifth Amendment, given the different treatment for male and female service members. Mr Levin and the Frontiero family lost the case at in District Court.

In its findings, the court sidestepped the real issue of gender discrimination, ruling that because men and women both had to prove they financed over 50 percent of an adult, child, or parents[10] to receive benefits for non-spouses, the rule was not based solely on sex, and therefore not discriminatory.[11] The court also provided in a footnote:

> We have concluded that Congress chose to employ a presumption of dependency in certain instances for reasons of administrative and economic convenience.[12]

Shocked but undeterred by the loss, Lieutenant Frontiero and Mr Levin were able to bypass the standard next stop at the Federal Court of Appeals as the issue at hand was the constitutionality of Federal Statutes. Therefore, they properly filed an appeal directly from the US District

---

[8] Board of Directors, Southern Poverty Law Center, Joseph J. Levin Jr. See https://www.splcenter.org/about/board-member/joseph-j-levin-jr

[9] 37 U.S.C. §§ 401, 403, Pay and Allowances of the Uniformed Forces, Definitions and 10 U.S.C. §§ 1072, 1076 Armed Forces, Definitions.

[10] *Frontiero supra*, note 6 at 207.

[11] *Ibid.*

[12] *Frontiero, supra* note 6 at footnote 1.

Court for the Middle District of Alabama to the Supreme Court of the United States, and certiorari was granted.

As they navigated their case forward, the American Civil Liberties Union (ACLU) was separately but simultaneously building the Women's Rights Project; a branch specifically to fight for gender equality. Leading the project was none other than Ms Ruth Bader Ginsburg,[13] who was, at the time, a professor and a civil rights lawyer who already had related experience both as a military spouse and having recently argued another landmark gender discrimination case, *Reed v. Reed.*[14]

Undoubtedly, she knew first-hand the challenges that come with military life and discrimination based on sex. Newly married, a younger Ruth Bader Ginsburg followed her husband to Fort Sill, Oklahoma where she worked in neighboring Lawton as a Claims Examiner for the Social Security Administration while her husband served in the Army.[15] It was in that role the eventual Supreme Court Justice was demoted – simply for being pregnant.[16] She felt not only the challenges of military life as a spouse but also of gender discrimination first-hand in the 1950s. With that experience she would fight for equality for the rest of her life. This time it would be in representation of a Service Member, Lieutenant Frontiero.

Mr Levin recognized the potential benefit of such expert assistance from the ACLU – an organization whose interests aligned with theirs. The two sets of counsel reportedly did not entirely agree on how to tackle and best present the case,[17] but ultimately, Mr Levin's team split the argument. Ms Ginsburg, and the ACLU filed its amicus brief as a 'friend of the court.'[18]

On 17 January 1973, oral arguments were heard, with possibly the

[13] Anna Claire Vollers "All Right to be a Hero: Meet the woman whose landmark case was the first Ruth Bader Ginsburg argued at the Supreme Court" Reckon, https://reckonsouth.com/all-right-to-be-a-hero-meet-the-woman-whose-landmark-case-was-the-first-ruth-bader-ginsburg-argued-at-the-supreme-court/ 20 September 2020.

[14] *Reed v. Reed*, 404 U.S. 71 (1971).

[15] Margaret Carlson "Ruth Bader Ginsburg Has Died. She Leaves Behind a Vital Legacy for Women — and Men" Time 24 September 2020 https://time.com/5660188/ruth-bader-ginsburg-dies/

[16] *Ibid.*

[17] Vollers, *supra* note 13.

[18] Ginsburg , Harnet and Williams, *supra* note 1 at 132.

best of both worlds. The Court heard from Mr Levin that an intermediate test would show the statutes violated the Fifth Amendment and resulted in substantive discrimination to the Frontiero family. They argued that the government's mere administrative convenience did not allow them to continue their disparate treatment of female service members.

The Court also heard the theory advanced by Ms Ginsburg that sex discrimination should be treated using the same strict scrutiny standard of review as racial, alienage, and national origin discrimination.[19] In other words, sex should be viewed as inherently suspect[20] for equal protection and due process. She explained, that like race, sex has no bearing on ability, and such repeated gender distinctions keep women in a place inferior to men. Therefore, a stricter standard of review should be applied by the Court.

Mr Samuel Huntington argued for the government and posited a rational basis to maintain the statutes as they existed under the then-current standard. He used statistics to highlight dual-military spouses were not entitled to benefits and that most female service members were married to other service members. Therefore, the only women treated differently are those married to civilians. He argued that because this number is so low, and the number of wives dependent on their service member husbands is so great, the administrative burden is appropriately placed on the female service members. Mr Huntington explained that because men statistically support their wives and rarely make less than their spouses, there is a rational basis for the statutes as they were written. In other words, these statutes reflected real differences between the genders.[21]

Fortunately, the Supreme Court found that history repeatedly discriminated against women, and this case was no different. Since gender does not bear on societal contributions, statutes should not create arbitrary sex-based distinctions. Even if some administrative burden was relieved by the statutes, in the *Frontiero* decision, the Court reminded us that the Constitution recognizes higher values than speed and efficiency.[22] Therefore, the statutes in question were inherently suspect; they

---

[19] *Frontiero, supra* note 7 (Oral argument transcript).

[20] *Frontiero, supra* note 7 (Amicus oral argument).

[21] *Frontiero, supra* note 7 (Mr. Huntington oral argument).

[22] *Frontiero, supra* note 7 at 677 (1973) citing *Stanley v. Illinois*, 405 U.S. 645, 656, 92 S.Ct. 1208, 1215, 31 L.Ed.2d 551 (1972).

were statutory classifications based on sex, discriminatory, and violated the Due Process Clause of the Fifth Amendment.[23]

While all this may seem merely history, it is worth reminding ourselves how culture can evolve and how quickly laws can be adjusted when injustice is raised, discovered, discussed, and contemplated. Looking back to 1973, it was a distinct year of change in United States history for so many reasons. We saw everything from the withdrawal of troops from Vietnam, the Watergate proceedings, and the Battle of the Sexes Tennis Match. While perhaps eclipsed by other changes, there is no doubt this case lifted discrimination and helped gain the traction that women, and specifically female service members, needed at the time.

While it took generations for women to serve without restriction in the United States military fully, this was arguably the first punch that landed on the female troops' glass ceiling. Over twenty years later, the *Frontiero* decision was followed by another, delivered by Supreme Court Justice Ginsburg, finding Virginia Military Institute's exclusion of all female students unconstitutional.[24] Almost twenty more years, the prohibition of women serving in combat arms roles was finally lifted in 2015, with the first females graduating from the US Army Ranger School.[25]

After a lifetime of service and a battle with pancreatic cancer, Supreme Court Justice Ruth Bader Ginsburg passed away in 2020. She was laid to rest at Arlington National Cemetery, alongside her husband. Perhaps appropriately, and in a full circle, Captain Shaye Haver, an Infantry Company Commander in the prestigious 'Old Guard' and one of the very first women to earn the coveted United States Army Ranger Tab, led the late Justice Ruth Bader Ginsburg's funeral procession.[26] In so many ways, Justice Ginsburg and the *Frontiero* decision paved the path for so many future leaders. She almost certainly would have been proud.

---

[23] *Frontiero, supra* note 7 at. 677, 682.

[24] *United States v. Virginia* et al. 518 U.S. 515 (94-1941) (1996).

[25] David Choi "First Woman Ranger on Ruth Bader Ginsburg Funeral" Business Insider, https://www.businessinsider.in/politics/world/news/it-was-an-honor-us-army-soldier-one-of-the-first-women-to-earn-ranger-tab-on-leading-ruth-bader-ginsburgs-lying-in-state-ceremony/articleshow/78562269.cms

[26] *Ibid.*

Colonel **Katherine Krul Stich** is an officer of the Judge Advocate General's Corps of the US Army. She is a graduate of St Bonaventure University and the University of South Carolina School of Law. She is a proud army wife, mother, sister, daughter, and soldier.

Women as Permanent Officers – Uncomplicated Logic, Impediments Galore

Aishwarya Bhati

Babita Puniya, India

The journey for equal opportunity of permanent commission (PC) for women officers of the Indian Army has been long and arduous. A large part of this battle has been fought and won before the constitutional courts of India. However, the success is unmistakably attributable only to the sheer grit, thorough professionalism, and proven track record of courage under fire of hundreds of extremely intrepid and valorous women officers of the Indian Army in service of the nation. It also makes for a fascinating case study for every law student.

Women were inducted into the Indian Army under the Women Special Entry Scheme (Officers) from 1992 onwards, on an experimental basis, initially for five years. After that, their tenure was extended from time to time, up to 14 years of service, and they were made eligible for varied branches and streams of the Army, in more and more numbers, over time. The experiment was working, and women officers proved their mettle as professional soldiers and equal stakeholders in the nation's service. However, the consideration for the grant of PC, at par with male short service commissioned (SSC) officers, eluded them.

In 2003, a Public Interest Litigation was filed by Babita Puniya, a lawyer, before the Delhi High Court for grant of PC to Short Service Commissioned Women Officers (SSCWOs) of the Indian Army. Some other petitions came to be filed by the affected women officers. They were all heard together and decided by a judgment dated 12 March 2010 of the Division Bench of the Delhi High Court titled *Babita Puniya v. Secretary and Another*.[1] The High Court, in emphatic words, held that the SSCWOs were entitled to be considered for PC on a par with SSC Gentlemen Officers with all consequential benefits. The High Court's judgment also dealt with the grant of PC to a category of then serving women officers of the Indian Air Force who had not been given the option of PC. Though the issues of women officers of the Indian Air Force and Indian Navy are not being discussed in this commentary, it is interesting to note anecdotally that the Air Force and Navy had decided to grant PC to SSCWOs between 2006 and 2008, albeit prospectively, excluding the women officers who had been inducted hitherto. The Army had also decided to grant PC prospectively to SSCWOs in two branches, i.e., Judge Advocate General and Army Education Corps. The rationale of the judgment of the High Court was that in the branches and streams that the defence forces had themselves considered women to be fit for grant of short service commission for 14 years, they had to be given the right of consideration for PC. The logic was uncomplicated – if they were good to serve for 14 years, they were good enough to serve for 20 years and more.[2]

A batch of appeals was filed by the Union of India in 2011, before the Supreme Court of India against the Delhi High Court's judgment dated 12 March 2010. In the preliminary hearings, notice was issued only after the Union assured the top court that it had decided to constitute a high-powered committee to consider the questions pertaining to grant of PC to SSCWOs and for them to be considered by the highest level in the Government. It also added that in the meanwhile, they would not release from service the women officers who had completed their term of 14 years of service.

Another important interim order was passed by the Supreme Court on 2 September 2011 when the Court stayed the contempt proceedings

---

[1] *Babita Puniya v. Secretary and Another* WP (C) No 1597 of 2003 (High Court of Delhi), can be accessed at https://www.casemine .com/judgement/in/56090d17e4b0149711178d98

[2] Under Short Service Commission, an officer can only serve for a maximum of fourteen years. However, under Permanent Commission, an officer has the right to serve as a career army officer till the age of superannuation. Twenty years is the minimum qualifying service required to earn a pension, which can only be attained under permanent commission.

that the original writ petitioners had initiated for non-compliance of the High Court judgment. However, it specifically directed that the operation of the impugned judgment had not been stayed at all. The appeals were pending for the final hearing and adjudication by the Supreme Court for almost a decade, delayed by the chronic and infamous backlog of cases across all tiers of the Indian judiciary (a problem of mammoth proportions that we, as a country, have been struggling with for over six decades), complicated with the fact that successive governments were dragging their feet in the name of taking well-considered policy decisions and requesting the Supreme Court not to hear the matter for final adjudication every time it was to be taken up for arguments.

Women officers continued to serve as SSCWOs, but with compromised seniority, promotions, honour, opportunities, pay and perks – everything that is sacred or important for a soldier. History has shown time and again how journeys of women, in hitherto male bastions, is fraught with insurmountable hardships and unparalleled adversity. These women that we are talking about are brave women who unflinchingly tread that path with nothing but sheer grit and determination. They define the path for hundreds, thousands and millions to follow suit till it becomes a normal way of life when nobody bats an eyelid.

Following an announcement by the then Prime Minister during his speech from the ramparts of the Red Fort on 15 August 2018, declaring that PC would be granted to the women officers of the Indian Army, a communication was issued by the Ministry of Defence on 25 February 2019, conveying the sanction of the President for grant of PC to SSCWOs in all the streams/corps that they had been inducted as SSCWOs. However, even after finally taking a policy decision at the highest level of Government, the modalities prescribed for grant of PC created further roadblocks and obstructions for women to be considered for grant of PC at par with gentlemen officers. The key problems were:

> The grant of PC would only be available prospectively. The proposal was to grant PC only to those women officers who had completed less than 14 years of service and to deny the same to all women officers who had completed more than 14 years of service by couching it in the form of a concession that they could serve till the pensionable service of 20 years, after which they would be released from service.

Women officers who were granted PC could only serve on staff appointments (as opposed to 'command appointments').

The women officers were required to exercise an option for the grant of PC before completing four years of commissioned service.

These three roadblocks would have rendered women officers as second-grade citizens in the Indian Army and were more like a consolation.

The final arguments of the appeals before the Supreme Court were undertaken in this backdrop. The Union of India defended its actions before the Supreme Court essentially on the grounds that grant of PC and the conditions thereof are policy decisions that have been taken after due consideration and could not be interfered with by a court of law. They also claimed that there was no discrimination between men and women SSC officers. The difference was essentially on account of occupational hazards inherent in military service not being suitable for women officers per se.

The written note and the arguments made on behalf of the Army constituted a classic example of how any attempt to justify a bad decision adds more fuel to the fire and insult to injury! The contentions raised ranged from exigencies of service, where women officers would face a greater challenge owing to their prolonged absence during pregnancy, motherhood and domestic obligations towards their children and families; to physical capabilities and lesser physical prowess of women soldiers to engage in combat; to infrastructure constraints in forward posts and small detachments; to physiological limitations of women officers, extenuated by the challenges of confinement, motherhood and childcare; and the fact that the rank and file of the Army consisted only of male soldiers, primarily coming from such a social structure where men would not be amenable to taking command from women officers, in addition to interfering with the inherent dynamics of an all-male environment.

The lawyers representing the women officers, invigorated with the passion and steel of their warrior clients, attacked each of the submissions advanced on behalf of the Union, on the strength of constitutional guarantees, facts and statistics and examples of how the situation on the ground was completely different than what was sought to be projected before the Court. The energy and environment in the courtroom during the days and weeks when these matters were being heard also needs special mention, as the courtroom comprised not just of regular lawyers appearing on both sides, but the court staff and other lawyers waiting for their matters too. The impeccable wood-panelled temple of justice was bejewelled with a strong strength of uniformed and decorated women officers, who stood in rapt attention during long hours of arguments with the discipline and decorum that is inherent to a professional soldier of one of the most respected armies of the world – the Indian Army. It was unmistakable that the eyes and hearts of these trained professional soldiers were impregnated with hope and aspirations, but there was no negativity or bitterness of a litigant embroiled in litigation for having been handed a raw deal.

As the word went around the majestic court corridors of the hot debates and fascinating issues being deliberated and considered in this batch of appeals, the hearing started to attract a large audience, seasoned and young lawyers and law interns. It was also interesting that while the bench consisted of Dr Justice DY Chandrachud and Mr Justice Ajay Rastogi, the court staff comprising court masters, stenographers, law clerks, court librarians, etc., were primarily women. Coincidently or otherwise, the charge on behalf of the women officers was also mounted by a team of women lawyers. The energy and vibe of the courtroom proceedings were extraordinary. The submissions and the cross-questions by the bench and arguments travelled seamlessly between constitutional principles, role and performance of women officers for the last almost three decades since 1992 and the stereotypes emanating from a patriarchal mindset. Equally fascinating were the eloquent expressions on the dozens of intent and curious eyes closely following the court proceedings.

Finally, after a marathon and comprehensive hearing, the arguments were closed, and the matters were reserved for judgment. Equipped with the knowledge of an extremely progressive bent of mind of the bench and a strong belief of the strength of their case, together with the redundancy of submissions made by the Union of India, the women officers were upbeat on the grand finale of the long battle that they had endured in the courts of law.

The judgment of the bench, authored by Dr Justice DY Chandrachud, titled *Secretary, Ministry of Defence v. Babita Puniya and Ors,*[3] was

[3] *Secretary, Ministry of Defence v. Babita Puniya and Ors,* Civil Appeals Nos. 9367-69 of 2011 with Nos. 1127-28 of 2013 and 1210 of 2020, can be accessed at https://indiankanoon.org/doc/

pronounced on 17 February 2020, days before the world was to recede into a global pandemic on account of COVID-19. The judgement was a watershed moment, a landmark like no other, a milestone not just for the women officers of the Indian Army and Indian defence forces, but for every woman, wading her way, grappling with the mindset of stereotype and bias. The judgement chronicles the entire evolutionary process of engagement of women officers in the Army. It also noted extensively the arguments raised by either side.

The Supreme Court completely demolished and discarded the submissions advanced by the Union as being based on gender stereotypes and premised on assumptions about socially ascribed roles of gender which discriminate against women. In no uncertain terms, the Supreme Court declared that the reliance on inherent psychological differences between men and women, rests in a deeply entrenched stereotypical and constitutionally flawed notion that women are the weaker sex and may not undertake tasks that are too arduous for them.

In paragraph 72 of the judgment, the Hon'ble Supreme Court noted some examples of highly meritorious women officers who had brought laurels to the forces. The Army had commended their distinction and celebrated it. These examples were important to demolish the baseless submissions that women had played a less important role than their male counterparts on account of their biological composition and social milieu.

The judgment proclaimed that the track record of service to the nation by women officers is beyond reproach and to cast aspersions on their abilities on the ground of gender is an affront not only to their dignity as women but to the dignity of the members of the Indian Army where men and women serve as equal citizens in a common mission.

The Supreme Court agreed with all the submissions made on behalf of the women officers and held that the decision of the Union to grant the benefit of PC prospectively and blanket restrictions on criteria and command appointments (confining the grant of PC to women only in staff appointments) suffered from grave legal infirmities and were in the teeth of fundamental constitutional guarantees strongly protected by the Indian Constitution. The judgement found that the proposal the Union had submitted to the Court to grant PC only to women officers who had completed less than 14 years of service and to deny the same to all women

---

117198144/

officers who had completed more than 14 years of service by couching it in the form of a concession that they could serve till the pensionable service of 20 years, after which they would be released from service, was farcical.

The judgement also declared that an absolute bar on women seeking criteria or command appointments would not comport with the guarantee of equality under Article 14 of the Constitution and that whether a particular candidate should or should not be granted criteria or command assignment is a matter for the competent authority to consider, having regard to exigencies of service, performance, merit and organisational requirement, and the absolute exclusion of women from all others, except staff appointments, is indefensible.

Finally, the Court directed all serving women officers on SSC to be considered for grant of PC, along with all consequential benefits, including promotion and financial benefits. The Court also held that all the choices for specialisation should be available to women officers on the same terms as for men SSCOs, and they shall be entitled to exercise their options for being considered for the grant of PC on the same terms as their male counterparts and for all appointments, including staff, criteria and command appointments. The Court went on to pass certain additional directions for women officers who had completed more than 14 years of service, on account of the long delay that had occasioned for no fault of theirs, but due to inaction by successive governments in not granting them PC, even after the judgment of the Delhi High Court in March 2010.

The matter was not to reach a culmination point so soon. Due to the inordinately long period taken by the Government to implement the original decision of the Delhi High Court on which there was no stay, there emerged some grey areas while considering SSCOs for PC essentially in the context of the criterion for annual confidential reports (ACRs) and medical categorisation standards. Aggrieved that while implementing the landmark decision, again, there were traces of tacit discrimination, many affected officers had to go back to the Supreme Court for relief.

The issue was finally decided in a recent judgment dated 25 March 2021 of the Supreme Court titled *Lieutenant Colonel Nitisha & Ors v.*

Union of India & Ors etc.,[4] where the Court examined the serious anomalies that had vitiated the implementation of the judgement in *Babita Puniya*. In this judgement, the Court employed the principle of indirect and facially neutral discrimination, where the intention (or the lack of it) is inconsequential. The following lines from the much-detailed dicta would provide a gist of its essence and its umbilical relationship with *Babita Puniya*:

> ...In rendering the decision in *Babita Puniya* (*supra*), this Court was mindful of the insidious impact on the generations of women who must have given up on their dreams to serve in the Armed Forces owing to the gendered roadblock on their aspirations, and of the women who must have chosen to opt-out of availing an extension to their SSC terms on similar grounds. We must not forget that those women officers who have remained in service are those with the tenacity to hold on and to meet the exacting standards of performance of which the Indian Army has made her citizens proud. It is also important for us to bear in mind that a career in the Army comes with a serious set of trials and tribulations of a transferable service with postings in difficult terrains, even in times of peace. This is rendered infinitely more difficult when society relegates functions of domestic labour, caregiving and childcare exclusively on the shoulders of women. The SSCWOs before us are not just women who have dedicated their lives to the service of the Army but are women who have persevered through difficult conditions as they trudged along a lengthy litigation to avail the simplest of equality with their male counterparts. They do not come to the Court seeking charity or favour. They implore us for a restoration of their dignity when even strongly worded directions by the Court in *Babita Puniya* (*supra*) have not trickled down into a basic assessment of not subjecting unequals to supposedly neutral parameters...

This judgement, too, would go a long way in demolishing the gender barriers and obstructions from the nooks, crevices and fringes of our world.

What a splendid victory and inspirational journey! Being one of the lead lawyers in this significant case, I believe that many such journeys of inspiring women are like relay-races. Every generation has to run its part

[4] *Nitisha v. Union of India*, Writ Petition (Civil) 1109 of 2020 (along with other similar cases), decided on 25 March 2021, can be accessed at https://indiankanoon.org/doc/190567716/

well and pass on the baton equally well to the future generations. None of us is in this alone. It is also largely agnostic of the geographies, nations, continents, forms of government, measures of development, et al. It is a universal journey, singing a universal tune.

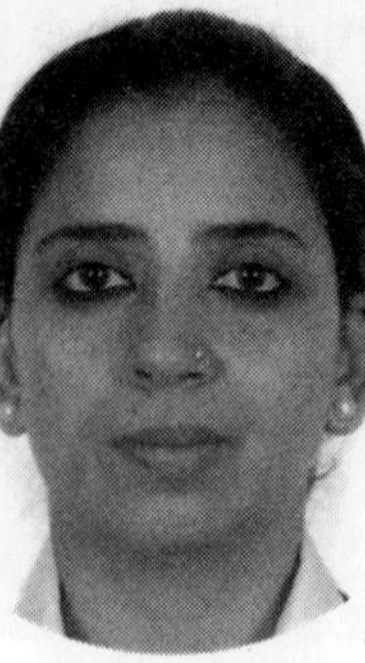

Ms **Aishwarya Bhati** is a practising advocate at the Supreme Court of India and is currently the Additional Solicitor General of India. She is the youngest woman lawyer to be designated Senior Advocate by the Supreme Court. She also has the distinction of being one of the youngest Additional Solicitors General of India and the fourth woman ever to occupy this distinguished position.

She has passionately fought for women's rights, children's rights, rights of persons with disabilities and has been a crusader in anti-tobacco litigation. She has led from the front for the rights of women officers of the Indian Army, Indian Air Force and the Indian Navy for consideration of permanent commission and command positions at par with male officers. She has been instrumental in leading the battle against the mighty tobacco industry on issues of larger pictorial warnings, plain packaging and stronger tobacco regulation.

The Saga of the Australian War Crimes Act

Kiran Mohandas Menon

Polyukhovich, Australia

Polyukhovich, War Crimes Acts and the Backstory

In many senses, *Polyukhovich v. Commonwealth*[1] (Polyukhovich) retains a sense of prescience, in that, in this period, when universal jurisdiction and domestic prosecution of international crimes have been summoned to the forefront, and are facing a quiet expansion,[2] the primary issues dealt with by its jurisprudence continue to remain timely, relevant and contentious. Perhaps this is an appropriate legacy considering that the case that was initiated, calling for the invalidation of the War Crimes Amendment Act 1988 (Cth), led to Australia's highest court, almost a decade before *that* now-iconic warrant was issued from Madrid against Pinochet,[3] deliberating on extraterritorial jurisdiction, retroactive criminalisation, their roles and limitations, and the contours of the powers of the Australian state itself.

---

[1] High Court of Australia, *Polyukhovich v. Commonwealth*, Order, 14 August 1991. Decision here: http://www6.austlii.edu.au/cgi-bin/viewdoc/au/cases/cth/HCA/1991/32.html

[2] Máximo Langer and Mackenzie Eason, *The Quiet Expansion of Universal Jurisdiction*, in The European Journal of International Law, 2019, Vol. 30 no 3, pp.779-819.

[3] House of Lords, *Regina v. Bartle and the Commissioner of Police for the Metropolis and others Ex Parte Pinochet* (on appeal from a Divisional Court of the Queen's Bench Division) *Regina v. Evans and another and the Commissioner of Police for the Metropolis and others Ex Parte Pinochet* (on appeal from a Divisional Court of the Queen's Bench Division), Judgments, 25 November 1998.

Mario Vargas Llosa once wrote that memory 'subtly rearranges the past to fit the present'.[4] Perhaps, this is also a risk that is present when courts evoke the past to form concluding narratives in a present that has been detached by time and change. In this regard, it speaks of the character of the Polyukhovich case that the term 'Nuremberg' featuring extensively and repetitively in the final order was neither a coincidence nor did it seem inappropriate.

The backstory that would lead to this case began with the passing of the Commonwealth War Crimes Act 1945, which 'provided for the establishment of military courts to conduct war crimes trials'.[5] Reports that individuals who may have been associated with Nazi war crimes have become Australian citizens or residents soon led to the initial act being amended and effectively replaced through the War Crimes Amendment Act 1988. The Preamble of the amended Act read:

> Whereas (a) concern has arisen that a significant number of persons who committed serious war crimes in Europe during World War II may since have entered Australia and became Australian citizens or residents; (b) it is appropriate that persons accused of such war crimes be brought to trial in the ordinary criminal courts in Australia; and (c) it is also essential in the interests of justice that persons so accused be given a fair trial with all the safeguards for accused persons in trials in those courts, having particular regard to matters such as the gravity of the allegations and the lapse of time since the alleged crimes.[6]

This legislation notably was aimed at acts committed in the context of the Second World War and pursuantly brought under its ambit 'war crimes committed between 1 September 1939 and 8 May 1945' and elaborated 'war' with the statement 'in so far as it occurred in Europe' during the aforementioned dates. Section 7 (1) detailed that a serious crime would be a war crime if it was committed: (a) in the course of hostilities in a war; (b) in the course of an occupation; (c) in pursuing a policy associated with the conduct of a war or with an occupation; or (d) on behalf

---

[4] See Mario Vargas Llosa, *The Storyteller: A Novel*, 1987.

[5] James A Thompson, 'Is it a Mess: The High Court and the War Crimes Case: External Affairs, Defence, Judicial Power and the Australian Constitution', 22 U.W. Austl. L. Rev. 197 (1992), p. 199.

[6] See https://www.legislation.gov.au/Details/C2018C00198

of, or in the interests of, a power conducting a war or engaged in an occupation.[7] Section 9 provided that:

> (1) A person who: (a) on or after 1 September 1939 and on or before 8 May 1945; and (b) whether as an individual or as a member of an organisation; committed a war crime is guilty of an indictable offence against this Act. (2) Sections 5 and 7, and paragraph 86(1)(a), of the Crimes Act 1914 do not apply in relation to an offence against this Act.[8]

Ivan Timofeyevich Polyukhovich was born in the village of Serniki in the Pinsk region of Ukraine. Having emigrated to Australia, he became a citizen in 1958. In January 1990, a case was brought against him for his 'alleged involvement in the mass killing of approximately 850 people from the Jewish ghetto in Serniki village and for killing 24 other people between August and September 1942'.[9] Relying on 'eyewitness testimony and forensic evidence' from a mass gravesite, near Serniki, Australian investigators belonging to a Special Investigation Unit set out to exactly recreate what had happened in the spot decades ago. Their efforts and the subsequent findings would be described as an 'endeavour that was both staggering in its scale and harrowing in its detail'. It was discovered that bullet wounds on the victims 'matched the 9 mm German ammunition scattered throughout the pit.'[10] Further, '553 bodies were examined. 407 were female. 80 were male. 48 were unknown. 63 bodies belonged to females aged birth to nine. 134 bodies were categorised between ages ten to nineteen. 410 suffered bullet wounds to the head'. Polyukhovich was arrested based on a warrant issued by Adelaide Magistrates Court in South Australia, accused of being responsible for the murder of 24 Jews, including women and children, and for being complicit in the murder of more than 850 others when Ukraine faced Nazi occupation.

The images of a frail old man, then in his seventies, who was accused of unspeakable horrors, including 'escorting three people to the pit and shooting them personally'[11] attracted sufficient media attention. It also

[7] *Ibid.*, Section 7.

[8] *Ibid.*, Section 9.

[9] See http://www.internationalcrimesdatabase.org/Case/1172

[10] See https://www.abc.net.au/news/2018-05-20/nazi-war-criminals-in-australia-and-the-case-of-polyukhovich/9756454

[11] See https://lsj.com.au/articles/the-case-that-changed-me-greg-james-qc/

re-awoke an ostensibly dormant conversation on whether Australian institutions had truly done enough to bring to justice those who had committed serious crimes, especially during the Second World War, before settling down with impunity in Australian cities and townships.

Polyukhovich and the Commonwealth Constitution

In September, the same year, the High Court of Australia (High Court) started hearing a 'challenge to the constitutional validity of the War Crimes Amendment under which Polyukhovich was charged',[12] the case that is the focus of this contribution. It also stayed the proceedings against Polyukhovich, who had shot himself, to determine whether he was, in fact, fit for trial. The High Court is Australia's highest court that retains original and appellate jurisdiction on matters related to and provided for within Australia's Constitution. It has a composition of seven judges and is headed by the chief justice. The Polyukhovich case was heard by a bench headed by Chief Justice Mason and further comprising of Justice(s) Brennan, Deane, Dawson, Gaudron and McHugh.

Whatever the individual fate of Polyukhovich would be, it was clear that this decision on the relevant constitutional questions would have a significant impact on the prosecution of war crimes in the country. The 'judicial discord and disunity'[13] that was ever-present in the decision would be an interesting assessment of how the Commonwealth of Australia viewed itself and the powers of its Legislature and External Affairs.

This was particularly the case as the primary questions that the High Court was concerned with, was stated thus:

> Is Section 9 of the War Crimes Act 1945, as amended, invalid in its application to the information laid by the second defendant against the plaintiff on two grounds? The first ground is that the section is beyond the legislative powers conferred upon the Parliament by s.51(vi) and (xxix) of the Constitution with respect to defence and external affairs, these being the only two powers which, according to the defendants'

---

[12] See http://www.internationalcrimesdatabase.org/Case/1172

[13] *Supra* note 6, 202.

> case, could sustain the validity of the law. The second is that the section, because it attempts to enact that past conduct shall constitute a criminal offence, is an invalid attempt to usurp the judicial power of the Commonwealth, that power being vested by the Constitution in Ch III courts.[14]

Deliberating on these questions, Chief Justice Mason noted:

> If 'a serious crime' committed by an individual 44 or more years earlier answering the statutory description of 'a war crime' was not itself an aspect of Australia's contemporary external affairs before 8 May 1945, does it make any difference to the character of the Act that the only persons who are liable to conviction must now be Australian residents or citizens?[15]

External Affairs and the Australian Constitution

The very nature and meaning of the term 'external affairs' came into question here as the relevant Section 51 of the Commonwealth of Australia Constitution Act, stated:

> The Parliament shall, subject to this Constitution, have power to make laws for the peace, order, and good government of the Commonwealth with respect to:
>
> ...
>
> (xxix) External affairs

Chief Justice Mason and Justices Deane, Dawson and McHugh concluded that 'externality per se is sufficient to invoke section 5 1 (xxix)' and that 'thus the external affairs power can support the validity of Commonwealth legislation applying to persons, relationships, matters and things outside Australia' and 'whether the external persons, relationships, matters or things had or have some identified connection with Australia' is, for constitutional law, irrelevant.[16]

The other justices disagreed for varying reasons, with Justice Brennan opining that 'the legislative powers of the Parliament are limited by

---

[14] *Supra* note 2.

[15] *Ibid.*

[16] *Supra* note 6, 204.

the terms of the Constitution, and the connotation of the phrase external affairs must be ascertained from its context and purpose.' He continued:

> ...Although affairs which exist or occur outside Australia may be described as 'external' in a geographical sense, I would not hold that the Constitution confers power to enact laws affecting affairs which, though geographically external, have nothing to do with Australia. There must be some nexus, not necessarily substantial, between Australia and the 'external affairs' which a law purports to affect before the law is supported by s. 51(xxix).[17]

In relation to this issue, by a majority of six to one, Judge Brennan dissenting, the Court held that the War Crimes Act was indeed a valid exercise of Australian external affairs power.

The Commonwealth Parliament and the Usurpation of Power

This led to the question of how it could be ascertained that a particular law was staying true to the requirement 'that Commonwealth laws be made for the peace, order, and good government of the Commonwealth', as noted in Section 51. Further, who would make this ascertainment? Was it the exclusive prerogative of the Parliament? Or could the High Court step in, and if so, under what circumstances? Was there a required nexus between Australia and the external realities, and if so, had it been satisfied in the Polyukhovich case?

That a certain dissonance existed among the justices regarding these issues was perhaps not unsurprising. However, Justice Deane's articulation remains noteworthy:

> ...It was argued that the words 'for the peace, order, and good government of the Commonwealth' introduce a requirement of some identified connection with Australia and that no such connection exists in relation to acts committed between 1939 and 1945 in Europe by a person who was not, at the relevant time, a citizen or resident of this country. There is a short answer to that argument. The words 'for the peace, order, and good government of the Commonwealth' in s.51 do not impose an objective qualification upon the subject matters of legislative power. They refer to the intended beneficial operation of laws made

---

[17] *Supra* note 2.

> with respect to those subject matters and simply express the fact that in 'a general and remote sense the purpose and design of every law is to promote the welfare of the community' for which the law is made.... It is for the Parliament, not for the Court, to decide whether a law will be or is 'for the peace, order, and good government of the Commonwealth'. Where the Parliament decides, by enactment, that a law is 'for the peace, order, and good government of the Commonwealth', that, of itself, provides sufficient connection between this country and the subject matter of that law for the purposes of s.51[18]

He further assumed the decision was for judges to make, and unhesitatingly held that in Polyukhovich the requisite connection existed, further noting:

> ... function of determining whether a person is in fact guilty of a crime against a law of the Commonwealth is a function which appertains exclusively to, and which cannot be excluded from, the judicial power which our Constitution vests solely in the courts which it designates. That being so, it is beyond the competence of the Parliament to declare, as s.9(1) of the Act purports to do, that a 'person ... is guilty' of a crime against a law of the Commonwealth by reason of having committed a past act which did not, when done, contravene any applicable Commonwealth law and was therefore not in fact such a crime.[19]

Here again, the majority by four to two rejected Polyukhovich's claim that the War Crimes Act 1945 was attempting to usurp the judicial power of the Commonwealth. While agreeing that a bill of attainder would cause such a usurpation, it was decided that the mere retroactive application of a law would not make it a bill of attainder.

Justice Dawson explored similar provisions in the United States Constitution and concluded that the 'Commonwealth Constitution contains no provision which corresponds to the bill of attainder clause in the United States Constitution. Nor does it adopt in its entirety the United States theory of the separation of powers.'[20]

---

[18] *Ibid.*

[19] *Ibid*

[20] *Ibid*

Polyukhovich and Universal Jurisdiction

Justice Toohey explored the universal jurisdiction aspect of the provisions, noting that 'since the Act focuses primarily (and, in practice, possibly entirely) on acts committed by non-nationals against non-nationals outside Australia, its likely basis for jurisdiction over war criminals from World War II is the principle of universal jurisdiction.'[21] He evoked Professor Baxter's commentary on the Eichmann case which opined that 'there could be no objection under international law to Israeli law's reaching out to "a person" of whatsoever nationality to the extent that the municipal law of that country merely incorporated in its law crimes under international law subject to universal jurisdiction...'[22]

Justice Brennan went further, stating that 'Australia's international personality would be incomplete if it were unable to exercise a jurisdiction to try and to punish offenders against the law of nations whose crimes are such that their subjection to universal jurisdiction is conducive to international peace and order.'[23] He continues in a paragraph that seems almost clairvoyant considering later developments:

> As the material drawn from international agreements and UNGA resolutions acknowledges, international law recognizes a state to have universal jurisdiction to try suspected war criminals whether or not that state is under an obligation to do so and whether or not there is any international concern that the State should do so...Even if there were an international obligation or concern as postulated by the Commonwealth, its content must be this: that states should try war criminals in exercise of their universal jurisdiction to do so, for there is nothing to suggest that the postulated obligation or concern was to be satisfied or met by a trial in exercise of a jurisdiction which is not conferred by international law.[24]

---

[21] *Ibid*

[22] *Ibid*

[23] *Ibid*

[24] *Ibid*

An Unfinished Saga and an Uncertain Legacy

The High Court's decision allowed for the Polyukhovich's trial to proceed, and in 1993, a jury acquitted Polyukhovich of all charges, citing lack of evidence. David Bewan, the author of *A Case to Answer,* which explored the impact of the circumstances of the case on Australian society, would later remark that the 'patchwork of evidence that the prosecution had to pull together to try and make a case...just wasn't strong enough'. To this day, Polyukhovich remains the only person to be tried under Australia's amended War Crimes Act.

Whether Polyukhovich offered a strong precedent and its pedigree will stand the test of future judicial scrutiny remains to be seen. The recent revelations that led to Australian soldiers themselves been accused of committing war crimes in Afghanistan[25] clearly show that the questions dealt with by this case have in no way become superfluous and that institutional reflection remains both an inward and outward need.

Perhaps, the only definite conclusion that can be made is that three decades later, it offers a fitting opportunity for reflection on the changing language, certainties, progressions and cyclical patterns faced by international criminal law, military law and related fields and that Polyukhovich's true moment as a flawed pioneer may yet be approaching.

---

[25] See https://www.bbc.com/news/world-australia-55088230

Kiran Mohandas Menon is a lawyer specialising in international law and international relations. He is currently a Doctoral Researcher at the Irish Center for Human Rights. From 2017–2021, he worked at the International Nuremberg Principles Academy, located at the historic Nuremberg Palace of Justice in Germany. Since 2020, he has also been affiliated with the Guernica Center for International Justice.

He has previously worked at the Spanish-Portuguese law firm, Cuatrecasas Goncalves Pereira, based in Madrid, the Center for Democracy and Reconciliation in Southeast Europe (CDRSEE) in Thessaloniki, Greece, the founding office of the International Nuremberg Principles Academy and the Office of the Chairman of Foreign Relations of the Bar Association of Sri Lanka in Negombo.

He has further worked on an Indian government project promoting the use of redressal mechanisms against domestic violence among the tribal communities in Kerala and for a Reporters without Borders sponsored newspaper run by Tibetan refugees in Dharamshala, India.

Kiran was also an Associate Editor for the foreign affairs website, *International Policy Digest*, and a writer for *The Diplomat* magazine.

Cementing the Primacy of Traditional Courts over Military Courts

Leslie Esbrook

Decision No 2012/125, Turkey

Finding a Turkish Constitutional Court case decision that has had a strong impact on military justice is harder than one might think. That is due to a confluence of three primary factors. First, until quite recently, the sharp historical separation between Turkey's military and political branches prevented military appeals from being heard at the Constitutional Court. Second, former Prime Minister and current President Recep Tayyip Erdogan has made extensive efforts to restructure large portions of the government by a constitutional amendment, and these executive-led reforms often prevent the Constitutional Court from having the first bite at the apple on consequential issues. Third, Turkey's longstanding preference for the European Court of Human Rights (ECHR) as an arbiter of individual rights issues, particularly those with internationally-based guidelines like military justice, further decreased the likelihood that the Constitutional Court would receive a case of lasting import.

Nevertheless, in the early 2010s, those same three factors converged to create conditions ripe for a Constitutional Court decision on military justice, namely, the curtailment of the use of military courts to try civilians. In 18 months, an executive-led constitutional referendum package paved the way for individuals tried in military courts to petition the Constitutional Court and limited 'non-military' personnel trials under military jurisdiction. Around the same time, the ECHR laid the legal groundwork on the issue of limited military jurisdiction when it ruled that a

Turkish civilian contractor had her rights to a fair trial violated by being tried in military court absent exceptional circumstances. Come September 2012, when a Turkish civilian contractor working for the Air Force petitioned the Constitutional Court for review of his case, Turkey's Constitutional Court, supported by these developments, ruled that civilian contractors must be tried in civilian courts. This piece reviews that Constitutional Court decision (Decision No 2012/125), which illuminates important clashes between Turkey's institutions of power and provides an example of the rare instance of the Turkish Constitutional Court influencing military justice for the better.

Constitutional Court Decisions on Military Justice in Context

The Separation of the Military and Political Branches

Since Turkey's founding in 1923, the military has acted as a self-proclaimed protector of the country's democratic institutions. On four separate occasions, the military has stepped in to take control of the government, all for short stints, to 'restore' what it considered the appropriate democratic balance of power in the nation. Each time, the military receded and handed control of the country over to a new civilian administration.[1] As one author has stated, to the majority of Turks, 'The military and military values still lie at the heart of any definition of what it means to be Turkish.'[2] Turkish society's near-universal support for the military extends even to the military's campaigns abroad. As recently as 2018, opinion polls showed over 90 percent of the Turkish population approved of the military's campaigns in Syria.[3]

Interestingly, the military's hold over the country directly led to the formation of the Constitutional Court. The military's first coup in 1960 ended with the installation of civilian leaders who favored judicial review of parliamentary decisions, something previously unavailable in the

---

[1] See *Timeline: A History of Turkish Coups*, Al Jazeera, 16 July 2016, https://www.aljazeera.com/news/2016/7/16/timeline-a-history-of-turkish-coups

[2] *The Military and Turkish Society*, 41 The Adelphi Papers 337, p. 9, 2001, https://www.tandfonline.com/doi/abs/10.1080/05679320108449652?journalCode=tadl19

[3] Turkish Study Shows Public Support for Military Campaign in Syria, *Voice of America*, 17 February 2018, https://learningenglish.voanews.com/a/turkey-poll/4257664.html

Turkish government. In 1962, the military's will manifested in the creation of the Constitutional Court, which would review laws and rules of procedure passed by the General Assembly for their compliance with the Turkish Constitution.[4] In sum, the military's role as a protector of democratic institutions against political excesses, and the deep and enduring popularity it has enjoyed, as a result, has generally resigned the political powers to allowing the military to function quasi-independently out of a begrudging mix of fear and respect.

The Turkish military's independence has bled into the structure and design of the country's judicial system. This design emanated first and foremost from the relevant Constitutional provision, Article 145. As enacted, Article 145 stated in relevant part that:

> Military justice shall be dispensed by military courts and military disciplinary organs. These courts and tribunals shall be responsible for conducting proceedings concerning offenses committed by military personnel which are breaches of military law or are committed against other military personnel, on military premises or in connection with military service and the related duties...

By 2012, this law had manifested in an entirely separate structure for adjudicating matters related to the military's interests parallel to the country's civilian courts. Turkish military courts encompassed courts of the first instance, a Military Court of Appeals, and a 'supreme' military court of administrative review known as the 'High Military Administrative Court.'[5] Military courts operated in military-restricted areas and had jurisdiction to try offenses connected with military service and duties, along with administrative issues related to the operation of the military. Lawyers and judges who appeared before military courts were all themselves military personnel, and cases heard before the highest courts in the military system were final.[6] Losing parties could not appeal to the country's Constitutional Court for review.[7]

---

[4] Kemal Baslar, *The Fifty Years of the Constitutional Court of Turkey (1962-2012), Justice and Law Review*, pp. 15-16, 2 November 2012, https://ssrn.com/abstract=2726460

[5] Ismail Aksel, *Turkish Judicial System: Bodies, Duties and* Officials ("Aksel Report"), pp. 13, 42-52 (The Ministry of Justice of Turkey 2013), https://rm.coe.int/turkish-judicial-system-bodies-duties-and-officials-by-ismail-aksel-ju/168078f25f

[6] *Id.*

[7] *Id.*

Prime Minister Erdogan's Reforms

Broad support of the military did not necessarily extend to support for bifurcated judicial systems. The separation of military and civilian courts began to be chipped away by the great pace of judicial and constitutional reform efforts spearheaded by Erdogan, who has been in power for nearly twenty years; he was first elected as Prime Minister of Turkey in 2003 and later elected as President in 2014. During his tenure, his party has proposed and successfully passed a dizzying array of reform packages that have fundamentally reshaped the Turkish judicial system (and general structure of government) for better and for worse. For example, while serving as Prime Minister in 2007, Erdogan's party proposed a successful constitutional referendum package that shifted power from the Prime Minister to the President of Turkey, extended the term limits of the President, and reduced the number of lawmakers necessary to pass legislation. What might have appeared generous was ultimately revealed to be self-serving. Erdogan is now President,[8] and, in 2017, he successfully proposed a similar constitutional referendum to abolish the Prime Minister's office altogether and consolidate its powers in the office of the President. That referendum too passed.[9]

Erdogan's constitutional changes have also had a direct impact on the judiciary. In 2010, his party proposed a successful constitutional referendum that allowed individuals to directly petition the Constitutional Court for review of their cases and 'strengthen(ed) the rights of women, children, workers, and civil servants.'[10] The referendum established a system for government employees to petition the courts for work-related grievances where previously employees could only seek administrative review and expanded the Constitutional Court to include elected, not just

---

[8] Orhan Coskun, Turkish party keeps term limit, hinting at Erdogan presidency, Reuters, 2 May 2014, https://www.reuters.com/article/us-turkey-election/turkish-party-keeps-term-limit-hinting-at-erdogan-presidency-idUSBREA410U820140502

[9] Patrick Kingsley, Erdogan Claims Vast Powers in Turkey After Narrow Victory in Referendum, New York Times, 16 April 2017, https://www.nytimes.com/2017/04/16/world/europe/turkey-referendum-polls-erdogan.html; see also Sinan Ekim and Kemal Kirisci, The Turkish constitutional referendum explained, Brookings, 13 April 2017, https://www.brookings.edu/blog/order-from-chaos/2017/04/13/the-turkish-constitutional-referendum-explained

[10] Sebnem Arsu and Dan Bilefsky, Turkish Reforms Pass by Wide Margins, New York Times, 12 September 2010, https://www.nytimes.com/2010/09/13/world/europe/13turkey.html

appointed, representatives. Tucked away in the 2010 constitutional reform package was Amendment No 5892 to Article 145 of the Constitution (Military Justice), stating:

> Military justice is administered by military courts and disciplinary courts.... Apart from in wartime, non-military people cannot be tried in military courts.

The referendum was passed in September 2010.[11] Following the passage of the 2010 constitutional referendum, by law, 'non-military people' could not be tried in military courts, and anyone, including individuals tried in military courts, could petition the Constitutional Court for review. These two changes created conditions ripe for Constitutional Court review of military court jurisdiction.

The European Court of Human Rights' Outsized Influence

The third contextual factor important to understanding Decision No 2012/125 is the outsized influence of the European Court of Human Rights on the Turkish judicial system. Since Turkey ratified the European Convention on Human Rights in 1954, it is a member of the European Court of Human Rights and has a national judge represented at the Court.[12] Since 1954, Turkey has consistently been among the countries at the Court with the most applications for review processed and, of those cases decided by judgment, among the countries with the most violations assessed against it.

In 2020, for example, Turkey accounted for nearly 20 percent of all cases brought to the Court, second only to Russia.[13] In the same year, it also received the second-highest number of adverse judgments, at least 88 percent of which concluded that the country had violated the Convention on Human Rights.[14] Turkey's activity at the ECHR is no mystery. Until the Constitutional referendum of September 2010, individuals whose

[11] Erdogan pulls it off, The Economist, 13 September 2010, https://www.economist.com/newsbook/2010/09/13/erdogan-pulls-it-off

[12] Press country profile: Turkey, European Court of Human Rights (last updated October 2020), https://www.echr.coe.int/Documents/CP_Turkey_ENG.pdf

[13] Analysis of statistics 2020, Council of Europe: European Court of Human Rights, p. 8 January 2021, https://www.echr.coe.int/Documents/Stats_analysis_2020_ENG.pdf

[14] *Violations by Article and by State, European Court of Human Rights*, p. 2, 2020, https://www.echr.coe.int/Documents/Stats_violation_2020_ENG.pdf

rights were violated could not petition the Turkish Constitutional Court to address their grievances, and even after the referendum was passed, Turkey's civilian courts were still disfavored as compared to the ECHR based in part on the difficulty of receiving damages from the Turkish Constitutional Court.[15]

Thus, it should come as no surprise that the first court to rule on the scope of Turkey's military court jurisdiction was the European Court of Human Rights.

In *Icen v. Turkey*, decided in 2011, a civilian translator petitioned the Court for violations of her right to a fair trial (Article 6 of the European Convention on Human Rights) after being sentenced in a Turkish military court to ten months imprisonment for disobedience and insulting a superior officer.[16] In its decision, the ECHR noted that international law applicable to the European Union (EU) held thus:

> Military courts should not, as a matter of principle, have jurisdiction to try civilians. In all circumstances, the state must ensure that civilians accused of any criminal offense, regardless of their nature, are tried in civilian courts.[17]

In accordance with this principle, the Court held that Turkey had violated the petitioner's right to a fair trial by trying her in a military court. While a military court may be within its rights to try a civilian with 'compelling reasons', the Court found no such applicable reasons in Ms Icen's case.[18] Since the use of military criminal courts raised doubts that were 'objectively justified' as to 'the independence and impartiality of military courts', their use in Ms Icen's case violated her right to a fair trial.[19]

---

[15] Orcun Cetinkaya, Sizing up the Turkish Constitutional Court and the ECHR, Commercial Dispute Resolution, https://iclg.com/cdr/litigation/5917-sizing-up-the-turkish-constitutional-court-and-the-echr

[16] Decision, *Icen v. Turkey* (Applicant No 45912/06), 2d Section, European Court of Human Rights, 28 November 2011 ("Icen Decision"), http://hudoc.echr.coe.int/eng?i=001-104969 (translations from Google translate).

[17] *Id.* 17.

[18] *Id.* 44.

[19] *Id.* 43. The ECHR had ruled in 2006 that peacetime prosecution of civilians in military trials more broadly violated other articles of the European Convention on Human Rights in the case *Ergin v. Turkey*. See *Ergin v. Turkey*, European Court of Human Rights, Appeal No 47533/99, 4 May 2006, Judgment, http://hudoc.echr.coe.int/fre?i=001-75327

Constitutional Court Decision No 2012/125

Description of the Case

That brings us to the Turkish Constitutional Court Decision No 2012/125. At the time of the case, the 2010 Constitutional referendum, which stated that 'non-military people cannot be tried in military courts' had already passed, but 'the regulations regarding the harmonization (of the legal code) with the Constitution had not yet become law.'[20] *Icen v. Turkey* had more or less clearly established that in the absence of compelling circumstance, Turkey could not continue to try civilians in military courts as a principle of international human rights law. The divide of the military and civilian spheres was beginning to crumble, but just barely.

Though it is hard to tell from its limited discussion of the facts, it appears that the circumstances underlying Decision 2012/125 mirrored those of Ms Icen's case. The appellant was a civil servant from the Turkish Air Force who was tried in military courts for extortion and disobedience. After being found guilty, the appellant filed suit in the Constitutional Court requesting the annulment of the law implementing Article 145 and allowing for civilians to be tried in military courts. That law, Law No 353 on the Establishment of Military Courts and Tribunal Procedure, broadly stated that 'military courts shall hear legal cases relating to' various offenses committed by 'military persons', and defined 'military persons' to include 'civilian personnel employed in the cadre and institutions of the Ministry of National Defense or the Turkish Armed Forces' and 'workers employed in military workplaces.'[21]

The Court found in favor of the appellant, though not unanimously. To reach its decision, the Court grappled with two major issues. First, it had to decide the import of the Icen decision on Turkish domestic law. The Court did not automatically accept the Icen decision as binding. It stated that, in cases where the ECHR decision would require a legislative change at the domestic level because it conflicted with domestic law, as

---

[20] Official Newspaper, Decision of the Constitutional Court, No 28484, 1 December 2012 ("Decision No 2012/125"), https://www.resmigazete.gov.tr/eskiler/2012/12/20121201-23.htm (translations from Google translate).

[21] Turkey: Law No 353 of 1963 on Establishment of Military Courts and Tribunal Procedure (Military Criminal Procedure Law), Arts. 9, 10, 25 October 1963, https://www.refworld.org/docid/3ae6b4d12c.html

with Icen, the legislative branch was required to heed the ECHR's instruction, not the judiciary. In short, the Court concluded that the appellant could not rely on the ECHR's decision. Any redress for the harms he suffered 'should be sought and found within the mechanisms of our domestic law.'[22]

The turn to domestic law brought the Court to its second major issue: whether the military courts had jurisdiction to try the appellant. On this, the Court was required to wade into the conflicting statutory landscape on military jurisdiction in the Turkish legal code. The 2010 constitutional reforms amended Article 145 of the Constitution to read:

> Except in the state of war, non-military persons cannot be tried in military courts...[23]

The law did not define 'non-military persons'. But Law No 353, which provided that civilian personnel working in the staff and organizations of the Ministry of National Defense or the Turkish Armed Forces were considered soldiers, i.e., military personnel, for purposes of military jurisdiction, was still in effect.

Reading these two laws together, the Court interpreted the new law amending Article 145 to include in the definition of 'non-military persons' civil servants working in military or defense-related positions. Though it ostensibly ruled based on the application of domestic law, much of its reasoning was grounded in international principles. For example, the Court noted that the national program developed to harmonize Turkish law with the EU had stated that it 'aimed to end the trial of civilians in military courts as much as possible,' and that the United Nations Human Rights Committee, of which Turkey was a member, had instructed members as far back as 1984 that circumstances to try civilians in military courts should be 'exceptional'.[24] It also recognized that Article 6 of the European Convention on Human Rights was principally concerned with 'independence and impartiality' of the judicial system and that those tenets could reasonably be called into question by a civilian tried before uniformed members of the branch of government in which they worked.

---

[22] Decision No 2012/125.

[23] *Id.*

[24] *Id.*

Questionable though its reasoning may be – particularly as to its effect on the future vindication of individual rights by reference to domestic law alone – a majority of the Court was ultimately persuaded by an amalgam of domestic and international law that military jurisdiction over civil servants was a violation of the Turkish constitution.

Six of the 17 judges dissented. Taking a more practical stance, the dissent reasoned that because civil servants were subject to the same working conditions and personal rights as soldiers, their disciplinary justice should be the same. The dissent also applied principles of statutory interpretation to bolster its position, comparing the language in the amended Article 145 with that of other statutes to demonstrate that, in their opinion, 'non-military persons' should be interpreted only as civilians, not civil servants.

The Meaning of Decision No 2012/125

Practically, Decision No 2012/125 affects a huge number of civilian-military personnel in Turkey. Aside from the profound respect Turks have for the military mentioned earlier, military service in Turkey is compulsory for all males. Every family has at least one member who has spent time completing military service. The large size of the military similarly means that support roles for civilian contractors are plentiful, too.

Decision 2012/125 was also rendered at a time when Turkey's hopes for inclusion into the EU were high, despite the country and bloc having reached an impasse in their accession talks in late 2012.[25] The Constitutional Court's affirmation of values from the ECHR and the UN Human Rights Committee on judicial independence, impartiality, and the right to a fair trial was certainly viewed by the EU at the time as a building block on the road to EU membership.[26] Decision No 2012/125 also

---

[25] See, e.g., Vincent L. Morelli, European Union Enlargement: A Status Report on Turkey's Accession Negotiations, 5 August 2013, Summary, https://fas.org/sgp/crs/row/RS22517.pdf; Sami Cohen, AKP Convention Spells Out Turkey's Foreign Policy Platform, Al-Monitor, 5 October 2012, https://www.al-monitor.com/pulse/politics/2012/10/akp-foreign-policy-congress.html

[26] See, e.g., Turkey: Opinion on the Amendments to the Constitution Adopted by the Grand National Assembly on 21 January 2017 and to be Submitted to a National Referendum on 16 April 2017, European Commission for Democracy Through Law (Venice Commission), Council of Europe, Opinion No 875/2017, March 13, 2017 (Venice Report), 112, 123, https://www.venice.coe.int/webforms/documents/default.aspx?pdffile=cdl-ad(2017)005-e

helped align Turkey with the principles of special rapporteurs at the United Nations governing the administration of military justice.[27]

That said, there remained skeptics within Turkey who saw any attempt by Erdogan's party to wrest control from the military as 'giving religious conservatives power' over one of 'the last independent guardians of the secular state.'[28] Such concerns reflected a view that, despite the international recognition of the benefits of civilians being tried in civilian courts, the Turkish civilian judicial system had serious flaws that required reform, and that placing hopes in the civilian judicial system engendered 'new controversies with respect to the independence of the judiciary as well as the quality of justice.'[29] Those concerns to date have largely gone unaddressed.

Even though Tukey's interest in EU membership has waned over time, the impact of Decision No 2012/125 lingers in the domestic political sphere, cementing the primacy of the traditional court system over specialized military courts. Whereas before the decision, it was nearly unthinkable for the military and civilian spheres to overlap, Decision No 2012/125's forced cross-over began a shift in that perception, at least for purposes of court jurisdiction. In 2013, shortly after the decision was published, reports by the Turkish Ministry of Justice continued to state that the 'main separation' in the Turkish judicial system was one between 'civilian judiciary and military judiciary.'[30] By 2017, however, the next successful omnibus constitutional reform referendum included a provision abolishing the military appeals courts altogether and funneling all military appeals into the traditional civilian appellate courts, a change that the European Commission for Democracy Through Law (Venice

---

[27] See Gabriela Knaul, Report of the Special Rapporteur on the Independence of Judges and Lawyers, report to the sixty-eighth session of the General Assembly, UN Doc A/68/285, 7 August 2013, https://undocs.org/A/68/285; Emmanuel Decaux, Draft Principles Governing the Administration of Justice Through Military Tribunals, report submitted by the Special Rapporteur of the Sub-Commission on the Promotion and Protection of Human Rights to the sixty-second session of the ECOSOC Commission on Human Rights, UN Doc. E/CN.4/ 2006/58, 13 January 2006; https://undocs.org/E/CN.4/2006/58; See also Leslie Esbrook, The State of Military Justice Reform in Turkey: 2014, Military Law and the Law of War Review 53/1, pp. 2-3 (2014).

[28] Arsu and Bilefsky, *supra* note 10.

[29] Ozgur Asik, Legal Reforms in Turkey: Ambitious and Controversial, p. 146, Turkish Policy Quarterly, 5 June 2012, see http://turkishpolicy.com/pdf/vol_11-no_1-asik.pdf

[30] Aksel Report, p. 9.

Commission) called 'certainly a step in the right direction.'[31] Decision No 2012/125 should thus be understood as a positive landmark in Turkish military justice.

---

[31] Venice Report, 112, 123. See also Kareem Shaheen, Turkish referendum: all you need to know, The Guardian, https://www.theguardian.com/world/2017/apr/10/turkish-referendum-all-you-need-to-know

Leslie Esbrook is an appellate and trial litigator at Robbins, Russell, Englert, Orseck & Untereiner LLP in Washington, DC, and an Adjunct Professor of Law at Brooklyn Law School. She is a graduate of Yale Law School and a former Fulbright scholar to Turkey. She has previously served as a Rapporteur to the Global Seminar on Military Justice Reform held at Yale Law School and has received an award from the National Institute of Military Justice for her published work on Turkish military justice.

Remaining Faithful to the Demands of Legality in the Face of a Violent Crisis

Shruti Bedi

Manipur Encounters, India

Introduction

The foil for my analysis of the *Manipur Encounters* case[1] is based on the use of the state power in preventing terrorism and insurgency as measured against the threat that these powers pose to constitutional or human rights. The effort to preserve the rule of law in times of crisis and emergency in a democracy usually defies normative coherence. In Shakespeare's play, *The Merchant of Venice*, Bassanio urges Portia to break the law to thwart Shylock – 'to do a great right, do a little wrong'.[2] This statement from the bard's time holds particular didactic value in the twenty-first century. The Armed Forces Special Powers Act, 1958 (AFSPA), empowers the forces to deal with terrorism and insurgency swiftly. With the aim of securing and protecting their own people, the forces act with

[1] *Extra-Judicial Execution Victim Families Assn. v. Union of India*, (2016) 14 SCC 536 (Bench: Madan Lokur & UU Lalit JJ.), popularly known as the Manipur Encounters case, can also be accessed at https://indiankanoon.org/doc/83144198/ (Note: The paragraph numbers in the weblink would be different than those of the above-mentioned citation).

[2] William Shakespeare, *The Merchant of Venice*, Act 4, Scene 1, available at: https://eg4.nic.in/jnv/DFILES/EBOOKS/IR/0780TheMerchantofVenice.pdf

expediency and sometimes their actions come under close scrutiny. This piece examines the judgment of the Supreme Court in *Extra Judicial Execution Victim Families Association (EEVFAM) v. Union of India* (the *Manipur Encounters* case, as stated earlier) from the point of view of questioning the rightness or wrongness of motives, ends and actions of a human soldier.

Background Facts

A public interest litigation was filed before the apex court by the Extra Judicial Execution Victim Families Association (EEVFAM) on the allegation that 1,528 people were killed in encounters by the security forces in the Indian north-eastern state of Manipur between 1979 and 2012 under the shield of AFSPA. In its defence, the Indian Army stated that it could not be subjected to First Information Reports (FIRs)[3] for carrying out anti-militancy operations in insurgency-prone areas, including Manipur.

On 8 July 2016, the Supreme Court, in the *Manipur Encounters* case, held that the Armed Forces could not claim blanket immunity from prosecution. Since the acts of commission by the security forces are too serious to be ignored by any democracy which thrives on the rule of law, the Supreme Court ordered an inquiry to be conducted into the killings by a Special Investigation Team (SIT). It concluded that the petitioners have a 'right to know' the truth under the ambit of the fundamental right under Article 21 of the Indian Constitution. Thereafter, in 2018, petitions were instituted by army personnel, objecting to the alleged dilution of AFSPA and praying for immunity for soldiers for actions carried out in 'good faith'. The Court did not think it appropriate to reopen the matter at the said stage and accordingly dismissed the petition.[4]

AFSPA has been enacted with the objective of empowering the Armed Forces to maintain public order in 'disturbed areas'. Under section 3 of AFSPA, an area can be declared as 'disturbed' by notification by

---

[3] A First Information Report is the report filed with the police whenever an offence first comes to notice; it is a part of criminal procedure in India.

[4] *Lourembam Deben Singh v. Union of India*, (2019) 12 SCC 346.

the Government on account of differences or disputes between members of different religious, racial, language, or regional groups or castes or communities. It can be invoked in places where 'the use of armed forces in aid of civil power is necessary'. The Armed Forces have the authority to prohibit a gathering of five or more persons in an area and can legitimately use force or open fire, after due warning, against a person who contravenes the law.

The Right to Know the Truth and to Lament

Searching for an end to impunity, the petitioners in the *Manipur Encounters* case did not simply seek accountability and punishment for the perpetrators; they wanted to fight for their right to lament the loss of loved ones and the right to the truth of enforced disappearances. The truth could restore dignity to people by allowing them to mourn for their dead, resulting in eventual personal and community healing. In Ackerman's words, lamentation is 'a language for dealing with, although not solving, the problem of suffering'.[5] Expressing pain is deeply human, and by contesting the untruth, the petitioners challenged the indifference to suffering and denial of justice. Thus, Justice Madan Lokur, speaking for the court, said, 'It is necessary to know the truth so that the law is tempered with justice.'[6]

The apex court had appointed a three-member Justice Santosh Hegde Commission to conduct an inquiry into six identified cases.[7] The report of the Commission was taken up by the Court on 4 April 2013, wherein the Court observed that the Commission had found that 'the killing of the victims was not in any true encounter with the police or the security forces.'[8] It further found that the victims did not have any crim-

---

[5] Ackermann, D M (2003), *After the Locusts: Letters from a Landscape of Faith*, (Grand Rapids: Eerdmans), p.100.

[6] *Manipur Encounters case, supra* note 1, para 86.

[7] *Extra-Judicial Execution Victim Families Assn.* v. *Union of India*, (2013) 2 SCC 493 (Bench: Aftab Alam and Ranjana P Desai, JJ).

[8] *Extra-Judicial Execution Victim Families Assn. v. Union of India*, (2016) 14 SCC 570 (Bench: Aftab Alam and Ranjana P Desai, JJ), reported within *Extra-Judicial Execution Victim Families Assn. v. Union of India, supra* note 1, para 19.

inal antecedents. The exercise for ascertaining the truth of the fake encounters was conducted to provide an answer to the question as to who the perpetrators were and what steps could be taken to commiserate with the kin of the victims. Resultantly, it was on the basis of the Commission's findings that the court called for a deeper probe to extract the truth on the alleged fake encounters.

Deployment of Armed Forces 'In Aid of Civil Power'

There are four situations that threaten the security of the country as envisaged under the Constitution, i.e., war, external aggression, armed rebellion and internal disturbance. Depending on the gravity of the situation, the President can proclaim emergency in the first three situations under Article 352 of the Constitution. In the case of internal disturbance, the Centre is duty-bound to offer protection to the states but cannot declare an emergency. Under Entry 1, List II, Schedule VII of the Indian Constitution, the maintenance of public order falls under the jurisdiction of a state.[9] However, the Centre may 'deploy armed forces in any state in aid of civil power' under Entry 2A, List I, Schedule VII[10] in a situation of internal disturbance. The point is that the armed forces can be deployed in the affected state but only in aid of civil power. In *Naga People's Movement of Human Rights v. Union of India,*[11] a constitution bench of the Supreme Court sought to explain the phrase 'in aid of civil power'. The court remarked that it 'implies that deployment of the Armed Forces of the Union shall be to enable the civil power in the state to deal with the situation affecting maintenance of public order' and that the armed forces do not 'supplant or act as a substitute for the civil power in the state.'[12] The conclusion drawn by the Court in the Manipur Encounters case, on a combined reading of Entry 2A of List I and Entry 1 of List II, was that

---

[9] Entry 1 – Public order (but not including the use of any naval, military or air force or any other Armed Force of the Union or of any other force subject to the control of the Union or of any contingent or unit thereof in aid of the civil power.

[10] Entry 2A – Deployment of any armed force of the Union or any other force subject to the control of the Union or any contingent or unit thereof in any state in aid of the civil power; powers, jurisdiction, privileges and liabilities of the members of such forces while on such deployment.

[11] *Naga People's Movement of Human Rights v. Union of India* (1998) 2 SCC 109.

[12] *Id.*, para 24.

the deployment of the armed forces is not limited only to a 'situation affecting public order', but that the forces were to 'operate in cooperation and conjunction with the civil administration' until the restoration of normalcy.[13] Resultantly, the court held that non-restoration of normalcy could not justify a prolonged and indefinite deployment of forces. The apex court observed that normalcy not being restored indicated either the failure of the civil administration or the armed forces, which makes a mockery of democratic values.[14] It is true that special powers enlisted to deal with crises invariably pose a host of difficult trade-offs between values such as life, liberty, equality on the one hand and those of security and safety on the other, especially in the face of delay in controlling the insurgency.

Immunity from Prosecution

Section 4(a) of AFSPA permits the use of force even to the extent of causing the death of 'any person who is acting in contravention of any law or order for the time being in force in the disturbed area prohibiting the assembly of five or more persons or the carrying of weapons or of things capable of being used as weapons or of firearms, ammunition or explosive substances'.

Section 6 of AFSPA grants immunity, inter alia, from prosecution to any person in respect of anything done or purported to be done in exercise of the powers conferred by AFSPA, except with the previous sanction of the Central Government.

A conjunctive reading of sections 125 and 126 of the Army Act, 1950, and sections 4 and 5 of the Criminal Procedure Code, 1973 (CrPC), provides that when both a criminal court and court-martial have jurisdiction in respect of an offence, the first option is with the Army to decide whether the accused should be tried before a criminal court or a court-martial. However, in case the criminal court is desirous of trying the matter, it may require the Army to send the accused to the nearest magistrate or make a reference to the Central Government in this respect. Therefore, if there is a conflict of jurisdiction between a criminal court

[13] *Manipur Encounters case, supra* note 1, para 173.

[14] *Ibid.*

(under CrPC) and a court-martial (under the Army Act), reference is made to the Central Government for passing an appropriate order. In the *Manipur Encounters* case, the state attempted to claim immunity for the armed forces from the criminal courts under CrPC and argued for the exclusive jurisdiction of the Army for offences committed by them. The court refused to accept the contention and held that the decision to prosecute does not lie exclusively with the Army and that in certain circumstances, a criminal court could also conduct a trial of the offender.[15]

Preservation of the rule of law even during an emergency is a desirable objective. Courts are the primary institutions to place a check on any abuse or misuse of power. Section 6, AFSPA grants protection from prosecution to any person in respect of anything done or purported to be done in exercise of the powers conferred by AFSPA, except with the previous sanction of the Central Government. In *Matajog Dobey v. HC Bhari*[16] the courts advocated that the grant of sanction to prosecute an official under CrPC should follow a cautious step-by-step approach. The first step is to ascertain whether the act complained of is an offence and thereafter to determine whether it was committed in the discharge of official duty.[17] Undoubtedly, killing a person is an offence; however, it is important to determine whether there exists a 'reasonable connection' between the death and the official act. In the case of AFSPA, to invoke protection from prosecution, the act under question not only has to be in the course of performance of duties but also with the intention of furthering a lawful objective. Interestingly, and appreciably, the version of AFSPA promulgated in 1990 for Jammu & Kashmir explicitly mentions that protection is only available to persons acting in 'good faith'.[18]

The Court in the *Manipur Encounters* case followed the principle laid down in the *Naga People's Movement* case[19] that in a case concerning the complaint against the conduct of the Armed Forces and misuse of their powers under AFSPA, a thorough investigation should be conducted and in case the allegation is proved, the 'victim should be suitably compensated by the state, and the requisite sanction under Section 6 of the

---

[15] *Id.*, para 246.

[16] *Matajog Dobey v. HC Bhari* AIR 1956 SC 44.

[17] *Id.*, para 17.

[18] Section 7, Armed Forces (Jammu & Kashmir) Special Powers Act, 1990.

[19] *Supra* note 12.

Central Act should be granted for the instruction of prosecution and/or a civil suit or other proceedings against the person/persons responsible for such violation.'[20] However, as far as the *Manipur Encounters* case was concerned, the apex court held that this position of law would not be applicable presently, as it was still to be determined if the 'deaths were in genuine encounters in counter-insurgency operations' and also 'whether the use of force was disproportionate or retaliatory or not'.[21] The Court also emphatically pointed out that if the killings were unjustified, the forces would not be given a 'blanket immunity' since nobody has the right to act with impunity. Consequently, the Court ordered an inquiry into the allegation of the use of excessive retaliatory force by the police and security forces in Manipur, regardless of the identity of the victims.

The Faceless 'Enemy'

Manipur has been facing a public order situation for the last 60 years, which effectively amounts to a state of internal disturbance and not a state of emergency or war-like situation. The question before the Court in the *Manipur Encounters* case was whether there was the use of excessive force by the Manipur police and Armed Forces in the said 1,528 cases during the period of internal disturbance in Manipur. Another answer that was being sought was whether the use of retaliatory force by the security forces was justified on the ground that the victims were 'enemy' as defined under the Army Act, 1950.

An 'enemy' under section 3(x) of the Army Act is inclusively defined as 'armed mutineers, armed rebels, armed rioters, pirates and any person in arms against whom it is the duty of any person subject to military law to act.' The state placed its reliance on this provision and contended that the militants and terrorists killed by the Armed Forces were covered by this definition of 'enemy' under section 3(x) as held in *Ratan Singh v. Union of India*.[22] The submission was that the deaths caused were justified,

[20] *Id.*, para 61.

[21] Manipur Encounters case, *supra* note 1, para 234.

[22] 1992 Supp (1) SCC 716, para 7. However, the court in the Manipur Encounters case stated that not all militants could be classified as 'enemy' in every situation (para 219).

being deaths of terrorists, militants and insurgents. Schedule 1 of the Unlawful Activities Prevention Act, 1967 (UAPA), lists some organisations operating in Manipur as terrorist organisations.[23] The Attorney General argued that under AFSPA, for maintaining public order in a disturbed area, the armed forces are empowered to cause the death of an 'enemy' which could include a militant, terrorist, insurgent who is or is likely to threaten the unity, integrity, security or sovereignty of India. Therefore, a person carrying weapons in violation of prohibitory orders in the disturbed area of Manipur is *ipso facto* an 'enemy'. The Court refuted this, stating that simply because a person was carrying arms in a prohibited area would not lead to a conclusion that he was an enemy or a member of a terrorist or unlawful organisation.[24] Any designation of a person as a militant or a terrorist ought to be justified by the commission or an overt act of violence.[25] Such determination of the exact identity of the 'enemy' could only be deciphered after a thorough inquiry.

Conclusion

The judgment of the apex court in the present case is well-reasoned and makes a great contribution to constitutional law by trying to balance the human rights of people along with the mandate of the security forces, especially in public order situations. The Court must be applauded for performing its constitutional duty by ordering a transparent, fair and detailed inquiry. The gravity of the acts of encounters is too serious to be ignored by any democracy and its rule of law. However, these situations of conflict between security and liberty raise unanswered questions which plague every government.

[23] The organisations which are listed as terrorist organisations or unlawful associations under UAPA include People's Liberation Army (PLA), United National Liberation Front (UNLF), People's Revolutionary Party of Kangleipak (PREPAK), Kangleipak Communist Party (KCP), Kanglei Yaol Kanba Lup (KYKL) and Manipur People's Liberation Front (MPLF). Manipur Encounters case, *supra* note 1, para 181.

[24] *Id.*, para 222.

[25] The court cited the cases of *State (NCT of Delhi) v. Navjot Sandhu*, (2005) 11 SCC 600; *Indra Das v. State of Assam*, (2011) 3 SCC 380; *Arup Bhuyan v. State of Assam*, (2011) 3 SCC 377 where the court held that mere membership of a banned organisation cannot incriminate a person.

The use of force by the armed forces is bound by the rules of preservation of the rule of law and protection of liberties. There was, in fact, a greater duty of care in the suspected fake encounters matter as the alleged 'enemy' were Indian citizens who were entitled to fundamental rights under the Constitution. Commenting on the irony of the situation, the Court observed that the armed forces have never been trained to raise arms against their own countrymen.[26] As remarked in the *Naga People's* case, the Army's primary task has always been to defend its borders against hostile forces. They are trained and oriented to face external aggression and not confront their own people in such a manner.[27] Consequently, a prolonged deployment of the forces ultimately has an adverse impact on their morale leading to an existential crisis. A soldier is trained to kill the external aggressor and protect the citizens of his own country. Any show of hesitation while carrying out such an act is termed as an act of cowardice. Hesitation, which could also mean losing the opportunity to kill a dreaded terrorist and defend his people, is not only looked down upon but is termed as a criminal offence. In such a situation, how does anyone (not just the soldier) assess the appropriate degree of force to be used and whether it exceeds the appropriate force?

Invoking the beginning of the Ten Commandments[28] issued by the Chief of the Army Staff for soldiers operating in such operations – 'Remember that people you are dealing with, are your own countrymen. All your conduct must be dictated by this one significant consideration' – is more easily said than done. Cowardice and abandonment of arms in the face of the enemy is a criminal act wherein the soldier can be punished with the death penalty. To disobey a direct order is an offence. Placing the forces in such a situation is a dilemma that defies a logical solution. The security forces are trained and directed to err on the side of imprudence, and to expect them to be cautious and use adequate discretion in killing the 'enemy' is a grey area. Understanding such directions in the fluid nature of such operations is a challenging task for a person in the midst of a situation who has to decide to 'kill' the enemy or save the lives

[26] *Manipur Encounters* case, *supra* note 1, para 224.

[27] Naga People's case, *supra* note 12, para 39.

[28] The Ten Commandments are issued by the Chief of the Army Staff under the caption "List of Dos and Don'ts" which restrain the Army from using excessive force while operating in disturbed areas. See Manipur Encounters case, *supra* note 1, para 232.

of his people in a fraction of a second. In this moment of challenge, the soldier then decides, what is at times perceived, 'to do a great right' and therefore 'does a little wrong'. This action is not an outcome of any mala fide intention. Can the soldiers, faced with a faceless enemy, take steps necessary to suppress the insurgency while remaining faithful to the strict demands of legality in dynamic operations and situations? No law and no court can give us the perfect answer.

Professor (Dr) **Shruti Bedi** is a Professor of Law at the University Institute of Legal Studies (UILS), Panjab University (PU), Chandigarh, India; Coordinator, Department of Law, University School of Open Learning, PU; and Director, Centre for Constitution and Public Policy, UILS, PU. She teaches the core course on Indian Constitutional Law and an elective course on Internal Security Law in addition to the master's course on Comparative Public Law (LLM). Her areas of research are constitutional law, counter-terrorism law and comparative public law.

She has authored two books: *Terrorism: Our World and Our Laws* (LAP Lambert, 2009) and *Indian Counter-Terrorism Law* (Lexis Nexis, 2016); and co-edited four books: *Judicial Review: Process, Powers and Problems* (Cambridge University Press, 2020); *Taking Bail Seriously: State of Bail Jurisprudence in India* (Lexis Nexis, 2020); *Law and Media (2019) and Electoral System: Democracy, Laws and Issues* (2019). She has published extensively in reputed journals, books, blogs and newspapers. In addition, she has lectured at international and national forums including universities in England, Canada, Indonesia, Brazil and Vietnam. She has also delivered a TEDx Talk on Justice: The First Promise.

Right to Silence in Brazilian Military Criminal Justice Procedure – Voracious Protection by the Courts

Justice Maria Elizabeth Guimarães Teixeira Rocha

Appeal No 2008.01.05099-3/RJ, Brazil

Introduction

The present legal reflection, relevant in the military criminal doctrine and jurisprudence, deals with the protection and interpretation of the fundamental right to silence by the Brazilian judiciary, especially its applicability in vexed issues in the *praxis* of Federal Military Justice.

Compelled by the Supreme Court, the Superior Military Court was forced to change its precedents to safeguard the right to silence of defendants and also witnesses, who, when questioned by the police or inquired by a judge, were to confess a crime or provide evidence against themselves, in light of Article 305 of the Military Criminal Procedure Code, the Decree No 1002, dated 21 October 1969, which provides as follows:

> Before starting the interrogation, the judge will observe to the accused that although he is not obliged to answer the questions put to him, his silence may be interpreted to the detriment of his own defense.

Certainly, the textual interpretation of the military code deviated and clashed with the constitutional precept inscribed in Item LXIII of Article

5 of the Constitution, which ensures non-self-incrimination to the accused:

> Litteris: the prisoner will be informed of his rights, including the right to remain silent, and assurance of family assistance and a lawyer.

Interpretative Evolution of the Federal Military Justice with respect to the Constitutional Right to Silence in the Context of Military Criminal Proceedings: The Repeal of Article 305 of the Military Procedural Code

The Federal Military Justice milieu had long argued about the affront of Article 305 of the Military Criminal Procedural Code to the right to silence guaranteed by the Constitution. The matter was brought before analysis of the judiciary in the judgment of Appeal No 2008.01.05099-3/RJ, in the Superior Military Court, according to the protocol of the 97th Judgment Session of 9 December 2009.[1]

The Superior Military Court, by a majority, accepted and declared the revocation of the offending provision, ruling that to keep silent is a guarantee of all defendants, and under no circumstances should the situation be interpreted to their disadvantage.

At the same time, in Habeas Corpus No 103.686/RJ,[2] the Brazilian Supreme Federal Court was urged to express its opinion on the matter, and although it did not explicitly confirm the revocation in the *ibid* appeal by the Superior Military Court, as the judgment remained restricted to appreciate the *meritum causae* of the writ, the Supreme Federal Court did not overrule the declaration of the Superior Military Court, and it was rather tacitly endorsed.

---

[1] Appeal. Repeal of Art. 305 of CPPM in the face of the Federal Constitution, 1988. Effect inter partes. Possibility. Prescript occurrence. Minor co-defendants. The effect of the lapse of time to impose a punishment has been observed in the case of the co-defendants who were minor at the time of the offense. In view of the incompatibility with the constitutional dictates, the repeal of Art. 305 of the Military Criminal Procedure Code was declared, since the accused's silence, during the interrogation cannot under any circumstances be interpreted to his detriment, according to the provisions of art. 5th, LXIII, of the Constitution. Concession of 'sursis'. – Preliminary accepted. Appeal partially allowed. Unanimous decision. (Appeal No 2008.01.050993-3/RJ. Rapporteur: Justice Maria Elizabeth Guimarães Teixeira Rocha. Publication: 16 December 2009).

[2] Federal Court of Justice. Habeas Corpus No 103.686/RJ. Rapporteur: Justice Dias Toffoli. Published in DJe 3 September 2012.

It is essential to note that the Supreme Federal Court, as an appellate and constitutional tribunal placed at the apex of the Brazilian judiciary, had been reiterating this guarantee for decades, both in the context of ordinary as well as military criminal proceedings. However, in doing so, it restricted the nullity of the criminal proceeding on a case-to-case basis, according to the principle 'pas de nullité sans grief' (no nullity without grievance). It held that the lack of warning about the right to silence does not lead to the automatic annulment of the interrogation or testimony, and it is necessary to observe the other circumstances of the specific case to verify whether or not there was an illegality, or a prejudice caused.

In a landmark case, the Supreme Court highlighted the importance of the concept and the impossibility of detrimental hermeneutics on the part of the magistrate against the defendant who remains silent. It was observed that the right to silence is a pillar of the system for the protection of individual rights and underscores one of the most important principles of human dignity. In the same breath, it was also held that the right of the accused to remain silent was an expression of the principle of non-self-incrimination and that it was legally applicable not only at the beginning but has been a concept that permeates the entire criminal process.[3]

For this reason, the presumption of innocence sculpted in item LVII of Article 5 of the Brazilian Constitution engages the criminal process not only during the formation of the evidence and the 'persecution criminis', but also until the verdict of guilt or innocence.

Ada Pelegrini Grinover, a respectable Brazilian proceduralist, points out that the State cannot disregard the defendant's presumption of innocence. As a result, the person can remain silent or even lie to prevent the production of evidence or prove against himself, and such prerogative, under no circumstances, can cause him legal prejudice.

Furthermore, the ample defense provided by Article 11(1) of the Universal Declaration of Human Rights provides that:

> Everyone charged with a penal offense has the right to be presumed innocent until proved guilty according to law in a public trial at which he has had all the guarantees necessary for his defense.[4]

---

[3] Supreme Federal Court, Habeas Corpus No 80,949, Rapporteur: Justice Sepúlveda Pertence, Published in the DJe of 12/14/2001.

[4] United Nations Organization. Universal Declaration of Human Rights. Adopted and proclaimed by the United Nations General Assembly (resolution 217 A III), 10 December 1948.

The principiology of the Brazilian Fundamental Law promulgated in 1988 established among judges and jurists the doctrinal consensus that the silence of the defendant cannot result in an adverse judgment by the judge because everyone has the right to be silent for their own benefit. In this regard, Justice Celso de Mello added:

> It is worth noting that the clause which legitimizes the right to silence, explicit in constitutional terms according to the postulate 'nemo tenetur', did nothing but consecrate this theme within the normative system established by the 1988 Charter of the Republic, a guideline proclaimed since 1791, by the Fifth Amendment that composes the North American Bill of Rights.[5]

The incompatibility of Article 305 of the Procedure of Military Code with the Brazilian Constitution was handled with judicial deftness. However, this is to be read in conjunction with the principle 'lex posterior derogat lex priori', meaning thereby that there is no automatic unconstitutionality of the actions taken prior to that date. This principle has also been endorsed by the Supreme Court earlier.[6]

Considering the contradiction over time and the normative hierarchy, the conflict of Article 305 with the Brazilian Charter was evident, which is why the Federal Military Court, based on law declared by the Supreme Court, was compelled to revoke it from the current procedural rules.

The Guarantee of the Right to Silence in the Inquisitorial and Judicial Processes to both Witnesses and Defendants

In the same vein, also to safeguard the same constitutional guarantee under analysis, the Supreme Federal Court decided to confirm the right to silence for witnesses too, and not only for the accused in the context of military criminal proceedings. Thus, they should also be warned about

---

[5] Supreme Federal Court, *Habeas Corpus* No 80530 / PA, Rapporteur: Justice Celso de Mello, Published in DJe 17 November 2000.

[6] The Supreme Court decision in the Action of Unconstitutionality No 74-8 / RN, supports the 'revocation' explained above, Rapporteur: Justice Celso de Mello, published in DJ 25 September 1992. RTJ 143/3. Other decisions: Appeal in *Habeas Corpus No* 122279/RJ, Rapporteur: Justice Gilmar Mendes, published in DJe 30 October 2014; *Habeas Corpus* No 79812, Rapporteur: Justice Celso de Mello, published in DJ 16 February 2001.

the right to remain silent when investigating during the inquisitorial phase and in the judicial process, when there is a possibility of confession, in order to preserve them from any type of self-incrimination.

It should be noted that this position was not the one originally adopted by the jurisprudence of the Superior Military Tribunal – a court with jurisdiction over processes and prosecution of military offenses committed by military or civilian personnel within the scope of the Armed Forces (Army, Navy and Air Force). It was a result of the federal criminal specialized justice, which integrates the Brazilian judiciary ever since the inception of the Constitution of 1934. In fact, the Military Court used to reject all preliminaries argued by the defendants' counsel in this regard. The parties systematically pleaded for the nullity of all criminal proceedings processed by the Military Prosecutor's Office due to the conviction being based solely and exclusively on a testimonial hearing provided without the warning of the constitutional guarantee of silence.[7] Paradoxically, the witnesses who deposed in military police investigations, under the commitment to tell the truth and without any warning of having the right to be silent, used to end up reporting facts that violated their own rights and even end up incriminating themselves.

In this context, the Public Defender's Office insistently postulated the procedural nullity, which was not accepted in appeal. It was held that the statements were signed by free will and were to be ratified in later inquiries and interrogation by the Court. Hence, this preliminary objection was rejected unanimously.[8]

---

[7] Superior Military Court. *Habeas Corpus* No 135-73.2010.7.00.0000/RN, Rapporteur: Justice Maria Elizabeth Guimarães Teixeira Rocha, published: 3 March 2011; Superior Military Court, *Habeas Corpus* No 132-21.2010.7.00.0000/RN, Rapporteur: Justice Maria Elizabeth Guimarães Teixeira Rocha, published: 18 February 2011; Superior Military Court, *Habeas Corpus* No 16-10.2013.7.00.0000, Rapporteur: Justice Maria Elizabeth Guimarães Teixeira Rocha, published:15 March 2013.

[8] Defense appeal. Art. 172 of the Penal Military Code. Preliminary: incompetence of military justice. Procedural nullity. Unconstitutionality of Art. 172 of Military Code. Rejection. Merit: atypicity. Absolution. Dismissal of the appeal. I – Preliminary of incompetence of the Federal Military Justice to prosecute and judge civilians. The matter has already been settled within the scope of the STM and the Supreme Court in order to recognize the competence of the specialized penal justice to judge military crimes perpetrated by civilians if the conditions of article 92, item I, of the Military Penal Code are satisfied, as well as art. 124, 'caput', of the Federal Constitution. Preliminary rejected, unanimously. II – Preliminary of procedural nullity. The assumption of defect in the phase of the Police Inquiry as a result of subpoena and the first statements as a witness, of those who came to confess the crime, does not hold, since the statements were signed freely,

The dispute ultimately reached the Supreme Federal Court in appeal since it involved constitutional rights, and it was recognized that the guarantee to remain silent would apply to both defendants as well as witnesses.[9]

It is interesting to note that even though the witness before a tribunal is legally obliged to declare the truth lest perjury is committed, certainly, it is not an absolute rule. Principles and values must be considered as a way of achieving practical aims of justice and harmonization with the constitutional standards, and hence laws must be interpreted and applied in a manner so as to serve the ends of justice.

As stated, the Lex Fundamentalis was responsible for expanding the list of obligations in the context of criminal proceedings. The Political Charter, a result of the National Constituent Assembly elected by the Brazilian people, dispelled divergences by establishing a long list of civil and criminal assurances. Thus, no one would be deprived of the defense of being silent for their own benefit.

Obviously, the exercise of non-self-incrimination is not restricted to the interrogation of a person formally accused; the spirit of the same is to apply throughout the investigative and procedural process within the parameters of the due legal process, in which it is ensured not only to the accused but to any person whose case may be harmed by eventual declarations, including the ones impelled to testify as witnesses. It is evident

---

with no defect of will and which came to be ratified in later inquiries as indicted as well as in the interrogation in court. Preliminary rejected, unanimously. III – Preliminary of unconstitutionality of article 172 of the CPM. The crimes foreseen in the military penal legislation were compatible with the article 124 of the Federal Constitution, as already declared by the Highest Court and by precedents of the Superior Military Court, adding in this case the literally of article 142, § 3 of the Magna Carta. In this case, the use of uniforms and patents are prerogative of members of the Armed Forces. Unanimous rejection. IV – On merit, the thesis of lack of intention to demonstrate the atypical nature of the conduct is not supported by law. The kind of deceit required by art. 172 of the Penal Code is generic, not specific, as it does not require any intentional complement to improve the crime of improper use of uniform. Appeal devoid of merits. Unanimous Decision. Appeal No 0000107- 80.2013.7.03.0303 / RS, Rapporteur: Justice José Coêlho Ferreira, published: DJe 8 April 2016.

[9] Habeas Corpus. Criminal procedure. Nullity. In observance to the right to silence. 'nemo tenetur detegere'. Flagrant illegality. Misuse of military uniform. Order granted I – It is settled law declared by the Supreme Federal Court that the investigated or accused person may remain silent, avoiding self-incrimination. II – The testimony of the patient, heard as a witness in the inquisitorial phase, was collected without observing her right to remain silent. III – Order granted. (HC No 136.331/RS, reporting by Justice Ricardo Lewandowski, judgment published on 13 June 2017).

that the concept of 'nemo tenetur se detegere' protects the witnesses too, with identical breadth and spectrum since its scope is to prevent the facilitation of his or her own conviction by the interrogation or production of evidence against himself or herself. It is a basic principle of the full exercise of guarantees peculiar to the Rule of Law in most democracies.

Therefore, despite the Superior Military Tribunal having revoked Article 305 (*supra*), when it rejected the preliminaries of nullity in cases where the witnesses were self-incriminating without being warned of the right to silence, and this testimony was the only means of proof on which the complaint was based, such a proposition explicitly violated the right protected by a magna clause, which reflects a cardinal rule of freedom that prevails in the Brazilian criminal process. In essence, the right to remain silent is related to:

> absence of duty to collaborate with the investigation or criminal procedural instruction;
>
> the right not to declare against oneself;
>
> the right not to confess; and
>
> the right not to speak the truth.

According to modern constitutional doctrine, the production of evidence and the search for truth cannot encroach upon the individual guarantees of a person and must be guided by the moral rules of society, which govern the activities of the State and citizens.

At last, in relation to the duty of flagging the right to silence as a norm that guides public agents, it is necessary to remember the Miranda Warning. It imposes imperative rules on the police officer who carries out the arrest of the citizen, and it emerged from the landmark judgment of the US Supreme Court in *Miranda v. Arizona*.[10] In the Miranda Warning, the concerned public or police official is supposed to inform about important aspects such as the right to remain silent and that whatever a person says can be used in a court of law, and further that there is a right to consult a lawyer, etc. The mere absence of this formality would be sufficient to invalidate the statements made by the person as evidence.

---

[10] More about the case can be read and accessed here: https://www.uscourts.gov/educational-resources/educational-activities/facts-and-case-summary-miranda-v-arizona

It is important to emphasize that only the evidence produced in a court of law by the criminal prosecution body under the aegis of an adversarial system of jurisprudence with a proper defense with constitutional guarantees can legitimize any punishment under criminal law. Although the unilateral and inquisitive elements obtained in police investigations might be sufficient to support a charge for the prosecutors, they are not enough for conviction by a criminal court.

Conclusion

In conclusion, the right to silence and non-self-incrimination are provided for in the Federal Constitution and are also internationally recognized in International Human Rights Agreements and Treaties adopted by Brazil;[11] as a result, these guarantees are mandatorily binding on the national courts.

Yes, the processes of criminal jurisprudence are an arduous mission for the judges and an ongoing organic feature, but then the unpredictable legal situations arising from time to time have to be taken head-on.

In the ultimate analysis, the system of Brazilian Military Justice safeguarding the right to silence, which is in any case, a measure imposed by the Federal Constitution, has established an equitable, fair, and reasonable judicial dispensation in the true spirit of a democracy where the Rule of Law is supreme and individual rights are precious.

---

[11] The American Human Rights Convention (San José of Costa Rica Pact) was internalized in the Brazilian legal context by Decree No 678, incepted on 6 November 1992, and is in force with the status of *supra* legal norm. Available: http://www.planalto.gov.br/ccivil_03/decreto/d0678.htm

Justice **Maria Elizabeth Guimarães Teixeira Rocha** is a judge of the Superior Military Court in Brazil. She is a PhD in Constitutional Law from the Federal University of Minas Gerais and Doctor *honoris causae* at Inca Garcilaso de la Vega Faculty, Lima, Peru. She also holds a master's degree in Legal and Political Sciences at the Portugal Catholic University, Lisbon, Portugal. She is also a Constitutional and Military Law Professor and has authored several books and legal articles published in Brazil and abroad.

She was assisted in the commentary by Mateus Schaeffer Brandão, a master's degree holder and a PhD student in Legal and Business Sciences from the Faculty of Law at the University of Lisbon, Lisbon, Portugal. He is a serving as a Brazilian Air Force officer and legal advisor to the Superior Military Court (STM), Brazil.

She was also assisted by Micheline Barboza Balduíno Ribeiro who is a specialist in criminal procedure from Potiguar University, Rio Grande do Norte and a Procedural Analyst at the Federal Attorney Office.

Trial of Civilians by Military Courts: Unfortunate Endorsement by the Supreme Court of Pakistan

Manmohan Sood

Constitution Petition 12/2010, Pakistan

President Abraham Lincoln famously summarised the spirit of democracy, stating that it is a government of the people, by the people and for the people. The essence of any democracy lies in the fundamental rights available to its common citizens. The members of the armed forces of any nation take an oath to protect the sovereignty of their country even to the peril of their lives, or to the same effect, and therefore the most valuable right to life is restricted in respect of members of the armed forces of any nation. Similarly, there are other restrictions on the fundamental rights of members of the armed forces to protect the sovereignty of their country and, in turn, protect the fundamental rights of their citizens. The members of the armed forces are generally governed by a special act to ensure the highest level of discipline in the armed forces. The Pakistan Army Act, 1952,[1] just like the Indian Army Act, 1950,[2] drew itself from the Indian Army Act, 1911. The primary purpose of the Pakistan Army Act, 1952, like any other Act relating to armed forces, is the maintenance of discipline of the members of the Pakistan Army. The Pakistan Army Act, 1952, came into force on 1 April 1955 through a gazette notification published in accordance with Section 1 of the Act. The boundaries of the

[1] Pakistan Army Act, 1952, can be accessed at http://nasirlawsite.com/laws/paa1952.htm

[2] Army Act, 1950 (India), can be accessed at https://www.mod.gov.in/dod/sites/default/files/TheArmyAct1950.pdf

Act as regards subjection of the persons governed by it were clearly demarcated in Section 2 of the Act. It was primarily applicable to the officers, junior commissioned officers and warrant officers of the Pakistan Army and to a limited extent to the civilians working with the Army during active service, in camp, and on the march under specified conditions. In the year 1958, sub-clause (bb) was inserted in Section 2, thereby bringing the seconded[3] persons of Navy and Air Force into the folds of the Pakistan Army Act, 1952. The scope of the subjection of civilians was further expanded in the year 1967 by including civilians seducing the persons subject to the Army Act from their duty and offenders under Official Secrets Act, 1923.

A Dastardly Attack on the Army Public School – A Trigger for Military Courts for Civilians

On 16 December 2014, a gruesome terror attack took place at the premises of the Army Public School, Peshawar, which resulted in the death of 151 innocent children and staff. Such a dastardly attack on innocent children shook the conscience of the entire country and also rightly caused global outrage, following which an all-party meeting was held at Peshawar on 18 December 2014. In the said meeting, the political leadership of Pakistan resolved to eliminate the scourge of militancy, terrorism, radicalisation and extremism. The leaders also resolved to establish speedy trial courts. The resolve to establish speedy trial courts was lost in the hurry to pass legislation, and finally, the resolve culminated in amendments to Pakistan Army Act, 1952. The state machinery worked overtime to bring the Constitutional (21st Amendment) Act, 2015, and Pakistan Army (Amendment Act), 2015. The 21st Constitutional Amendment and the bill of Pakistan Army (Amendment Act), 2015, were together introduced in the National Assembly. They were passed by the National Assembly and Senate on 6 January 2016, received Presidential assent on 7 January 2016, and accordingly, the Pakistan Army (Amendment Act), 2015, came into force on 7 January 2016. The controversy later erupted during the course of arguments before the Supreme Court of Pakistan in (the already pending) Constitution Petition No 12 of 2010

---

[3] The term 'seconded' refers to personnel who are permanently deputed to a different service.

titled *District Bar Association, Rawalpindi v. Federation of Pakistan & others,*[4] which is the subject of this piece, and which is discussed in the succeeding paragraphs, wherein, it was challenged by the petitioners that if Presidential assent to the constitutional amendment did not precede the amendment to the Army Act, then the said amendments made to the Army Act were without any force. The said contention was taken note of by the bench but was found to be without any force.

Constitutional Provisions

The Constitution of the Islamic Republic of Pakistan, in Part-II, deals with the fundamental rights and principles of policy. Article 8 of Part-II declares that the laws inconsistent with or in derogation of the fundamental rights are void. Article 8(3)(b)(i) excludes the laws contained in the First Schedule of the Constitution of Pakistan from provisions of Article 8. Accordingly, the First Schedule in Sub-Part III of Part I was amended by the 21st amendment and entries 6, 7, 8 and 9 were added after entry 5. The said entries related to the Pakistan Army Act, 1952, Pakistan Air Force Act, 1953, Pakistan Naval Ordinance, 1961 and Protection of Pakistan Act, 2014, respectively. Article 175, dealing with the establishment and jurisdiction of the courts, was also amended by adding a proviso that excluded the application of the said article to the newly inserted entries 6, 7, 8 and 9 in the first schedule in accordance with Article 8 of the Constitution of the Islamic Republic of Pakistan. The said proviso to Article 175 effectively excluded the jurisdiction of the courts in Pakistan as regards persons triable by military courts, who claimed, or were known to belong, to any terrorist group or organisation using the name of religion or a sect of religion. A corresponding amendment was made in Section 2 (d) of the Pakistan Army Act, 1952, and sub-clauses (iii) and (iv) were added vide Pakistan Army (Amendment) Act, 2015. Thus, after the amendment of 1967, the subjection of civilians under the Pakistan Army Act, 1952, was further expanded to include the civilians

[4] The full text of the judgment in *District Bar Association, Rawalpindi v. Federation of Pakistan & others,* along with other clubbed cases can be accessed at https://studylib.net/doc/8786492/text-of-detailed-sc-judgment-on-18th-21st-amendments

of various descriptions contained in the amended Section 2 of the Pakistan Army Act, 1952. In order to give effect to the said amendment, another amendment was made in Section 60(k) of the Pakistan Army Act, 1952 by adding the words 'and any other law for the time being in force', thereby applying the punishments prescribed under the concerned act to the class of civilians included in subjection clause. However, the sunset clause contained in Section 1(3) of the Constitution (21st Amendment) Act, 2015, limited the application of the amendments to a period of only two years.

The Challenge Before the Supreme Court of Pakistan

The 21st Constitutional Amendment and the Pakistan Army (Amendment) Act, 2015 were challenged before the Supreme Court of Pakistan. The petitions challenging the 18th and 21st amendments to the Constitution were clubbed and heard together by a 17-judge Constitution bench since the two sets of cases involved a common constitutional question as to 'whether there were any limitations on the powers of the Parliament to amend the Constitution and whether the Courts possess jurisdiction to strike down a constitutional amendment'. The main contention of the petitioners in the case was that there were certain basic features of the Constitution which were unamendable and that notwithstanding ostensible conferment of unlimited power on the Parliament by clause (6) of Article 239 and ouster of jurisdiction of the Courts by clause (5) thereof, the Parliament is not empowered to bring about changes in the basic structure of the Constitution. Professor Conrad's theory of the unamendable basic structure of the Constitution followed by the Supreme Court of India in various judgments was discussed in detail by the Supreme Court of Pakistan. It was argued that extension of powers of the Pakistan Army Act, 1952 (as amended) over the civilians abridges the fundamental right of access to justice. It was further argued that persons tried by the military courts were denied the essential elements of justice, that is, an independent court, independent procedure and the right to engage a counsel of choice. As regards the sunset clause, it was argued that it indicated the hesitation of legislators in granting unchecked powers to the military. There was a near unanimity with the petitioners' lawyers that the Constitutional Amendment was a clear denial of justice to the persons tried under the amended Pakistan Army Act. On the other hand, it was argued by the State that the courts being a creature of the Constitution, derive their power and jurisdiction from it and limits of such power are also set by the Constitution itself. It was argued that Article 245, read with Entry 1 and Entry 55 of the Federal Legislative List, grants the Federal Government the power to legislate on creating military courts for the defence of Pakistan during times of war. The Constitutional Amendment merely included the Pakistan Army Act, 1952, in the first schedule and had not made any other amendment to the Constitution, touching or affecting the basic structure.

The View Taken by the Supreme Court of Pakistan and the Departure from the Law Laid Down Earlier

The Supreme Court of Pakistan, while disagreeing with the theory of the basic structure of the Constitution relied upon by the Supreme Court of India in various judgements, observed that there are no limitations, express or implied, on the powers of the Parliament in Pakistan to amend the Constitution and the amendments brought about in exercise of such power are not liable to be challenged on any ground, whatsoever, before any court. However, the decision to select and refer the case of any accused of trial under the Pakistan Army Act, 1952, and any order passed or decision taken or sentence awarded in such trial was held to be subject to judicial review on the limited grounds of *coram non-judice*, being without jurisdiction or suffering from *mala fide*. Accordingly, the petition was dismissed by Supreme Court by a majority of 11 to 6 on 5 August 2015. The judgment was also a departure from the earlier landmark dicta of the same Court in Constitution Petition No 37 of 1998 *Liaquat Hussain v. Federation of Pakistan*,[5] wherein the Supreme Court of Pakistan had declared unconstitutional that part of the Pakistan Armed Forces (Acting in Aid of the Civil Power) Ordinance, 1998, which provided for the establishment of military courts to try civilians charged with offences mentioned in Section 6 and the schedule to the said ordinance and held the

[5] The full text of *Liaquat Hussain & others v. Federation of Pakistan & others* can be accessed at https://www.scribd.com/document/419506969/Liaquat-Hussain-PLD-1999-SC-504

same to be without authority and any effect. The Court had also impressed upon the independence of the judiciary and held that military courts would not fall within the purview of the category of 'courts' provided under the Constitution, and military personnel could not staff courts or perform judicial functions. The Court, however, in the *District Bar Association, Rawalpindi* case (rather feebly) expressed an opinion that civilians cannot be tried by courts-martial or other military courts as held in the *Liaquat Hussain* case when called out in aid of civil power, but where the Armed Forces are to deal with 'external aggression or threat of war', they can be tried by military courts since the alleged offence has a direct nexus with the armed forces or the defence of Pakistan.

As per the sunset clause, the Pakistan Army (Amendment) Act, 2015, came to an end on 6 January 2017. To continue with the trials of civilians under the Act, another Pakistan Army (Amendment) Act, 2017, was brought into force with effect from 7 January 2017. The said amending Act of 2017 brought one important amendment in the subjection clause at Section 2(1)(d)(iv), which permitted engagement of the defence counsel for the persons being tried under the amended Act. Pursuant to the 2015 amendment to the Pakistan Army Act, 1952, eleven military courts were established in four provinces till December 2016. The military courts functioned from 7 January 2015 till 6 January 2017, convicted 274 allegedly hardcore militants, of which 161 were sentenced to death, whereas 113 others were awarded prison terms, mostly life imprisonment.[6] Therefore, on average, 2.66 days were taken to try and convict each of the persons so sentenced. Thus, it is apparent that the civilians termed as 'hardcore militants' and awarded the harshest of the punishments under the Pakistan Army Act, 1952, had been tried without any opportunity of engaging a defence counsel of their choice since there was no such provision in the said Act and convicted in a trial averaging 2.66 days which anyway displays the sham nature of the trial since it is humanly impossible to provide an effective and fair trial in such a short span.

---

[6] The Dawn article, by Waseem Ahmad Shah, titled *Changes in Army Act to Ensure Transparency in Military Courts*, can be accessed at https://www.dawn.com/news/1324499/changes-in-army-act-to-ensure-transparency-in-military-courts

The Proactive Approach of High Courts Within the Limited Jurisdictional Scope

The glaring discrepancies in the justice delivery system in respect of civilians convicted by various military courts pursuant to the amendment become apparent from a judgment of the Peshawar High Court dated 16 June 2020 in a case titled Writ Petition 5265-P of 2018 *Masoom Jan v. Federation of Pakistan.*[7] It was observed by the High Court that all the said cases of conviction were cases of 'no evidence' and based on the malice of facts and law. Interestingly, the convictions of Masoom Jan and others were based solely on their own confessional statements made by them during their military custody. What is more perplexing is that the said confessional statements were made before persons who were neither competent nor notified to do so. The eminent English jurist, William Blackstone, once wrote, 'Better that ten guilty persons escape than that one innocent suffer.' The said basics of criminal jurisprudence appear to have been thrown to the wind in the trials set aside by the Peshawar High Court. The Court came down heavily upon the concept of justice followed by the military, and it observed that the witnesses, prosecution, investigators and the court itself were all the same and wearing the same uniform. All documents for hundreds of accused persons were the same with the same language and identical applications, depositions etc. The Court also observed that the names, dates, witnesses and signatures in documents were erased 'reflecting the attitude of military authorities towards Courts of Law'.

The Scope of Legal Challenge to Military Action in Pakistan as Compared to India

The civilians made subject to the Pakistan Army Act,1952, and tried by Field General Courts Martial had only the remedy of appeal before the

---

[7] The full text of *Masoom Jan v. Federation of Pakistan* along with a related article can be accessed at https://globalmjreform.blogspot.com/2020/07/landmark-decision-of-peshawar-high-court.html

Court of Appeal consisting of the Chief of Army Staff or any officer designated by him, in terms of Section 133 of the Pakistan Army Act, 1952. Generally, the Court of Appeal is headed by an officer of the rank of a brigadier. As per Section 133B(3), after exhausting the remedy of appeal, no other appeal lies before any other court. Thus, even after trial and conviction, the civilians so tried and punished under the Pakistan Army Act, 1952 never got a fair opportunity to appeal before a civil criminal court since the sentence had been awarded by a military court.

In India, the situation is different.

Firstly, there is no such power vested with the military authorities to try civilians under the provisions of the Army Act, 1950.

Secondly, even in the case of military personnel tried under the Army Act, 1950, by any type of courts-martial prescribed under the Act, the person can file a petition under the Army Act, 1950. If the person is still aggrieved by the decision of the competent authority to whom he or she had petitioned and represented, he/she has a right to challenge the court-martial proceedings before the Armed Forces Tribunal (AFT) which has the power to re-appreciate the evidence, take additional evidence and adjudicate upon the issue. The judicial member in the AFT is a retired judge of the High Court, whereas the administrative member is a retired senior officer from the Armed Forces. The Armed Forces Tribunal Act, 2007, attempts to provide for a tribunal independent of the Armed Forces, and the members of the tribunal are in no manner connected with the military hierarchy. The decisions of the Armed Forces Tribunal are further amenable to judicial review before the High Courts or appeal before the Supreme Court in certain limited cases.

However, in the case of Pakistan, in the absence of any opportunity of appeal against the decision of the Court of Appeal before a forum outside the Army, the conviction attains finality within the military without any recourse to independent courts. Therefore, the aspect of *command influence* cannot be offset when the matter is challenged before the Court of Appeal, which is also under the military hierarchy. Even as per the decision of the Supreme Court of Pakistan above, a civilian convicted by a military court can invoke the powers of judicial review under Article 199(3) of the Constitution of the Islamic Republic Pakistan on very restricted grounds, as discussed in the preceding portion (*Coram non-judice*, lack of jurisdiction, *mala fide*). Hence, by bringing civilians within the ambit of the Pakistan Army Act, 1952, some of the basic rights to challenge the conviction or State action and effective justice have been snatched away from them. Needless to state, the said rights are not available to military personnel in any case.

Not just in trials under military law, but even otherwise, the courts in India do not shy away from striking down policy or administrative decisions by military or governmental authorities whenever a case is made out, and the rights of citizens are always kept at a sacred pedestal, irrespective of the might of the State.

The Preciousness of Judicial Intervention and Independent Judicial Functioning in a Democracy

While the initial resolution, passed in the all-party meeting held at Peshawar on 18 December 2014 in the aftermath of the Army Public School attack was for the establishment of speedy trial courts, but somewhere down the line, in a hasty manner, citing incapability of the lower judiciary, the aspect of speedy trial courts took the colour of military courts under the Army Act. The spirit of the resolution could have been upheld by designating special courts for the trial of such offences under the existing criminal laws with time-bound trials. It is perplexing to see that the *seducers* of persons subject to the Pakistan Army Act, 1952, could as such be tried for an offence under Section 131 of the Pakistan Penal Code, 1860, in any case. Similarly, the offences under the Official Secrets Act, 1923, when committed by civilians, were punishable under the said Act. Thus, it was not that the State was helpless or remediless and that the only way out was to bring civilians under the ambit of Pakistan Army Act, 1952, by the amendment of 2015. Holistically observing, there appears to be an increasing trend of bringing civilians under the scope of the Pakistan Army Act, 1952, despite the availability of adequate legal mechanisms under the existing laws as applicable to the citizenry.

In any democracy, the armed forces have curtailed fundamental rights vis-a-vis their civilian counterparts for valid reasons relating to discipline expected out of them. However, civilians are not expected to have such stringent requirements of military discipline, and thus, they are governed by the regular set of laws that are required by the society at large to flourish. By virtue of the sunset clause, the amendments in the Pakistan Army Act, 1952, remained in force till 2019 as no further extension was granted, but the four-year era leaves a lot to learn for the democracies around the world on how *not* to treat their citizenry.

Colonel **Manmohan Sood** (Retired) was commissioned in the Judge Advocate General's Department of the Indian Army in the year 1985. During his 32 years of service in the Army's judicial wing, Colonel Sood served in serval important positions at the Army Headquarters as well as at different command and corps headquarters. He also handled numerous cases relating to human rights. He was also called upon to address students on various aspects of military law at prestigious institutions such as the Defence Service Staff College, Wellington and Institute of Military Law, Kamptee. He also served as a judge advocate in innumerable courts-martial under the Army Act. For his distinguished service, he was awarded the Commendation of the Chief of the Army Staff once and thrice by the General Officer Commanding-in-Chief. After retiring from the Indian Army, he is working as the registrar at Armed Forces Tribunal, Chandigarh. The views expressed by him in this piece are personal.

Progressive, but Definitely not Revolutionary

Preston Lim

Martin, The United Kingdom

In several landmark cases during the 1990s and 2000s, the European Court of Human Rights (ECHR) scrutinised various aspects of the British military justice system.[1] Parliament responded with wide-ranging reforms, civilianising key aspects of the military justice system through legislation – namely, the Armed Forces Acts of 1996 and 2006.[2] One key case that reshaped the British military legal landscape was the case of *Martin v. The United Kingdom (2006)*. The ECHR found that the trial of the applicant – Mr Alan Martin – contravened Article 6 of the European Convention on Human Rights, which guarantees the due process of law.

The facts of *Martin* are grisly. Mr Alan Martin's father was a British Army Corporal serving as part of the Support Unit of the Rhine Garrison. Following the Second World War, the British had established the Army of the Rhine to shield Europe from the threat of a Soviet invasion; despite budget cuts in 1993, the British presence in Germany at the close of the last century remained significant. Mr Martin's father served as part of the Rhine Garrison, and in keeping with common practice, had brought his family to Germany with him. Mr Martin, a 17-year-old, was

[1] See e.g.: *Findlay v. United Kingdom* (1997) 24 E.H.R.R. 221; *Grieves v. United Kingdom* (2004) 39 E.H.R.R. 2; *Martin v. United Kingdom* (2007) 44 E.H.R.R. 31, henceforth *Martin v. UK*, can be accessed at http://hudoc.echr.coe.int/fre?i=001-77661

[2] Armed Forces Act 1996, c. 46; Armed Forces Act 2006, c. 52.

found guilty of murdering Vanessa Chappell, a civilian computer expert working as part of the Support Unit.[3] Chappell's body was found in the woods, and the German police initially assumed that a German civilian had committed the crime.[4] Military authorities charged Alan Martin on 8 February 1994.

The British Armed Forces can exercise jurisdiction over certain categories of civilians who are subject to service discipline. The Army Act of 1955 applied to Martin since it brought within its ambit certain civilians living outside the United Kingdom, including:

> Persons forming part of the family of members of any of her Majesty's naval, military or air forces and residing with them or about to reside or departing after residing with them.[5]

Martin's court-martial began on 21 April 1995 and ended with his conviction on 3 May 1995. Martin spent the bulk of the period between the murder and the court-martial in England. Since his father had been posted back to England in March 1994, military authorities determined that Martin ought to be 'returned so as to be near his family.'[6] He was detained at the Military Corrective Training Centre at Colchester, and then returned to Mönchengladbach, Germany, to face court-martial.

The court-martial that convicted Martin of murder was a general court-martial. The court-martial scarcely resembled an English jury trial: it was composed of a president and six ordinary members – four of whom were senior military officers and two of whom were civilian civil servants who had come from the UK solely for the trial. In a civil trial, a majority of 10 to 2 jury votes would have been necessary to convict Martin; in the case of a general court-martial, however, all that was required was a simple majority vote. Martin's lawyer, Mr Blades, argued that the trial of Martin by 'court-martial was inherently unfair and oppressive and thus an abuse of process.'[7] The Vice-Judge Advocate General, who exercised a supervisory role over the court-martial, rejected Mr Blades' submissions

---

[3] *Case by Case: How Europe's Human Rights Court Has Made a Mockery of British Justice*, DAILY MAIL (10 February 2011), https://www.dailymail.co.uk/news/article-1355403/Prisoners-vote-EU-human-rights-court-mockery-UK-justice.html

[4] *R v. Martin* [1998] AC 917 (HL) (Lord Hope of Craighead) (appeal taken from HM Court-Martial App. Ct.) (UK).

[5] Army Act 1995, c. 18, Fifth Schedule, para 5 (Eng.).

[6] *R v. Martin* [1998] AC 917 (HL) (Lord Lloyd of Berwick).

[7] *Martin v. UK* at para 16.

and allowed the court-martial to proceed.

Following the court-martial conviction, Martin appealed to the Courts Martial Appeal Court, which had the limited 'power to quash the conviction if it considered it unsafe.'[8] The Appeal Court could declare the conviction unsafe if the proceedings 'leading to what would otherwise have been a fair trial...[were] such as to threaten either basic human rights or the rule of law.'[9]

Lord Bingham of Cornhill, delivering the Court's judgment in July 1996, dismissed Martin's appeal. He expressed 'considerable sympathy' for Martin's complaint, suggesting that 'it would have been preferable if this young appellant...had been tried [in the UK] with all the procedural safeguards which procedure in the ordinary criminal courts affords.'[10]

Yet, Lord Bingham specified that the proceedings were not abusive, that there was no 'attempt to overreach or oppress or prejudice the appellant,' and that military authorities had good reason to favour court-martial in Germany: namely, the availability of German factual witnesses.[11]

The case then proceeded to the House of Lords. The Appeal Court certified the following question of law to the Lords:

> Whether proceedings by way of a court-martial which are regularly constituted and conducted according to provisions of the Army Act 1955 may nevertheless be stigmatised as an abuse of process.[12]

The House of Lords unanimously dismissed the appeal. Lord Slynn of Hadley concluded succinctly that:

> I do not consider that it has been shown that there was any breach of the rules required to be followed or that there has been any abuse of process entitling the Courts Martial Appeal Court or your Lordships' House to interfere.[13]

Lord Lloyd of Berwick emphasised the limited powers of the Courts Martial Appeal Court below. The Court was limited by statute and could only dismiss the appeal if the conviction was unsafe; abuse of process, in

---

[8] *Martin v. UK* at para 18.

[9] *R v. Martin* [1998] AC 917 (HL) (Lord Hope).

[10] Quoted in *Martin v. UK* at para 18.

[11] *Ibid.*

[12] *R v. Martin* [1998] AC 917 (HL) (Lord Lloyd).

[13] *R v. Martin* [1998] AC 917 (HL) (Lord Slynn of Hadley).

contrast, did not constitute sufficient grounds for the Court to dismiss the appeal.[14] Lord Hope of Craighead delivered the most wide-ranging opinion, concluding that prosecution in the English courts was not practicable in this case. Thus, the only way to secure the ends of justice 'other than returning the case to the German prosecutor' was to try Martin by court-martial. Lord Clyde similarly concluded that the lack of a jury trial was not 'so serious a factor...as to render [Martin's] eventual conviction unsafe.'[15] Despite some confusion in the various opinions of the two concepts of abuse of process and an unsafe conviction, the verdict was clear, and the House of Lords dismissed Martin's appeal.

In the centuries before the birth of the ECHR, Martin's case would have ended after the House of Lords' disposition. The European Convention, however, gave Martin fresh grounds to appeal his conviction. His appeal to the ECHR focused on Articles 3 and 6 of the Convention. The former provides that '[n]o one shall be subjected to torture or to inhuman or degrading treatment or punishment.'[16] The Court dismissed Martin's Article 3 claim quickly, noting that he had 'failed to substantiate his complaint.'[17] The key to Martin's appeal revolved instead around Article 6, which provides that 'in the determination of his civil rights and obligations...everyone is entitled to a fair...hearing...by an independent and impartial tribunal established by law'.[18]

In other words, Article 6 guarantees the due process of law. Article 6 mandates that a tribunal be both independent and impartial. Impartiality has both a subjective and objective component: Martin's court-martial not only had to be 'free of personal prejudice or bias' but also had to offer sufficient guarantees to exclude any doubt of impartiality.[19] Military courts are not 'absolutely' excluded from trying civilians. Yet the Court warned that the existence of such jurisdiction should be subjected to particularly careful scrutiny, since only in very exceptional circumstances could the determination of criminal charges against civilians in such courts be held to be compatible with Article 6.[20]

[14] *R v. Martin* [1998] AC 917 (HL) (Lord Lloyd).

[15] *R v. Martin* [1998] AC 917 (HL) (Lord Clyde).

[16] Article 3, European Convention on Human Rights.

[17] Martin v. UK at para 32.

[18] Article 6, European Convention on Human Rights.

[19] *Martin v. UK* at para 42.

[20] *Martin v. UK* at para 44.

That is, the ECHR, while refusing to articulate a blanket ban on the trial of civilians by court-martial, articulated the application of careful scrutiny to such scenarios. In the immediate case, the Court held that the 'composition, structure and procedure' of Martin's court-martial were 'in themselves sufficient to raise in him a legitimate fear as to its lack of independence and impartiality.'[21]

The Court criticised two aspects of Martin's court-martial. Crucially, the Court noted that all six members of the general court-martial were subordinate in rank to the convening officer – in this case, the commanding officer of the Rhine Garrison Support Unit, who had been responsible for convening the court-martial. Such an arrangement was problematic for it gave rise to concerns about the members' independence; the fact that two of the six members were civilians did not alter the Court's reasoning, since the civilians did not 'have sufficient influence over the proceedings as a whole…to satisfy the independence and impartiality requirements of Article 6.'[22]

Second, the Court considered the Government's argument that the presence of a civilian Vice-Judge Advocate General (VJAG) rendered the proceedings impartial. The VJAG had considered and rejected Martin's preliminary submissions – specifically, the submission that his trial by court-martial was an abuse of process as well as his application for an adjournment for the purposes of judicial review.[23] The ECHR determined that, notwithstanding the VJAG's civilian status, his influence and involvement was insufficient to 'guarantee the independence and impartiality of [Martin's] court-martial.'[24]

Having found a violation of Article 6 of the Convention, the ECHR then considered the question of reparations. The Court did not quash Martin's conviction but did award him EUR 8,370 in costs and expenses.[25]

What effect did *Martin* have on the British military justice system more broadly? Colonel Stephen Strickey, a Canadian legal officer, has argued that the modern view of discipline in the UK has 'resulted in the

---

[21] *Martin v. UK* at para 45.

[22] *Martin v. UK* at para 52.

[23] *Martin v. UK* at para 17.

[24] *Martin v. UK* at para 52.

[25] *Martin v. UK* at para 59.

military justice system trending closer towards a civilianised model.'[26] He contends that *Martin* sounded the 'death knell for the traditional British military justice system.'[27] On the one hand, Colonel Strickey's overall argument is correct: *Martin,* along with other key ECHR judgments, forced the civilianisation of key aspects of the British military justice system. On the other hand, it bears noting that various aspects of the British system remain quite traditional: Parliament's reforms in the Armed Forces Acts of 1996 and 2006, while progressive, arguably did not go far enough. To take one example, Judge Blackett, then British Judge Advocate General, argued before the Constitutional Affairs Select Committee in 2005 that the judge advocate, rather than the military panel, ought to be responsible for sentencing, yet conceded that 'I do not think the services are yet ready for us to move to that position.'[28]

The Armed Forces Act, 2006, tabled just prior to the *Martin* decision, came into force in October 2009. The Act introduced several important reforms. Certain serious charges, such as mutiny and criminal conduct offences, were no longer to be dealt with by commanding officers; instead, if faced with serious offences, a commanding officer had a duty to inform service police of allegations. The consequential reduction in a commanding officer's power represented the triumph of the civilianised model. In addition, the Act created a single Service Civilian Court. Prior to the Act, Standing Civilian Courts could try civilians who had contravened the Army Act or the Air Force Act. Thus, the creation of the new Service Civilian Court extended rights to those civilians subject to the Naval Discipline Act. The Service Civilian Court is equivalent to a domestic Magistrates' Court and is neither designed nor equipped to deal with serious offences. More serious offences, as in Martin's case, proceed to court-martial.

Other provisions of the Act, however, only underscored traditional aspects of the British system. The Act extended the jurisdiction of courts-martial to include 'more serious offences committed in the UK, such as murder or manslaughter.' Thus, just as a court-martial had jurisdiction

---

[26] Stephen S. Strickey, *'Anglo-American' Military Justice Systems and the Wave of Civilianization: Will Discipline Survive?* CAMBRIDGE J. INT'L & COMP. L. 763, 764 (2013).

[27] *Id.* at 769.

[28] *The Armed Forces Bill: Bill 94 of Session 2005-2006,* House of Commons Library 30 (2005), https://researchbriefings.files.parliament.uk/documents/RP05-86/RP05-86.pdf

to try Martin for the murder abroad of Vanessa Chappell, so too could a court-martial try an individual subject to service discipline for the domestic commission of a serious offence. Most tellingly, despite the ECHR's warning in *Martin* that courts-martial should try civilians only in 'very exceptional circumstances', the 2006 Act retained military jurisdiction over civilians.[29] The Parliamentary Joint Committee on Human Rights, which reviewed the Act, was sufficiently worried to question the Ministry of Defence's approach. The Committee warned that:

> The compatibility of the trial of civilians in a military context, including in the service civilian court, with the right to a fair hearing...is far from clear.[30]

In other words, the response of the British Government and Parliament more broadly to the ECHR's holding in *Martin* was progressive but not as revolutionary as some have implied: rather than removing or curtailing military jurisdiction over civilians, the British response was to increase procedural safeguards. To this day, the British Armed Forces retain jurisdiction over civilians subject to service discipline. Ultimately, *Martin* represented a key example of the gradual civilianisation of the British military justice system. Comparatively speaking, however, the British system remains traditional in certain key respects.

---

[29] *Martin v. UK* at para 44; Armed Forces Act 2006, c. 52.

[30] Joint Comm. on Human Rights, *Legislative Scrutiny: Armed Forces Bill*, UK PARLIAMENT (2011), https://publications.parliament.uk/pa/jt201012/jtselect/jtrights/145/14510.htm

Preston Jordan Lim is a graduate of Yale Law School. He graduated *summa cum laude* from Princeton University and went on to represent Canada as a Schwarzman Scholar at Tsinghua University, where he received a master's in Global Affairs. He has written and published widely on British and Canadian military history. He is the author of *The Evolution of British Counter-Insurgency During the Cyprus Revolt, 1955-1959* (Palgrave Macmillan, 2018).

Protection of Good Faith Acts from Abuse of the Process of Law

Alok Shukla

GOC v. CBI, India

(Disclaimer: All views expressed and the suggestions made in this article are solely of the author in his personal capacity and do not have any official endorsement. Attributability of the contents lies purely with the author.)

The soldier is the army. No army is better than its soldiers. The soldier is also a citizen. In fact, the highest obligation and privilege of citizenship is that of bearing arms for one's country.

– George S Patton

Introduction

Deployment of soldiers in a counter-insurgency (CI) environment requires the regular conduct of military operations to maintain the security and sovereignty of the country. In few cases, the military operations are contested and scandalized by the vested elements alleging human rights violations. In such a scenario, the military authorities are often faced with the delicate situation whereby, on the one hand, it is necessary that the soldiers are kept motivated amidst the gruelling and hostile CI environment despite any harassment owing to the vexatious litigation and, on the other hand, ensure that every operation is conducted within the four corners of law and any infraction, howsoever minor, is dealt with promptitude, fairness and firmness. To strike a balance between the aforesaid two seemingly divergent goals, it is of utmost importance that due bonafide protection to the soldiers, as accorded by the law of the land, is maintained.

In the above backdrop, a landmark decision in military jurisprudence was pronounced on 1 May 2012 by the Supreme Court of India, in the case *General Officer Commanding v. CBI & Another,*[1] which stands as an authoritative pronouncement, particularly in the context of adjustment of the conflict of jurisdiction between a regular criminal court and court-martial. It also lays down another important facet of military jurisprudence regarding the entitlement and extent of protection to a soldier against the institution of any suit or other legal proceedings for anything done, or purported to be done, in the exercise of the powers conferred by the Armed Forces (Special Powers) Act, 1990[2] and 1958[3], (hereinafter called AFSPA, 1990 and AFSPA, 1958) and the need for sanction for prosecution from the Central Government for such purposes, if so required.

Factual Backdrop

The origin of the litigation, which came to be ultimately decided by the Supreme Court, was in two military operations that occurred in Jammu & Kashmir (J&K) and in the north-eastern sector of India in the counter-insurgency environment. The factual matrix of the first case was that in Village Chittising Pora, District Anantnag, J&K, 36 innocent citizens were killed by terrorists on 20 March 2000. Immediately thereafter, search for the responsible terrorists started in the entire area, and five people identified to be terrorists were killed at Village Pathribal, District

[1] Criminal Appeal No 257 of 2011 titled *General Officer Commanding v. CBI and Another* decided on 1 May 2012, can be accessed at https://indiankanoon.org/doc/40133779/

[2] Armed Forces Special Powers Act, 1990, can be accessed at https://www.mha.gov.in/sites/default/files/The%20Armed%20Forces%20%28Jammu%20and%20Kashmir%29%20Special%20Powers%20Act%2C%201990_0.pdf

[3] Armed Forces Special Powers Act, 1958, can be accessed at https://legislative.gov.in/sites/default/files/A1958-28.pdf

Anantnag, J&K, by the Indian Army on 25 March 2000 in a military operation. On the other hand, there had been processions to protest the killing of the five terrorists alleging they were civilians and had been killed by certain Army personnel in a fake encounter. This led to an investigation by the Central Bureau of Investigation (CBI). The CBI, after its investigation, filed a charge-sheet in the court of the Chief Judicial Magistrate-cum-Special Magistrate (CJM), CBI, Srinagar, wherein it was alleged that it was a fake encounter wherein criminal conspiracy was hatched by certain officers and troops.

In sum, the CBI alleged commission of offences under Section 120-B read with Sections 342, 304, 302, 201 of the Ranbir Penal Code (a penal code then applicable to J&K) by the said military personnel. The CJM held that veracity of the allegations made in the charge-sheet and the analysis of the evidence could not be gone into as it would then mean assuming jurisdiction that was not vested in him, given the provisions of AFSPA, 1990, by virtue of which protection to persons acting under the said Act was accorded. However, the CJM, Srinagar, giving regard to the provisions of Section 125 of the Army Act, 1950 (hereinafter called the Army Act), allowed the Army authorities to exercise the option as to whether or not the competent military authorities would like to exercise their inherent jurisdiction to try the case by way of a court-martial under the Army Act by taking over the case.

Army officers, in response thereto, filed an application before the CJM stating that in view of protection as accorded vide Section 7 of the AFSPA, Act 1990, no prosecution could be instituted except with the previous sanction of the Central Government and that the case be closed, and the charge-sheet be returned to the CBI. However, the CJM dismissed the application on the ground that the said court had no jurisdiction to go into the merits of the case and the veracity of the documents filed by CBI, and it was for the trial court to find out whether the action complained of fell within the ambit of the discharge of an official duty or not. The aforesaid order of the CJM was challenged before the Sessions Court, Srinagar, and the High Court but with a similar fate. This led to the filing of an appeal in the first case before the Supreme Court.

The second case, which was also tagged with the above case in the Supreme Court, arose out of Criminal Appeal No 55 of 2006 wherein some Army officers, who were the appellants, were aggrieved by an order of the Guwahati High Court in Criminal Revision No 117 of 2004 wherein the High Court upheld the order of the Special Judicial Magistrate (SJM), Kamrup. In the aforesaid order of the SJM, the application of the Army officers seeking protection of Section 6 of the Armed Forces Special Powers Act, 1958, for the north-eastern region (analogous provision to Section 7 of the Armed Forces Special Powers Act, 1990), was rejected. Hence, Criminal Appeal No 55 of 2006 was filed before Supreme Court. Both cases were clubbed together for hearing and decision. In both cases, the appellants were confronted with whether to let the soldiers face trial by court-martial for their purported bona fide duty once the Army authorities took over the case under Army Act Section 125, and thus, to let go of the protection of sanction for prosecution, which was being statedly a matter of evidence to be unfolded before the trial court, or to appeal against the order of the High Court before the Supreme Court to ensure protection of good faith acts of soldiers in the line of their duty from prosecution.

Issues Before the Supreme Court

The prime issue before the Supreme Court was whether the court, after the charge-sheet was filed, could entertain the same and proceed to frame charges without the previous sanction of the Central Government. Section 7 of Armed Forces (Jammu & Kashmir) Special Powers Act, 1990, provides for umbrella protection to the Army personnel with respect to anything done, or purported to be done, in the exercise of powers conferred by the Act. The Supreme Court identified that the whole issue in the said case was regarding the true meaning and interpretation of Section 7 of the AFSPA, 1990, (almost *pari materia* to Section 6 of the Armed Forces Special Power Act, 1958, for the north-eastern regions of the country), as to whether the term 'institution' used therein means filing/presenting/submitting the chargesheet in the court or taking cognizance and also whether or not the court can proceed with the trial without the previous sanction of the Central Government.

Since the moot issue revolved around Section 7 of the Armed Forces (Jammu & Kashmir) Special Powers Act, 1990, it would be apposite to reproduce the same as under:

> Protection of persons acting in good faith under this Act – No Prosecution, suit or other legal proceedings shall be instituted, except with the previous sanction of the Central Government, against any person in respect of anything done or purported to be done in exercise of the powers conferred by this Act.

The appellants presented their case stating that 'institution' of prosecution is a stage prior to taking 'cognizance' and, therefore, the word 'institution' is different from the word 'cognizance'. Thus, the scheme of the AFSPA, 1990, mandates that any legal proceeding 'instituted' against any Army official working under the AFSPA, 1990, has to pass the test of Section 7 of the AFSPA even before the institution of any such proceeding, much less taking cognizance thereof; and that the legislative intent of providing special powers is to meet the special conditions, i.e., use of the armed forces in aid of civil administration to prevent activities involving terrorist acts directed towards overawing the Government of India or striking terror in citizens of India.

The Ruling of the Supreme Court

'Institution' of a Case

The Supreme Court, after navigating the legal position of various laws and judgments, held that the expression 'institution' has to be understood in the context of the scheme of the Act as applicable in a particular case and that so far as criminal proceedings are concerned, 'institution' does not mean filing, presenting, or initiating the proceedings. Rather, it means taking 'cognizance' as per the provisions contained in the Criminal Procedure Code (CrPC).

This meant that the protection on 'institution' of any prosecution, suit, or other legal proceedings, as accorded by AFSPA, 1990, shall apply only from the stage of cognizance and not from/during the stage of the investigation. The fallout of this ruling is that the member of the Armed Forces, while operating in the disturbed area, becomes prone to multiple and vexatious litigations, including lodging of First Information Reports with the police in old matters where even the records of the cases were not held being very old. In other words, members of Armed Forces were exposed to the long-drawn and gruelling process of investigation for acts done or purported to be done in exercise of the powers conferred by the AFSPA Act, 1990, without the protection of Section 7 of the said AFSPA, 1990, until the matter could reach its cognizance stage. This got accumulated further when such members retired or got posted out from the area and stood quite disabled to even answer the basic queries of investigators from the records as the same were not held with them and the military unit concerned had also not preserved the said records or not taken efforts to dig them out.

Stage of Sanction for Prosecution and its Necessity

The Supreme Court, while considering the issue of the sanction for prosecution under Section 197 CrPC and/or Section 7 of the AFSPA, 1990, dealt with two sub-issues. Firstly, whether such sanction is necessitated or not under the aforesaid laws, and if yes, at what stage such sanction can be legally pressed? That is, can they be legally pressed at the time of taking cognizance of the offence, or during enquiry or investigation. With respect to the first issue, the Supreme Court clarified that the stage of prosecution starts when the cognizance of offence is taken and not from the time when the investigation commences. The Supreme Court also underlined that cognizance is taken of the offence and not of the offender. Thus, from the above, what is evident is that the stage of the sanction for prosecution should be before taking cognizance of the offence after filing of the charge-sheet.

Prior Sanction is a Condition Precedent for Institution

On the issue of the necessity of the sanction for prosecution, the Supreme Court clarified that the sanction of the appropriate authority is necessary to protect a public servant from unnecessary harassment or prosecution and that such a protection is necessary as an assurance to an honest and sincere officer to perform his public duty honestly and to the best of his ability. The Supreme Court also noted the specific legislative intent stating that use of words like 'no' and 'shall' in Section 7 of the AFSPA, 1990 denotes the mandatory requirement of obtaining prior sanction of the Central Government before the institution of the prosecution, suit, or legal proceedings and that, Section 197(2) CrPC and Section 7 of the AFSPA, 1990, makes it clear that prior sanction is a condition precedent before the institution of any of the aforesaid legal proceedings.

Act Done in Good Faith or Not

The Supreme Court held that in order to offer protection, it is necessary that firstly, the act has to be official and not private as it has to be distinguished from the manner in which it has been administered or performed, and secondly, such duty should have been performed in 'good faith'. The Supreme Court, while dwelling upon the term 'good faith', clarified that it covers such acts which are based on genuine belief and command a loyal performance, which proceeds on reliable authority, and is accepted as truthful. The Supreme Court further elaborated the term 'good faith' by stating that it is the opposite of the intention to deceive, and duty performed in good faith is to fulfil a trust reposed in an official and which bears allegiance to the superior authority which should be honest in intention, and sincere in professional execution.

Presumption of an Official Act in Good Faith and its Onus

The Supreme Court clarified that the presumption of good faith could be dislodged only by cogent and clinching material, and so long as such a conclusion is not drawn, a duty in good faith should be presumed to have been done or purported to have been done in exercise of the powers conferred under the statute. There must be the existence of material to attribute or impute an unreasonable motive behind an act to take away the immunity clause and that when the authority empowered to grant sanction is proceeding to exercise its discretion, it has to take into account the material facts of the incident complained of before passing an order of granting sanction or else official duty would always be in peril even if performed in a bonafide and genuine manner.

Construe the Protection Widely Lest it Becomes Sterile

In the aforesaid backdrop, a very important legal dictum was pronounced by the Supreme Court that the protection granted by the AFSPA, 1990, has to be widely construed in order to assess the act complained of; that this would also include the assessment of cases like mistaken identities or an act performed on the basis of a genuine suspicion; that such immunity clauses have to be interpreted with wide discretionary powers to the sanctioning authority in order to uphold the official discharge of duties in good faith and a sanction, therefore, has to be issued only on the basis of a sound objective assessment and not otherwise.

Scope of Protection of AFSPA, 1990, vis-a-vis Protection under Section 197 CrPC and Section 19 of the Prevention of Corruption Act, 1988

The Supreme Court held, after making a comparative chart, that under the provisions of CrPC and Prevention of Corruption Act, it is the court which is restrained from taking cognizance without the previous sanction of the competent authority; that under the AFSPA, 1990, the investigating agency/complainant/person aggrieved is restrained from instituting the criminal proceedings; suit or other legal proceedings; and that there is a marked distinction in the statutory provisions under the Act 1990, which are of a much wider magnitude and are required to be enforced strictly. It is evident that the Supreme Court ruled authoritatively that the protection provided to a member of the Armed Forces by the AFSPA, 1990, is of much wider magnitude and is operable against the investigating agency/complainant/person aggrieved. On the face of it, this creates a conflicting situation, as on the one hand, the term 'institution' has been held at par with 'cognizance' and, on the other hand, the mandate of restrain from the institution has been held to be operable against investigating agency/complainant/person aggrieved, which have no role in taking cognizance of the matter. In other words, the legislative intent of the ASFPA, 1990, and the usage of the term 'institution' in Section 7 of the Act, 1990, was always meant to accord protection of persons acting under the Act from the vexatious investigation/complaint from any person either at the behest of the person aggrieved or otherwise. In the backdrop of the aforesaid analysis, the Supreme Court concluded that sanction of the Central Government is required in the facts and circumstances of the case and the Court concerned lacked jurisdiction to take cognizance unless sanction is granted by the Central Government.

Applicability of Sanction for Prosecution in Trial by Criminal Court or by Court-martial

The Supreme Court held that undoubtedly, the court-martial proceedings are akin to criminal prosecution, and this fact has been dealt with elaborately by the Supreme Court in the case titled *Union of India & Ors. v. Major A. Hussain*. However, once the matter stands transferred to the Army for conducting a court-martial, the court-martial has to be as per the provisions of the Army Act. The said Act does not provide for sanction of the Central Government. In other words, the Supreme Court ratified an extremely profound and existential question relating to the Army Act, 1950, that it is a special law which is a self-contained code and the proceedings under the Army Act shall always be governed by the provisions of the Army Act and not by the CrPC. However, what is important to note is that the Supreme Court used the words 'once the matter stands transferred to the Army authorities, which means that till transferred, the issue of sanction for prosecution as accorded vide AFSPA, 1990, and 1958, shall be fully applicable and alive.

Impact Analysis

To sum up, the Supreme Court held that 'institution' as contained in Section 7 of the Act 1990 means taking 'cognizance' of the offence and not mere presentation of the chargesheet by the investigating agency and that prior sanction is a condition precedent before institution (i.e., taking cognizance) of any of the legal proceedings and to proceed with the criminal prosecution/trial.

The Supreme Court also laid down the guidelines commanding that when the authority empowered to grant sanction is proceeding to exercise its discretion, it must consider the material facts of the incident complained of before passing an order of granting sanction or else official duty would always be in peril even when performed with bonafide and genuine intentions.

With respect to the stage of pressing the aforesaid sanction, the Supreme Court ruled that the competent military authority has to exercise discretion to opt as to whether the trial would be by a court-martial or by a criminal court after filing of the chargesheet and not after the cognizance of the offence is taken by the court.

The major interpretational error that is often made while understanding the aforesaid law with respect to the requirement of prosecution sanction is that the competent authorities are expected to exercise their option under Army Act Section 125 without insisting on the issue of prosecution sanction. While it is undoubtedly true that the issue of sanction is inapplicable once the matter stands transferred to the Army for trial by court-martial, it would be perverse to hold that the Supreme Court commanded that the option has to be exercised by the authorities before the issue of prosecution sanction. In other words, the adjustment of jurisdiction between a regular criminal court and a court-martial is also a pre-cognizance stage requirement and the issue of sanction for prosecution too is the same – a pre-cognizance stage requirement. Both the requirements are mandatory. As a matter of fact, the magistrate can only call upon the military authorities and seek to adjust the jurisdiction with court-martial once the issue of sanction is decided and the concerned magistrate has derived the jurisdiction.

It is for this reason that the Supreme Court used the term such as 'once' and 'in case' while stating that 'once' the matter stands transferred to the Army for conducting a court-martial, the court-martial has to be as per the provisions of the Army Act and that the Army Act does not provide for sanction of the Central Government. Such reading of CrPC Section 197/Section 7 of the AFSPA, 1990, read with the 'Adjustment of Jurisdiction Rules' would not render the protection of sanction meaningless for the person subject to the Army Act.

In effect, if protection under Section 7 of the AFSPA, 1990, has been accorded by the legislature, it cannot be fettered by misreading the stage at which the option is to be exercised by the Army authorities. It is in this context the Supreme Court, while summing up the law on the stage of exercising the option, clarified that the option should be after the filing of the chargesheet and not after the cognizance of the offence is taken by the court, and the Supreme Court nowhere commands that the option should be exercised before the issue of sanction has been decided. To visualise a situation, we may imagine a case that did not deserve grant of sanction, but the Army authorities have prematurely exercised the option to try a person subject to the Army Act by a court-martial and thereby rendering the requirement of sanction inapplicable, the accused person had to face the ignominy of entire trial even when the accused had a right to be protected from a vexatious trial. It is a settled law that if the objects of the two statutory provisions are different and the language of each statute is restricted to its own objects or subject, then they are generally intended to run in parallel lines without meeting, and there would be no real conflict though apparently, it may appear to be so on the surface.

Therefore, it can be safely stated after the judgment that while the Army Act, a special law, does not require sanction for trial under the said Act, the said law cannot be invoked in the manner to defeat another special law such as AFSPA, 1990, and the harmonious construction must be resorted to so that both the Special laws (AFSPA, 1990/1958) and the Army Act, 1950, could coexist. Thus, competent military authorities are well within their power to utilise the bracket period, particularly the right part of the bracket, whereby they can exercise their option only after the issue of sanction for the institution of prosecution/launching of prosecution has been decided by the Central Government and this judgment does not come into the way of this approach in any manner whatsoever.

It also highlights a very important point of law that the conduct of a military operation would necessitate the sanction of Central Government for prosecution and that prior sanction is a condition precedent before the institution of any of the aforesaid legal proceedings under the Armed Forces Special Power Act. The aforesaid conundrum is buttressed by the Supreme Court in acknowledging another foundational fact that under the AFSPA, the investigating agency/complainant/person aggrieved is restrained from instituting the criminal proceedings; suit or other legal proceedings and that there is a marked distinction in the statutory provisions under the Army Act 1990, which are of much wider magnitude vis-à-vis the protection provided under the criminal procedural code, i.e., Section 197 or Section 19 of the Prevention of Corruption Act. We have seen that often, the protection of sanction for prosecution is viewed with an existing template available under Section 197 of the CrPC and/or Section 19 of the Prevention of Corruption Act. While the protection under Section 7/6 of the AFSPA, 1990/1958, may seemingly look congruous, but their legislative standing is quite different since, firstly, the protection of AFSPA is provided by a substantive act of the Parliament instead of a procedural code, and secondly, that the use of words 'no' and 'shall' provide the loud and clear intention of the legislature with regard to the extent of protection from vexatious litigation. It is in this context that the Supreme Court ruled herein that the protection provided under the statutory provisions of AFSPA, 1990/1958, are required to be enforced strictly.

To conclude, the aforesaid judgment has gone down in the annals of the military jurisprudence as a landmark judgment which has laid down the law on a crucial question of adjustment of jurisdiction between a regular criminal court and a court-martial and the extent of protection to soldiers operating in a counter-insurgency environment. Simultaneously, as the law is dynamic and meant to grow, the judgment has also paved the way for the settlement and further development of law on the aspect of unexplained and unresolved bracket period from the time of registration of FIR till the filing of the police report before the cognizance. Further, since the issue of sanction for prosecution and the issue of exercising of option under the 'Adjustment of Jurisdiction Rules' and Army Act Section 125, both are pre-cognizance stage functions, what is important is that both of such powers should be exercised in the manner that the mandate of Section 7 of AFSPA is fulfilled. This assumes greater significance since the *vires* of AFSPA, 1958, have been upheld by the Constitution Bench judgment of the Supreme Court in *Naga People's Movement of Human Rights v. Union of India*[4] in no uncertain terms. Hence, the option under Army Act Section 125 cannot be expected to be prematurely exercised at such stage and manner that the issue of sanction for prosecution as accorded vide AFSPA becomes redundant and inapplicable. Thus, neither the Army authorities can be denied of the benefit of the decision of the Central Government on the grant of sanction (or otherwise) nor can military personnel be denuded of the protection provided to them by the law of the land. In other words, the judgment is *sub-silentio* on this pertinent point but gives an amply wide bracket period on the aforesaid aspect, which must be read and interpreted correctly till a more authoritative pronouncement on this precise issue is rendered by the Supreme Court. Indubitably, this judgment paves the way for further settlement of

---

[4] Writ Petition (Criminal) 550 of 1982 *Naga People's Movement of Human Rights Etc v. Union of India*, decided on 27 November 1997, can be accessed at https://indiankanoon.org/doc/1072165/

this important question of law which is absolutely necessary so that the Armed Forces of the Union can continue performing their sovereign functions in accordance with the law with full adherence to human rights, but without fear of abuse of the process of law.

Colonel **Alok Shukla** holds varied and rich experience in multifarious appointments in the Judge Advocate General's Department of the Indian Army. Colonel Shukla, in his more than two decades of military service, has dealt with various issues involving service, penal, procedural, contractual, and constitutional law, besides arbitration, conciliation and mediation. During his tenures in Jammu & Kashmir and the north-eastern sector, he had the opportunity of extensively dealing with the operational law cases involving the Armed Forces (Special Powers) Act, 1958 and 1990.

For his contribution, he has been awarded Commendation by the Chief of the Army Staff, and also on four occasions by the General Officer Commanding-in-Chief. He was also decorated with the Presidential award of Vishisht Sewa Medal (VSM) on 15 January 2021.

The Principle of Truth in Danish Military Law

Lars Stevnsborg

Case No 139/2011, Denmark

Abstract

The obligation of truth – the duty not to provide false or misleading information – is one of the central and fundamental duties of a public servant. A breach of that duty would be a dereliction of duty unless the public servant is in a situation where he will be able to assert self-incriminating views. This is, in particular, of vital importance and a fundamental requirement in the military command system, which requires that legal orders be complied with. The present essay analyses an important Supreme Court ruling on disclosure of untrue information to superiors by a highly trusted and experienced senior officer.

Introduction

Military cases in the Supreme Court of Denmark are very scarce. The case at hand was heard by the Supreme Court in 2012 and concerned the application of the general principle of truth and the interpretation of a recent justice reform.

The Law

A Very Brief Introduction to the Danish Military Justice System

Although the Danish military justice system has origins in the sixteenth century, the development was accelerated by the extensive codification of civil and military law adopted in the late seventeenth century by King Christian V.[1] The King passed laws in two parallel jurisdictions, one for the citizens of the kingdom in general and one for military personnel and their dependents. This legislation was amended over the years, but the latter formed an important part of the military justice system until the general justice reform in 1919.[2]

The 1919 reform inter alia abolished the military courts (courts-martial) and directed that all military criminal cases would be heard by the ordinary courts. Military criminal cases have since then been heard by the District Court either by a single judge presiding alone or with a panel of two lay judges or jurors, or by three judges presiding with a panel of six jurirs, depending on the nature and severity of the case. A District Court ruling may be subject to appeal to a Court of Appeals (that would sit with three judges presiding alone or with a panel of lay judges or jurors). A judgment of a Court of Appeals may, only with a special leave from the Appeals Permission Board, be heard by the Supreme Court in particular where the case is of a fundamental nature.

The Military Justice Reform of 2005

A comprehensive reform of the Danish military justice system was passed in Parliament in 2005. The key driver for the reform was the issue of whether military personnel would be subject to (the stricter) military criminal law in peacetime. A select committee had submitted a report based on lengthy and thorough deliberations proposing to uphold a system in peacetime but in the form of a new model separating the military

---

[1] King Christian V was an absolute Monarch ruling from 1670 to 1699. For further information, see the booklet published on the occasion of the 350 Anniversary of the Office of the Military Prosecutor General in 2009 at www.fauk.dk

[2] King Christian V *Danish Law* 1683 and King Christian V *War Articles for the Army and the Navy* 1683.

criminal cases from the military summary proceedings. The division between the two strands of military justice would limit criminal liability to apply only to aggravated acts committed intentionally or as a result of gross negligence, thus resulting in significant decriminalisation. The view was that minor offences and lesser degrees of negligence would not constitute a criminal offence but might be sanctioned within a non-criminal (administrative) framework of summary proceedings governed by the military commanders, whereas the criminal cases would be investigated and prosecuted by the Military Prosecution Service. Both strands of the military justice system apply to military personnel only.

The Minister of Defence presented a draft bill to Parliament based on the recommendations which were adopted by Parliament and came into force on 1 January 2006.[3]

The 2005 Military Criminal Code includes several service offences that are unique to military service, such as disobedience of a lawful command, mutiny and absence without leave. It also comprises a number of offences that would be prejudicial to good order and discipline, such as insubordinate behaviour, abuse of position, degrading rituals and abuse of alcohol and controlled substances, as well as a specific set of 'War Articles' that are applicable in armed conflict only.

In the case at hand, the question before the courts was whether to apply the general provision on the negligent performance of military duties. This reads as follows:

> § 27. Anyone who, moreover, grossly disregards his service duties shall be punishable by a fine or imprisonment of up to three months.
>
> (2) The sentence may be increased to one year in prison where the dereliction of duty is of a particularly serious nature or when it has caused significant harm or danger.
>
> (3) During armed conflict, the penalty for intentional violation may be increased to imprisonment for 3 years.

[3] The reform legislation comprised three acts of Parliament: Act no 530 of 24 June 2005 Military Criminal Code, Act no 532 of 24 June 2005 Military Disciplinary Act and ACT no 531 of 24 June 2005 Military Administration of Justice Act. The acts were revised by Act no 1550 of 19 December 2017 after the reorganisation of the Danish Defence in 2015. For additional information, see the publication (in English) The Danish Military Justice System at www.fauk.dk

Disciplinary measures may be imposed where there has been a dereliction of duties, and disciplinary reasons call for such a sanction, but where there is no legal basis or need for criminal sanctions. The dual strand military justice system offers a series of parallel sections in the Military Disciplinary Act for acts of a less severe and less negligent nature that would not constitute a criminal act. In the case at hand, the relevant section would be Section 4 (9), which reads:

> Disciplinary measures according to § 6 may be imposed on a person who ... is in any other way guilty of dereliction of duty.

The Case

The Course of Events Around the Publication of a Book on a Deployment to Afghanistan

In December 2001, the Danish Parliament decided to support the American-led war against terror by sending special forces to Afghanistan. In January 2002, soldiers from the Danish Army and Navy Special Forces were deployed to participate in Operation Enduring Freedom. Amongst those deployed was an Army Special Forces soldier who, after having left this service some years later, decided to write his memoirs, including references to some of his covert operations.

The publishers had planned to launch the book, which was titled *Ranger – In War with the Elite,*[4] on Wednesday, 9 September 2009. The project immediately gave rise to considerable concerns and discussions regarding security issues within the Defence Command Denmark (DCD) and the Ministry of Defence. In the ensuing three weeks, events accelerated.

News of the book's release was published by the major Danish news outlets on Friday, 11 September. The following Monday, 14 September, the head of the DCD Secretariat, Colonel N, thought that he had seen references to the book translated into Arabic language on the internet and asked the head of the DCD IT department, Navy Captain A, to investigate the matter.

Simultaneously the DCD initiated proceedings to have an injunction

---

[4] In Danish, 'Jæger – I kamp med eliten'.

order against the publication of the book as it was assessed that it posed a security risk. Nevertheless, on 16 September, the daily newspaper, *Politiken,* chose to publish the unpublished book in its entirety in an appendix.

The Copenhagen Bailiff's Court ruled on the injunction case on 21 September. The Court held that the Ministry of Defence had made it probable that the book contained confidential information and supported the assessment of the security aspect. The public should therefore not have access to the information. The court refused to issue an injunction order, however, as the book had already been made available to the public and had been quoted widely in the press in connection with the extensive media coverage and was already on the internet. An injunction would, therefore, no longer prevent the unwanted retransmission of the information in the book.

On 24 September, Captain A, after having searched for a translation in vain, decided to produce a translation of the book into Arabic language using the Google Translate tool and presented a hard copy of the translation to Colonel N and a digital copy of the translation to the head of the DCD Communications Secretariat, Lieutenant Colonel B (LTC B). Captain A did not reveal that the translation was false and that he had produced it himself. The same day the Minister of Defence informed the Parliament's Foreign Policy Committee about the translation. LTC B did later, on his own initiative, send a digital copy to a news reporter at the daily newspaper, *BT*, who published the translation on the media's website (from where it was presumably quickly removed again).

In the late afternoon that day, the media provided evidence that the Word document with the translation was indeed produced in DCD, and it all blew up.

The fact that the translation was on *BT*'s website for a short period of time meant that DCD had to find out where the translation had come from. LTC B and other communications professionals were asked about this. In the period from 24 to 30 September, LTC B was interviewed twice by the Chief of the Defence Staff, Lieutenant General NN, and once by the Chief of Defence, Admiral NN, whether he knew anything about who had sent the translation to *BT* LTC B replied in the negative.

On 29 September, Captain A was interviewed by the Chief of the Defence Staff about his knowledge of the translation. He stated that he had found it on the internet and denied having been responsible for the translation. On 30 September, he was interviewed again and repeated his statement, but later that day, Captain A admitted that he himself had produced the false translation. On 2 October, LTC B admitted to having sent the translation to *BT*.

The political and public attention on the case created a lot of pressure on the Defence, and, on 4 October, the Chief of Defence decided to resign. Captain A and LTC B later resigned from the Defence as well.

The Indictment and Court Proceedings[5]

They were both indicted for dereliction of duty of a particularly serious nature. Captain A with four counts for having presented the translation to Colonel N and LTC B without revealing that it was false and knowingly having given false information upon the direct request of the Chief of the Defence Staff and the Chief of Defence. LTC B was indicted with one count for denying, on direct request and contrary to the truth, that he had sent the digital file.

The Court of First Instance agreed that the defendants, by their actions, had failed to fulfil their duties in the service, but the incorrect information had related more closely to case management in the DCD than to information relevant to the security of the service. To establish criminal liability under the rules of gross negligence under the Military Criminal Code, the Court found that the incorrect information must relate to information relevant to the security of the service. On the basis of an overall assessment, the Court found that the facts to which the charge related were not of a nature punishable by Section 27(2) of the Military Criminal Code and acquitted the defendants.

The prosecution appealed the ruling to the Eastern Court of Appeals, which found both guilty as charged with the votes five to one. The Court held:

> As regards the question whether that dereliction of duty can be characterised as serious in that it is contrary to Paragraph 27(2) of the Military Criminal Code, [the majority] notes that the military leadership

---

[5] Court rulings in the case: Supreme Court ruling delivered on 25 April 2012. Judgments in the previous instances were delivered by the City Court of Copenhagen on 10 September 2010 and by the Eastern Court of Appeal on 28 February 2011.

> and the Minister of Defence were at that time under severe pressure following the publication of the book [–]. The book was seen both by the military leadership and by the Defence Minister as a possible security risk to the Danish forces in Afghanistan. This was an important reason why the Danish Defence Command tried to have the publication of the Danish edition of the book banned. In view of this and the course of events described above, it must have been particularly clear to the defendants that the provision of the Arabic translation, regardless of the existence of a Danish version of the book on the internet, and the transmission of the translation to the daily newspaper BT by the military leadership and by the Minister of Defence were given great security and political importance. Finally, it should be noted that the events contributed to the departure of the Defence Chief...
>
> Based on the preparatory work on the concept of unlawful conduct in the Military Criminal Code as described in the District Court's judgment, and on the nature and extent of the defendants' conduct, [the majority] consider, on an overall basis, that the defendants' actions in accordance with the content and purpose of the military duties, constitute a breach of fundamental requirements of the service which can be characterised as a particularly serious dereliction of duty within the meaning of Section 27 of the Military Criminal Code paragraphs 1 and 2. The majority then find the defendants guilty of the charge...

Captain A was sentenced to 30 days imprisonment (suspended due to the impact the case had had on him), and LTC B was to pay a fine of 8,000 DKK. Both were ordered to pay the (extensive) legal costs for the hearings in the Court of First Instance and the Court of Appeal.

Upon application, the Appeals Permission Board granted both defendants leave to have the case heard by the Supreme Court. Shortly before the hearing in the Supreme Court, the co-defendant and instigator of the plot, Captain A, decided to abandon his appeal.

The Supreme Court

Legal Issues in the Case Concerning LTC B

The issues before the Supreme Court in the case were the following:

> Was it indeed a formal interview?

Was LTC B under the circumstances obliged to tell the truth?

Were the criteria set out in Section 27 met, and did LTC B's behaviour constitute a criminal offence or a disciplinary offence?

Was it a particularly serious offence due to the specific obligations of a senior military officer?

Counsel for the defence argued inter alia that section 27 would only apply to specific military conduct contrary to military service. LTC B's communications with journalists as head of the DCD Communication Secretariat had not taken place in fulfilment of such duties. Nor did his reporting to his superiors about his communication with journalists happen to fulfil specific military duties and could not be characterised as official, and his statements could not be attributed to him as negligence of a particularly serious nature.

Furthermore, it was argued that it would be unreasonable to impose costs on him as was the case. According to the Court's judgment, he was ordered to pay DKK 260,125.[6] The obvious political significance of the case for the Government, Parliament and the population should be clarified in the form of a commission or similar which would have been economically neutral for him. In addition, the case against him had become more expensive by being brought together with the much larger case against Captain A. The costs of the case should therefore be paid in full or in part by the Treasury.

The prosecution inter alia argued that section 27 is not limited to specific military conduct contrary to military service but applies to all types of negligence and is not dependent on the subject of the untrue information. LTC B deliberately disclosed untrue information to his superiors during official interviews, and the information about who had sent the Arabic translation of the book to *BT* was at that time important to the DCD and attracted considerable political attention.

The prosecution also underlined that LTC B was not the subject of a criminal or a disciplinary investigation at the time. He was obligated to speak the truth, and the issue of a prohibition against self-incrimination had not been invoked at any point in the proceedings. It would constitute gross neglect of a particularly serious nature covered by section 27 (2)

---

[6] Approximately USD 44,000.

when a high-ranking officer directly and repeatedly submits untrue information to his superiors on such important matters as was the case.

The fact that the costs of conducting the case before the lower courts had been significant was due to LTC B's own circumstances and should not lead to the Treasury being ordered to pay legal costs. He had, throughout the course, pleaded not guilty.

The Supreme Court Ruling[7]

The Supreme Court ruled in favour of the military prosecution:

> A key issue in the case is whether section 27 is limited to military duties that are relevant to the security of the service. According to its wording, the provision is not limited to duties that are important for security, and the preparatory work for the Military Criminal Code clearly states that the provision corresponds to sections 156 and 157 of the Civilian Criminal Code and covers all types of military service. This view is also based on case law.[8]
>
> The obligation of truth is of fundamental importance in service matters, and breach of this duty is, in principle, a gross breach of the duties that apply in the service.
>
> In deciding whether there is a breach of duty of a particularly serious nature pursuant to section 27, subsection 2, emphasis may be placed on whether a commander has to a large extent failed to meet the requirements that must be placed on him according to his position [–].[9]
>
> The question then is whether there are grounds for punishing [LTC B].
>
> The Court of Appeal has found it proven that [LTC B] shortly after receiving the Arabic translation of the book [–] forwarded the transla-

[7] Published in the Law Journal (*Ugeskrift for Retsvæsen*) 2012, page 2387 pp. Also available at the Supreme Court's website. Can be accessed at https://domstol.fe1.tangora.com/media/300016/files/139-2011.pdf

[8] Section 27 in the Military Criminal Code has a parallel in the Civilian Criminal Code Section 157, a section rarely used in a civilian context as a contravention would, in general, be subject to disciplinary measures.

[9] Official Journal of the Parliament 1972-73, Appendix A, column 13.

> tion to journalist [–] on the newspaper BT, and that he during conversations with the Chief of the Defence Staff, Lieutenant General [–], on 24 and 30 September 2009 and during conversations with the Chief of Defence, Admiral [–], on 29 September 2009 on direct inquiry[10] and in violation of the truth denied having done so. Based on the evidence presented, it must also be assumed that the clarification of who had sent the translation to BT was a matter to which the Defence leadership attached significant importance and that this was clear to [LTC B].
>
> LTC B knowingly provided, as a senior officer and commander in the Defence Command, the said false information to the Chief of Defence and the Chief of the Defence Staff in a service capacity. The Supreme Court agrees that this is such gross neglect of the duties that follow from the position that the matter is covered by section 27 (2) of the Military Criminal Code...

The Supreme Court found no basis for changing the imposed fine of DKK 8,000 and no basis for limiting LTC B's cost liability to the present case.

Conclusion

The Supreme Court's statement in this landmark case on the seriousness and fundamental importance of a breach of the obligation to tell the truth and the reference to the General Criminal Code indicates that the precedential value of the judgment goes beyond military personnel.

---

[10] In a recent case, the Western Court of Appeal, on 19 May 2020, came to the conclusion that it had *'not been proven that the Chief of Defence's inquiries whether* [former Chief of the Army, Major General –] *had unjustifiably promoted* [his girlfriend's] *career in the Danish Armed Forces had such a precise and concrete nature that the defendant's response to his superior constituted gross dereliction of duty'* and concurred with Court of First Instance's acquittal of the defendant in that part of the charge. Criminal Law Review (Tidsskrift for Kriminalret) 2020, page 958 pp. An abstract on this judgment: *Global Military Justice Reform* Blog 23 December 2020.

Lars Stevnsborg is the Military Prosecutor General of Denmark since 2007. Prior to his current appointment, he was Deputy Director of Public Prosecutions and prosecutor at the Danish Supreme Court, where he participated in over 100 cases. He has *inter alia* been a long-standing member of the Danish Ministry of Justice Committee on the Administration of Criminal Justice and a member of the Danish Ministry of Defence Select Committee on the Military Justice Reform. He is presently on the Board of Directors of the International Society for Military Law and the Law of War.

Strengthen the System, Restore Confidence!

UC Jha

Fonseka, Sri Lanka

Sri Lanka, formerly called Ceylon,[1] got independence from the British in 1948. During the colonial era, parts of Sri Lanka came under the control of three European colonial powers: the Portuguese in the sixteenth century, the Dutch in the seventeenth century and the British in the eighteenth century. The entire island came under British control in 1815, which integrated the locals into the British defence forces. There was no regular armed force in colonial Ceylon, except for the Ceylon Defence Force, which consisted of regulars from the British Army stationed for service in Ceylon, together with a local volunteer force that was trained and called upon for duty only when necessary. Sri Lanka has not been governed by a military regime, though it has experienced an unsuccessful military coup in 1962. It has deployed the military to maintain law and order during labour and communal unrest and in operations against the Liberation Tigers of Tamil Eelam (LTTE).

The President of the Republic is the head of the state, the head of the executive and the Government, and the Commander-in-Chief of the Armed Forces.[2] In addition, the President may lead any ministry at his

[1] Until the name was changed under the 1972 Constitution, Sri Lanka was formerly called the Republic of Ceylon.

[2] The Constitution of Sri Lanka, Article 30(1) provides, 'There shall be a President of the Republic of Sri Lanka, who is the Head of the State, the Head of the Executive and of the Government, and the Commander-in-Chief of the Armed Forces.'

discretion. The President is empowered to appoint the heads and judges of the Supreme Court and Courts of Appeal, chiefs of the Army, the Navy, the Air Force and the Police. There is no restriction on the President appointing close family members in such positions.

The armed forces are divided into the Sri Lanka Army, the Sri Lanka Navy, and the Sri Lanka Air Force. The Army is the oldest and largest of the three armed services. The British military justice system is the progenitor of the military legal systems followed in Sri Lanka. The Army Act was enacted by Parliament on 10 October 1949, which is recognised as the day that the Ceylon Army was raised. The Sri Lankan Constitution restricts the fundamental rights of the armed forces personnel. Article 15 (8) provides:

> The exercise and operation of the fundamental rights declared and recognised by Articles 12 (1), 13 and 14 shall, in their application to the members of the Armed Forces, Police Force and other Forces charged with the maintenance of public order, be subject to such restrictions as may be prescribed by law in the interests of the proper discharge of their duties and the maintenance of discipline among them.

General Sarath Fonseka was the commander of the Sri Lanka Army from December 2005 to July 2009. He led the Sri Lankan army to its 2009 victory over the LTTE, ending its 37-year separatist conflict. After the war, Fonseka became the first and only serving Sri Lankan officer to be appointed as Chief of Defence Staff. However, Fonseka quit service in November 2009, complaining the job was designed to sideline him and that President Rajapaksa had wrongly accused him of planning a coup. Fonseka was elected as a Member of Parliament at the General Elections of 2010. However, Rajapaksa defeated him in the presidential election, although Fonseka claims that electoral results were manipulated.

Retired General Fonseka was taken into military custody by the military police on 8 February 2010 and was charged for committing alleged fraudulent acts and military offences. He was kept in custody until the court-martial. The former army commander denied all the allegations, saying they were politically motivated.[3] However, the international press

[3] Retired General Fonseka claimed that he was invited by the major political parties in the opposition to contest the 2010 Presidential Election as the 'common candidate'. Ever since his nomination as a common candidate, there was a coherent, systematic and discernible course of events,

viewed his arrest as a means of getting rid of the only real opponent of President Rajapaksa in the elections. Under section 57 of the Army Act, till the period of six months after an officer or soldier resigns or retires from the Army, he remains subject to the Act.[4]

A summary of evidence over five charges against retired General Fonseka was ordered, and evidence from 35 individuals, inclusive of 22 army personnel, seven police officers, and six civilians, was recorded. This was followed by the assembly of two courts-martial for the trial of Fonseka at the Naval Headquarters in Colombo. Reporters were banned from attending the courts-martial proceedings.[5]

In the first court-martial, Fonseka was charged that he had engaged in political activities whilst being subject to military law. He was convicted of the charge and was imposed the sentence of cashiering from the Army. Fonseka petitioned the Court of Appeal, challenging the court-martial decision which stripped his rank and pension. The second court-martial was convened on 17 March 2010, which considered four charges, all related to Fonseka having served as chairman of the Tender Board pertaining to the procurement of certain equipment.[6] The charges alleged that tenders were awarded to a company in which his son-in-law had an interest or concern. It was alleged that Fonseka concealed or failed to disclose that his son-in-law had such intent or concern, thus committing a fraudulent act, punishable under section 109 (e) of the Army Act.[7] The court-martial convicted Fonseka on 17 September 2010 and sentenced him to 30 months of imprisonment. The sentence was confirmed by the

amounting in law to targeted malice. Further, his security cover was totally removed, the armed forces surrounded the hotel which he had occupied on the day of the Presidential Election.

[4] Section 57 of the Army Act provides, 'Where a person subject to military law commits any offence and thereafter ceases to be a person subject to military law, he may be taken into and kept in military custody and be tried and punished for that offence by a court-martial: Provided that he shall not be so tried after the lapse of six months from the date of the commission of such offence unless such offence is the offence of mutiny, desertion, or fraudulent enlistment.'

[5] See https://www.theguardian.com/world/2010/mar/16/sri-lankan-general-court-martial

[6] The equipment included 234 day-vision binoculars, 50 12v maintenance-free batteries, 50 5KVA generators, and Three VHF direction finders.

[7] Section 109(e) of the Army Acts states, 'Every person subject to military law who commits any other fraudulent act hereinbefore not particularly specified, or any act of a cruel, indecent or unnatural kind, shall be guilty of a military offence and shall, on conviction by a court-martial, be liable to suffer simple or rigorous imprisonment for a term not exceeding three years or any less severe punishment in the scale set out in section 133.'

President of Sri Lanka on 29 September 2010. As a result of this sentence, Fonseka became ineligible to continue as a Member of Parliament, and his seat was declared vacant.[8]

Fonseka thereafter approached the Court of Appeal, making various allegations of biases and injustices. He alleged that the members of the court-martial were specially selected and had either personal interest in the matter or were those against whom he had taken action as the Army Commander. Further, the members of the court-martial were not in the command stream of the Army and were junior to him in rank.[9] In addition, both the courts-martial failed to give reasoned decisions.[10] The Judge Advocate of the Sri Lankan Navy, who was not in the country when the court-martial was ordered, was specially flown from the United Kingdom to be the Judge Advocate for both courts-martial. The Army has a regular Judge Advocate of the rank of major general, but he was not detailed for the trial. Fonseka alleged that the conduct of the Judge Advocate was suspicious and questionable during the trial. It was also stated that the award of a sentence of 30 months of imprisonment was severe and disproportionate. When a person is imposed a sentence of six months or more, he is disqualified from being elected as President or as a Member of Parliament. Fonseka pleaded that imprisonment of 30 months was imposed on him to keep him away from challenging the President.[11]

The government denied most of the allegations and stated that

---

[8] Article 89(d) of the Sri Lankan Constitution dealing with disqualifications of the Members of Parliament provides, 'No person shall be qualified to be an elector at an election of the President, or of the Members of Parliament or to vote at any Referendum if he is subject to any of the following disqualifications, namely; (d) if he is serving or has during the period of seven years immediately preceding completed serving of a sentence of imprisonment (by whatever name called) for a term not less than six months imposed after conviction by any court for an offence punishable with imprisonment for a term not less than two years or is under sentence of death or is serving or has during the period of seven years immediately preceding completed the serving of a sentence of imprisonment for a term not less than six months awarded in lieu of the execution of such sentence…'.

[9] A writ application bearing No 350/2010 was filed by General Fonseka in the Court of Appeal against the decision of the officers detailed as the President and Members in second Court Martial II. However, it was dismissed by the Court of Appeal by an order dated 29 June 2010.

[10] Supreme Court in G.S.C. *Fonseka v. Dhammika Kitulegoda* [No 1/210 CA. (Writ) Appl No 676/2010 S.C.M. 10.1.2011] has held that the court-martial should act judicially and therefore should give reasons for its decision.

[11] *Fonseka v. General Jagath Jayasuriya and five others,* The Sri Lanka Law Reports, [2011] 2 SRI L.R.- Part 14, pp. 372–392.

Fonseka had suppressed material facts and misrepresented to mislead the court, which the Court of Appeal found true. The Court was of the view that the Fonseka was guilty of non-disclosure of material facts and therefore not entitled to any remedy from the Appeal Court. His petition was dismissed in limine.[12]

Fonseka filed another writ application on 12 October 2010 in the Court of Appeal and sought mandates in the nature of certiorari to quash the decisions made to declare that his seat as a Member of Parliament had fallen vacant, as well as a mandate in the nature of mandamus to enable him to sit and vote in Parliament and to exercise his powers, privileges and immunities as a Member of Parliament. The Court of Appeal referred the following question to the Supreme Court:[13]

> Whether the words 'any court' referred to in Article 89(d) of the Constitution refer to the Supreme Court, Court of Appeal and the other Courts of First Instance, to the exclusion of tribunals and institutions or whether the words 'any court' include courts-martial.[14]

In his petition, General Fonseka argued that the term "any court" referred to in Article 89(d) does not include courts-martial. Further, the court-martial is not a 'court' for the reason that it is convened by and comprises of the executive, requires certification by the convening officer for validity, does not follow set procedures as a civil court, is not manned by a judicial officer as per Article 170, is not subject to the Evidence Ordinance, is not a designated institution of justice under the Constitution,[15] lacks permanency of regular courts, is limited to military matters, consists of ad hoc appointments, does not adhere to the principles of a fair trial and is in conflict with several other provisions of the Constitution.[16]

---

[12] *Fonseka v. General Jagath Jayasuriya and five others*, The Sri Lanka Law Reports, [2011] 2 SRI L.R.- Part 15, pp. 393-415.

[13] The Court of Appeal referred to Articles 24(5), 105 and 13(4), of the Constitution, and to Section 2 of the Judicature Act No 2 of 1978, as amended.

[14] Article 91 (1) (a) of the Sri Lanka Constitution states: 'No person shall be qualified to be elected as a Member of Parliament or to sit and vote in Parliament – (a) if he is or becomes subject to any of the disqualifications specified in Article 89.'

[15] Article 105(1) of the Sri Lankan Constitution.

[16] Article 24 of the Constitution, which deals with the language of the Courts, has in an inclusive application including tribunals and other institutions within its limited purview. As such, tribunals and other institutions are not 'courts' with reference to the rest of the Constitution. Further, Article 13(4) provides, 'No person shall be punished with death or imprisonment except by order

The Supreme Court, referring to a few earlier decisions,[17] observed that certain provisions of the Constitution[18] had preserved the validity of all existing laws at the time of its enactment and the jurisdiction of the Supreme Court, in terms of Article 125, is limited to the interpretation of the Constitution. Accordingly, courts-martial in terms of the Army Act are valid and operative, and the petitioner (Fonseka) never challenged the validity of courts-martial during his trial. Further, the interpretation of a constitutional provision cannot be made in a vacuum – such interpretation should coincide and be comfortable with the rest of the Constitution. The Supreme Court held that the concept of court-martial is a valid and operative aspect of law, and it cannot strike down existing legislation. A court-martial is empowered to impose sentences of death and/or imprisonment,[19] and therefore, a sentence of death or imprisonment handed down by a court-martial is valid until and unless overturned by a court of competent jurisdiction. The power of courts-martial to impose sentences of death and imprisonment under section 133 of the Army Act is to be read with Article 13(4) of the Constitution, wherein it provides that such sentences may be imposed only by competent courts.[20]

The bench of the Supreme Court headed by the Chief Justice ruled that the court-martial is a court accepted under Article 89(d) of the Sri Lankan Constitution. The words 'any court' in Article 89(d) should be construed in a manner so as to include all courts which are created and established or otherwise recognised by the Constitution as being competent to impose the punishments envisaged by that Article, including a court-martial. It ruled that a court-martial verdict in September 2010 that found him guilty of arms procurement offences meant that he was no longer qualified to be a Member of Parliament. The implication of the Supreme Court's judgment is that courts-martial have been placed on the

---

of a competent court, made in accordance with the procedure established by law.' In addition, a Court Martial does not comprise judicial officers as in the interpretation clause of the Constitution with reference to Article 170.

[17] *Bribery Commissioner v. Ranasinghe*, Privy Council (1964) 66 NLR 73, *Walker Sons & Co. Ltd. and others v. Fry (1965)* 68 NLR 73, *Liyanage and others v. The Queen (1965)* 68 NLR 265, *Panagoda v. Budinis Singho (1966)* 22 July 68 NLR 490, and *Gunaseela v. Udugama* (Major General and Commander of the Army) (1966) 22 July 1969 NLR 193.

[18] Article 16, 105(2) and 168 (1) of the Sri Lankan Constitution.

[19] Under section 133 of the Army Act, the court-martial is empowered to impose sentences of death and/or imprisonment, besides other punishments.

[20] *Supra* note 10.

same footing as civilian courts under Article 89(d) of the Constitution.

Justice Saleem Marsoof, in his concurring opinion, held that the institution of court-martial controlled by the executive is not a court, tribunal or institution set up as described in Article 105 of the Constitution, and has no place in Chapter XV of the Constitution because a member of the armed forces who sits on a court-martial does not fall within the definition of 'judicial officer' under Article 170 of the Constitution. Justice Marsoof, however, concurred with the majority that 'competent court' in Article 13(4) includes any court (regular or extraordinary) capable of imposing punishments. Since the court-martial was capable of imposing punishment, it must be taken to be within the ambit of 'competent court.' Thus, Article 89(d) should be interpreted to include a court-martial.[21]

The detention of the General had caused an uproar within and outside the island nation, and the government was under pressure from several quarters to immediately release Fonseka and have a transparent probe into the allegations levelled against him. After spending nearly two years in prison, President Mahinda Rajapaksa pardoned him from serving the remainder of his sentence, and Fonseka was released in May 2012. In March 2015, Fonseka was conferred the highest military rank of the Field Marshal. Later in June, the Appeal Court dismissed his petition, which pleaded the Court to issue a mandatory order to re-appoint him to the Colombo district seat as a Member of Parliament. The Court said that there were no legal provisions in the Constitution to allow reappointment of members to Parliament subsequent to a presidential pardon.

Some of the major issues which these courts-martial had brought out are holding two trials against the accused at a short interval; allegations of biases against the Judge Advocate who remain under the direct chain of command of the officer who convened the court-martial; and double jeopardy, i.e., the second trial of a military accused by a civil court who has been convicted by court-martial on the same charge.[22] Since the same sovereign is responsible for both the civil and criminal process, this provision surely violates the principle of double jeopardy.[23] The only solace

---

[21] Opinion of Justice Saleem Marsoof in *Fonseka v. Kithulegoda & Others*, SC Ref 1/2010, SCM 10-01-2011, LST review, Vol. 21, Issue 283, Pay 2011, pp. 21-32.

[22] Section 77(2), Army Act.

[23] Fidell Eugene R., *The Fonseka Courts-martial: An Opportunity for Law Reform, Law and Society Trust Review*, Vol. 21, issue 283, May 2011, p. 1.

is that the civil court will take into account the punishment awarded by the court-martial while awarding a sentence. The composition of the court-martial was another important issue in this case as a former general of the Army was an accused. This could be problematic in any military justice system to find officers senior to him to constitute such a court. Whatever may be the reason, Fonseka's trial by officers who were junior to him, besides having served under his command, was an embarrassment to the former commander of the Army. In a similar situation, the Supreme Court of India has recently held that a retired lieutenant general cannot be tried in a general court-martial (GCM) consisting of members below his rank.[24] The Court held:

> Merely because the appellant had retired in the meantime cannot be a ground to discard and give a go by to the provisions of Rule 40(2) of the Army Rules...[25] It is a travesty of justice that a person holding the rank of a lieutenant general is tried by the GCM which consisted of members below his rank. Such a composition cannot be countenanced in law. We are, therefore, of the opinion that the GCM was not validly constituted. Once that finding is arrived at, entire proceedings held by the said GCM stand vitiated.

The Sri Lankan President, in the opinion of this author, should have referred the case of Fonseka to the civil court for trial for this reason.

Fonseka's case has brought out glaring deficiencies in the Sri Lankan military justice system when compared to international standards of a fair trial. The 1949 Army Act, so also the 1949 Air Force Act, and the 1950 Navy Act of Sri Lanka are descendants of British legislation of the year 1881 and are totally out of date. A court-martial constituted under military law determines both the findings and the sentence. The members of a court-martial are neither legally qualified nor trained in the administration of justice and are exposed to varying degrees of command influence. The judicial branch of the military, consisting of judge advocates (JA), is

---

[24] In this case, one lieutenant general and four major generals constituted the general courts-martial for the trial of the accused of the rank of lieutenant general. *Ex. Lt. Gen. Avadhesh Prakash v. Union of India*: Criminal Appeal No 140 of 2019, decided on 4 February 2019.

[25] Under the Rule 40 (2) of the Army Rules, 1954, members of the GCM for the trial of an officer shall be of a rank not lower than that of the officer [accused] unless, in the opinion of the convening officer, officers of such rank are not (having due regard to the exigencies of the public service) available. Such opinion shall be recorded in the convening order.

placed under the administrative and functional control of the same executive who orders trial by Court Martial and reviews the proceedings. Under the Sri Lankan military law, the courts-martial are not required to provide any reason in support of their conclusions, even in cases where they enforce the death sentence. The officers of the Judge Advocate department are not independent and cannot be expected to render a just opinion. Independence of the judiciary is essential in maintaining the rule of law and the notion of a fair trial.

The laws of Sri Lanka provide for the issue of writs of mandamus, certiorari and prohibition in respect of courts-martial; however, there is no independent judicial forum where the aggrieved person can appeal against the final order passed by a court-martial.[26] This is a serious lacuna in the military justice system. Sri Lankan Supreme Court judgment has, in general, negative implications in regard to the competence of a court-martial even in trying civilian abuses by military personnel. A court-martial may impose the death penalty but does not guarantee the right to a fair trial. The UN Human Rights Committee is of the opinion that in cases where the death penalty is imposed, scrupulous respect of the guarantees of a fair trial is particularly important. Failure to respect and guarantee the provisions of Article 14 is a violation of the right to life under Article 6 of the International Covenant on Civil and Political Rights.[27] The world has moved forward in the last two decades, and there have been major changes in the military justice systems of other democracies. It is time the Sri Lankan Parliament strengthens its military legal system to restore the confidence of the public in the quality of military justice.

---

[26] Sri Lankan legislature Act No 56 of 2007 gives effect to International Covenant on Civil and Political Rights. Section 4 (2) of the Act No 56 of 2007 enshrines that 'every person convicted of a criminal offence under any written law shall have the right to appeal to higher court against such conviction and any sentence imposed.'

[27] UN Human Rights Committee, General Comment 32, Article 14: Right to equality before courts and tribunals and to a fair trial, UN Doc. CCPR/C/GC/32 dated 23 August 2007.

Dr **UC Jha**, a former wing commander of the Indian Air Force, has extensive field and academic experience in international humanitarian law, military law, and human rights law. He was invited by the UN High Commissioner for Human Rights, Geneva, in November 2014, to make a presentation during a thematic session on the independence, impartiality and competence of the judiciary, including military courts. In addition, he has been invited by the Parliamentary Standing Committee on Defence on quite a few occasions. He was a visiting fellow at the Centre for the Study of Law and Governance, Jawaharlal Nehru University, New Delhi, during 2008-2009. His work comprises 25 books and over 125 articles on subjects relating to military legal systems, international humanitarian law and human rights.

The Constitutional Court of Georgia – Conscientious Objection to Military Service

Nino Nikolaishvili

Public Defender of Georgia Case, Georgia

Introduction

This chapter broadly reviews values, national security (international disputes) and the issue of military service for Georgia, a unique country situated at a strategically important crossroad which is part of the European and Euro-Atlantic space.

The chapter then considers the concept of conscientious objection to military service. In particular, the chapter analyses the applicable international standards and jurisprudence of Georgia related to conscientious objection. This was addressed in the judgment of the Constitutional Court of Georgia in the case *Public Defender of Georgia v. The Parliament of Georgia*[1] dated 22 December 2011, which declared anti-constitutional the normative content imposing the duty to serve in military reserve for citizens who object to compelled military reserve service on the ground of freedom of belief. This decision ushered in a new era, as the country became obliged to implement conscientious objection to military service and permit other forms of alternative service.

[1] *Public Defender of Georgia v. The Parliament of Georgia*, judgment of 22 December 2011; Available at: https://constcourt.ge/en/judicial-acts?legal=450.

A Pertinent Overview of Georgia

Strategically, Georgia's geopolitical location has been both a burden and a blessing. On the one hand, it sits at vital crossroads in Eastern Europe. On the other hand, its location has caused it to be a centre of political attention by others. Georgia's stated goal is to become part of European and Euro-Atlantic structures. This goal is envisaged by its Constitution and reflects the will of the society,[2] which will be a huge step towards the consolidation of its democracy and strengthening its national security.

In the twentieth century, Georgia saw 70 years of Soviet occupation. In 1991, Georgia regained its independence which was followed by political and economic instability. At the beginning of the 1990s, aggressive separatist movements triggered an armed confrontation with military forces of the Russian Federation who aligned with local groups. In order to infringe upon the sovereignty and the territorial integrity of Georgia and to limit its free and democratic choice, in August 2008, the region saw further military aggression, accompanied by a new wave of ethnic cleansing.[3]

In response to all the aforementioned threats and massive violations of human rights, Georgia referred to all available international legal means.

Among other actions, Georgia lodged two inter-state applications to the European Court of Human Rights (ECHR) that relate to the armed conflict of 2008 and the subsequent situation in and around the occupied territories of Georgia.

On 21 January 2021, Georgia celebrated a historical victory over Russia at the Strasbourg Court on the August 2008 war case, *Georgia v. Russia (II)*.[4] The Grand Chamber of 17 judges ruled that Russia was responsible for the mass violations committed against the Georgian population since Russia exercised effective control over the Tskhinvali region

---

[2] Constitution of Georgia, Article 78 – 'Integration into European and Euro-Atlantic structures –The constitutional bodies shall take all measures within the scope of their competences to ensure the full integration of Georgia into the European Union and the North Atlantic Treaty Organisation'.

[3] National Security Concept of Georgia, p. 7; Available at: https://mod.gov.ge/uploads/2018/pdf/NSC-ENG.pdf

[4] ECHR, Case of *Georgia v. Russia* (II); Available at: http://hudoc.echr.coe.int/eng?i=001-207757

and Abkhazia. Accordingly, the Court upheld Georgia's claim that the Tskhinvali region and Abkhazia are integral parts of Georgia's territory and are occupied by Russia. Furthermore, the European Court's acknowledgement of these violations confirms the ethnic cleansing of Georgians during the August 2008 war.

On 22 August 2018, the Government of Georgia lodged a new inter-state application under Article 33 (inter-state cases) of the European Convention on Human Rights, which is currently pending before the Court.[5]

Apart from the aforementioned cases, on 27 January 2016, Pre-trial Chamber I of the International Criminal Court (ICC) granted the prosecutor's request to open an investigation *proprio motu* in the situation in Georgia. The ICC investigations focus on alleged crimes committed in the context of an international armed conflict between 1 July and 10 October 2008 in and around South Ossetia, including crimes against humanity and war crimes.[6]

Georgia is actively engaged in cooperation with the investigation of the Prosecutor's Office of the International Criminal Court into the August 2008 conflict. Georgia desires to bring justice to the victims of the most heinous crimes committed against ethnic Georgians.

Concept of Conscientious Objection

The aforementioned challenges and international threats create the necessity of robust military service from the Georgian population. According to international standards, some exclusions are envisaged from this service, among others, the right to conscientious objection to military service.

In a number of states, conscription laws require that adult citizens have a legal duty to undertake a period of military training or service. For some individuals, such a duty conflicts with their conscience due to religious or philosophical beliefs, and they assert the right to refuse to un-

---

[5] New inter-state application brought by Georgia against Russia available at: http://hudoc.echr.coe.int/eng-press?i=003-6176209-8005403

[6] *Situation in Georgia – Investigation*, information; Available at: https://www.icc-cpi.int/georgia

dertake military service. International human rights standards are evolving in the direction of accepting that such refusal is a manifestation of the individual's conscience and should be protected under the guarantee of freedom of thought, conscience, and religion.[7]

The right to conscientious objections to military service has been recognised by the Human Rights Committee and other UN bodies. The Committee has recognised that a state may instead require an individual to undertake alternative service. Such service must not be punitive in nature. Rather, it must be a real service to the community and compatible with respect for human rights. Similarly, the European Union (EU) Charter of Fundamental Rights and Freedoms recognises a right to conscientious objection to military service.[8]

Conscience, generally, is one of the important rights based on the 'Right to Freedom of Thought, Conscience and Religion', which is guaranteed in the Universal Declaration of Human Rights (UDHR),[9] as well as in the International Covenant on Civil and Political Rights (ICCPR)[10] and the European Convention on Human Rights.[11]

While the above Covenant does not explicitly refer to a right to conscientious objection, in its general comment No 22 (1993), the Human Rights Committee[12] stated that such a right could be derived from Article 18, since the obligation to use lethal force might seriously conflict with the freedom of conscience and the right to manifest one's religion or belief.

The 'Right to Freedom of Thought, Conscience and Religion' as set out in Article 18 of the ICCPR is a non-derogable right under Article 4 (States of Emergency) of the Covenant, even during times of a public emergency threatening the life of the nation. The right to manifest one's religion or belief may be subject 'only to such limitations as are prescribed

---

[7] *International Human Rights Law*, Daniel Moeckli, Sangeeta Shah, Sandesh Sivakumaran, David Harris, second edition (Oxford, 2014), p. 224.

[8] *Ibid*, p. 225.

[9] Universal Declaration of Human Rights, Article 18; Available at: https://www.ohchr.org/EN/UDHR/Documents/UDHR_Translations/eng.pdf

[10] International Covenant on Civil and Political Rights, Article 18 (1); Available at: https://www.ohchr.org/EN/ProfessionalInterest/Pages/CCPR.aspx

[11] European Convention on Human Rights, Article 9; Available at: https://bit.ly/2PLsEJh

[12] UN Human Rights Committee (HRC), CCPR General Comment No 22: Article 18 (Freedom of Thought, Conscience or Religion), 30 July 1993, CCPR/C/21/Rev.1/Add.4, available at: https://www.refworld.org/docid/453883fb22.html

by law and are necessary to protect public safety, order, health, or morals or the fundamental rights and freedoms of others'.[13] The Human Rights Committee has emphasised the limited nature of permissible restrictions to the right to freedom of religion and belief in its general comment No 22 (1993).

The Human Rights Committee has been critical of states that allow conscientious objection only during peacetime. In its concluding observations on a state report by Finland, it stated that it:

> Regrets that the right to conscientious objection is acknowledged only in peacetime. The State party should fully acknowledge the right to conscientious objection and, accordingly, guarantee it both in wartime and in peacetime [...].[14]

The Human Rights Committee reaffirmed its position in *Min-Kyu Jeong et al. v. The Republic of Korea,* in which the authors claimed that their rights under Article 18 of the Covenant had been violated because there was no alternative to compulsory military service since their failure to perform military service had resulted in their criminal prosecution and imprisonment. The Committee noted that the Republic of Korea

> Reiterate[d] arguments advanced in response to the earlier communications before the Committee, notably on the issues of national security, equality between military and alternative service, and a lack of a national consensus on the matter.

The Committee stated it could find no reason to depart from its earlier position as set out in *Yoon et al. v. the Republic of Korea.*[15] It concluded that the state was under an obligation to provide an effective remedy, including compensation, for the violation of Article 18 and to avoid similar violations of the Covenant in the future.[16]

Article 9 of the Convention also does not explicitly mention the right to conscientious objection, whether in the military or the civilian sphere.

---

[13] International Covenant on Civil and Political Rights, Article 18 (3).

[14] *Conscientious Objection to Military Service,* (United Nations Publication, New York and Geneva, 2012), p. 26; Available at: https://www.ohchr.org/Documents/Publications/ConscientiousObjection_en.pdf

[15] UN Human Rights Committee (HRC), Jung, Oh, Yeom, Nah, Lim, Lim, Goh v. *The Republic of Korea;* Available at: https://www.refworld.org/cases,HRC,4c19e0322.html

[16] *Conscientious Objection to Military Service,* (United Nations Publication, 2012), p.13.

Nevertheless, the Strasbourg Court has ruled that the safeguards of Article 9 apply, in principle, to opposition to military service when it is motivated by a serious, insuperable conflict between compulsory service in the army and an individual's conscience or his or her sincere and deeply held religious or other convictions. The answer to the question of whether, and to what extent, the objection to service military falls within the ambit of Article 9 will vary according to the specific circumstances of each case.[17]

With respect to conscientious objection, one of the landmark judgments of the ECHR is the Grand Chamber judgment of 7 July 2011, *Bayatyan v. Armenia,*[18] in which the Court examined the issue of the applicability of Article 9 of the Convention to conscientious objectors. The Court stated:[19]

> [...] Article 9 [of the European Convention on Human Rights] does not explicitly refer to a right to conscientious objection. However, it considers that opposition to military service, where it is motivated by a serious and insurmountable conflict between the obligation to serve in the army and a person's conscience or his deeply and genuinely held religious or other beliefs, constitutes a conviction or belief of sufficient cogency, seriousness, cohesion and importance to attract the guarantees of Article 9 [...] Whether and to what extent objection to military service falls within the ambit of that provision must be assessed in the light of the particular circumstances of the case.

In the case *Papavasilakis v. Greece,*[20] the Court expanded the concept of conscientious objection and ascertained that generally, it is not necessary for a person to be a member of practising religion or pacifist organisation to be recognised as a conscientious objector. The Court held that there had been a violation of Article 9 of the Convention, finding that the applicant did not enjoy the necessary procedural safeguards in having his request for alternative civilian service examined.

---

[17] Guide on Article 9 of the European Convention on Human Rights – Freedom of Thought, Conscience and Religion (updated on 31 December 2020), p. 24; Available at: https://www.echr.coe.int/Documents/Guide_Art_9_ENG.pdf

[18] ECHR, Case of *Bayatyan v. Armenia*; Available at: http://hudoc.echr.coe.int/eng?i=001-105611

[19] *Ibid*, § 110.

[20] ECHR, Case of *Papavasilakis v. Greece*; Available at: http://hudoc.echr.coe.int/eng?i=001-166850

On the other hand, in the case of *Enver Aydemir v. Turkey*,[21] the Court concluded that the applicant's opposition to military service did not trigger Article 9 of the Convention. There, the applicant complained that, *inter alia*, he had been repeatedly detained, prosecuted and convicted because he had claimed the status of conscientious objector.

The Court found that the applicant's objection to performing compulsory military service for the benefit of the secular Republic of Turkey did not fall within the scope of Article 9 of the Convention, given that the arguments he had put forward for claiming the status of conscientious objector were based on political grounds and not on religious beliefs which were in serious and insurmountable conflict with his obligation to perform military service. The Strasbourg Court, therefore, declared this complaint inadmissible.

Thus, all the above international bodies have recognised the right to have a conscientious objection to military service as a legitimate exercise of the right to freedom of thought, conscience and religion.

Judgment of the Constitutional Court of Georgia

In the light of the aforementioned findings, building strong military forces for Georgia, as with other countries, is a top national priority that is in some tension with human rights norms. For example, the concept of conscientious objection confronts various legal interests, but the internationally established standard, as well as the case-law of the Constitutional Court of Georgia, balanced the above interests from the human rights standpoint, which will be discussed below.

The subject matter of the landmark judgment of the Constitutional Court of Georgia, *Public Defender of Georgia v. Parliament of Georgia*,[22] was the constitutionality of Article 2, clause 2 of the Law of Georgia 'On Military Reserve Service', which declared the duty of each and every citizen of Georgia to serve in military reserve pursuant to this norm. The Court considered this rule in light of Article 14 (Right to Equality) and

---

[21] ECHR, Case of *Enver Aydemir v. Turkey*; available at: http://hudoc.echr.coe.int/eng?i=001-163940

[22] *Supra*, note 1.

Article 19 (Freedom of Belief, Religion and Conscience) of the Constitution of Georgia.

According to the Constitutional claim, compulsory military service recruits enjoyed the right to good faith resistance and the right to request alternative military service based on the good faith resistance. However, the same exception did not apply to persons who were subject to serving in Reserve Military Service. In the said judgment, the Constitutional Court extended the right of good faith resistance based on religious or non-religious (pacifist) beliefs to Reserve Military Service as well.

The claimant stated that:

> Reserve service comprises preparation for a fight. Therefore, people who are obliged to serve in military reserves can have a conscientious objection to that service in view of religious or non-religious beliefs. (...) according to the law of Georgia on Military Reserve Service, individuals and students have no right to refuse to serve in military reserve on the ground of conscientious objection, and when they are called to serve in reserve, people with conscientious objection have no possibility to demand non-military, alternative labour service.

The Court explained that freedom of religion guaranteed by Article 19 of the Constitution includes a right to claim conscientious objection to military service. In other words, the right to refuse to perform military service for religious or other beliefs and perform military service as required by the Constitution in other alternatives (non-combatant) civilian forms. The disputed norm coerced a conscientious objector to act against his/her conscience, beliefs and ethics, which constitutes an unjustified interference with freedom of religion.

The Constitutional Court noted that Article 14 of the Constitution prohibiting discrimination requires a legislator to follow a main principle of equality – not to allow unequal treatment of people in equal conditions, not to adopt such legislative norms which do not take into account the differences existing between various religious, ethnic, social and gender groups and establishes equal requirements and obligations for them.

The disputable norm, which does not consider exceptions regarding the persons who are conscientious objectors to military service for religious or ethical beliefs, violates the requirements stipulated by Article 14 of the Constitution prohibiting discrimination.

Taking into account all the aforementioned, the Constitutional Court recognised the prohibition provided by the law against a good faith resistance, with no available alternative for military reservists, as unconstitutional since it conflicted with Articles 14 and 19 of the Constitution.

The Constitutional Court of Georgia noted the complexity of the issue in question and ascertained that several factors should be taken into consideration while discussing a conscientious objection of a person (or a group) on each case.

Thus, the judgment of the Constitutional Court of Georgia is in line with international standards of human rights. The Court relied on the landmark case of the ECHR of *Bayatyan v. Armenia* (see above) and referred to some important rulings in that case.

To sum up, Georgia's Constitutional Court's judgment should be regarded as a progressive and commendable decision that reflects national priorities, and that is in full compliance with the UN Human Rights Committee, other UN human rights institutions, and the recent caselaw of the European Court of Human Rights.

Conclusion

Military service is regarded as one of the core values of every country. The present chapter briefly reviewed geopolitical location, threats and ongoing occupation issues concerning Georgia, which aspires to become a member of European and Euro-Atlantic structures.

After a brief examination of international documents and bodies that recognise a right of objection, it can be concluded that the right to conscientiously object to military service should be regarded as an important human right. Conscientious objection to military service is frequently connected to freedom of religion or belief, as many conscientious objectors are motivated by deeply held religious beliefs. This right has achieved a certain degree of international consensus and is compatible with the practice of many states. To protect the rights of these individuals, some states maintain laws that exempt them from compulsory military service. Often, objectors are required to participate in an alternative national service.

This chapter analysed the international standards, decisions of the UN Human Rights Committee and the judgments of the European

Court as well. According to all pertinent sources, it is crystal clear that states must universally ensure the right to object to military service based on genuinely held religious beliefs as an integral part of the absolute right to hold beliefs.

The chapter reviewed the judgment of the Constitutional Court of Georgia, which is vital in the context of fulfilling the above obligation. The Constitutional Court agreed with the claimant's averments and considered that the freedom of religion guaranteed by the Constitution of Georgia gives any person the right to conscientious objection.

The provision that imposed the duty for even objectors to serve in the military reserves was declared unconstitutional. According to this judgment, a person, in accordance with his/her own beliefs, has a right to request alternative labour service. This decision may be regarded as a positive example for the development of military law in other countries.

To sum up, compliance of national legislation and case-law of the highest domestic courts (as in the present case of Georgia) with international human rights standards will further decrease complaints lodged before international/regional human rights bodies and ensure universal protection of human rights worldwide.

As a scholarship holder, **Nino Nikolaishvili** completed her LLM degree in International Human Rights Law at the University of Nottingham (UK) and graduated from the Hague Academy of International law and the International Nuremberg Principles Academy. Her LLM dissertation in Nottingham, *The Determination of Inter-State Cases at the European Court of Human Rights*, was awarded a distinction.

Nino has worked in various positions in the judicial system and at the Ministry of Justice of Georgia. Currently, at the Ministry, she holds the position of Head of the Department representing Georgia before all international courts, UN Human Rights Treaty Bodies and the bodies of the Council of Europe.

She holds certificates of appreciation from the Ministry of Justice for her successful career at the Ministry and her special contribution in preparation and proceedings of the August 2008 war case [*Georgia v. Russia (II)*] before the European Court of Human Rights.

She has participated in various conferences and workshops as an expert in Georgia and worldwide. Since 2019, she is involved in various projects related to Ukraine and the International Criminal Court. She received a certificate of appreciation from the Embassy of the United States of America in Ukraine in 2019.

She is also a visiting trainer for Georgian law enforcement bodies and teaches at the Ivane Javakhishvili Tbilisi State University and Tbilisi Open University.

How Nepal's Supreme Court Shaped the Country's Military Tribunals

Prem Chandra Rai

Iman Singh Gurung, Nepal

Introduction

Nepal has a long history of legal developments involving the military. The current constitution of Nepal recognises the military as a mainstay for safeguarding independence, sovereignty, territorial integrity and national unity. Nepal's army has been actively participating in various United Nations peacekeeping missions soon after the country became a member of the UN in 1955. Until 1990, when the King was the active ruler under a party-less political system, the Army was accountable only to the King. After the advent of democracy in 1990, an effort was made to bring the then Royal Nepal Army under civilian control. Then, the military justice system of Nepal, which was hitherto in isolation, became a subject matter of public discourse, especially through litigation in the Supreme Court of Nepal. During the last three decades, several issues with respect to the reformation of the military justice system have come to the forefront. Great improvement has been made, but work still remains to be done.

This essay examines efforts made in reforming the military justice system through the judicial intervention of Nepal's highest court. A quick history of army organisation in Nepal will be observed, followed by the turning point that propelled the public debate over the issues relating to the military tribunals. To give the readers a picture of the existing scenario, the main part of this writing starts with the current system of military justice. The heart of the writing then covers one after the other, the issues of debate with reference to the Supreme Court judgments and the changes brought about thereafter. Based on the analysis and findings, the author proposes further reform of the military justice system.

A Brief History of the Military Justice System in Nepal

Nepal has had a long history of existence as a distinct territorial state where several rulers have ruled and have been overthrown by subsequent rulers. History shows that the Kirants have ruled the territory from the eighth century BC to the fourth century AD and were thereafter replaced by the Lichchhabi dynasty.[1] Then the Mallas came to rule the territory during whose time Nepal was divided into several tiny states and principalities and was conquered by a Shah King from the Gorkha state who unified the territory in the form of today's Nepal in 1769.[2]

The recorded history of Nepal shows that the institution of the army was only initiated after 350 AD,[3] and by the seventh century, it was already taking considerable shape.[4] As regards military justice, the Lichchhabis vested the army commanders with the power to adjudicate the case involving their soldiers.[5] Until the Malla era, the religious texts were the fundamental sources of the laws, according to which the king

---

[1] The Government of Nepal, *History of Nepal*, information sheet published online by the Ministry of Foreign Affairs. Available at: https://mofa.gov.np/about-nepal/history-of-nepal/ Also: Adhikari BB, *An Easy History of Nepal*, (Kathmandu, Swades Publication Pvt. Ltd., 2019), p. 46.

[2] *Ibid.*

[3] *History of the Nepal Army*, published on the official website of the Nepal Army. Available at: https://www.nepalarmy.mil.np/page/history (accessed on 1 January 2021).

[4] In the year 647, King Narendra Dev extended the cooperation of 7,000 cavalry and 3,500 infantry troops at the request of China to attack the Southern Kingdom. See *History of the NA, ibid*

[5] Brigadier General Lawati HK (Judge Advocate), 'Military Justice System: An Overview', *The Judge Advocate Journal* (2012), 19-26, 19. According to Gen Lawati, there were laws even during Kirant rule, which was in 17 sections, out of which seven sections were related to the fighting force.

was the supreme power including in the administration of military justice.[6] During the earlier Shah rules, different court systems were developed, of which Daphterkhana was established to handle the dispute relating to the soldiers.[7] It was only in the nineteenth century that the military justice system made significant changes from its historical religious traditions when Junga Bahadur Rana, the first prime minister of Nepal, introduced the military code in 1854.[8] During the third Nepal-Tibet war in 1855, the military code designated certain acts as military crimes to maintain military discipline.[9] In 1939, when Nepal dispatched its army to support the British Government during WWII, a military code was introduced under which Nepali army officers were vested with the power to punish the guilty soldier.[10] In the subsequent decades, other statutes governing the operation of the Nepal Army, namely the Military Law Applicable to Our Soldiers Serving Abroad, 1944, and the Army (Special Management) Act, 1958, were adopted.[11]

In 1959, the above-mentioned legislations were repealed by the Army Act 1959. For the first time in the history of the Nepal Army, this legislation formally established the military justice system in Nepal. Section 117 of the Act incorporated the provision relating to the Judge Advocate General's (JAG's) Department, a concept that originated in the English military justice system in the seventeenth century.[12] Standing on that legal ground, the Government of Nepal duly established the JAG's Department on 21 September 1962.[13] The 1959 Act remained in force for almost six decades until it was replaced by current legislation, the Army Act, 2006. Initially, the JAG was established with one officer of

---

[6] Major Pyakurel A (Judge Advocate), 'The Historical Aspect of Military Justice System, and the Judge Advocate General's Department', *The Judge Advocate Journal* (2012), 46-52, 46.

[7] Other courts were: Kotiling, Itapachali, Taksar, Dhansar, Kokhi, Kumarichauk and Chhedbhel. See: *Ibid*, at 48.

[8] *Ibid*, at 48.

[9] Mutiny, looting the property of the enemy or enemy soldiers, defecting or escaping from the battleground, questioning the commander's orders etc. were listed as military crimes. See: *Ibid*, at 48.

[10] *Ibid*.

[11] *Ibid*.

[12] See the introductory webpage of the Judge Advocate General's Department on the official website of the Nepal Army. Available at: https://www.nepalarmy.mil.np/legal/index.php?page=in troduction

[13] *Ibid*.

the rank of major as the judge advocate at the army headquarters, which continued till 1973.[14] Since then, to meet the demand of the times, it has been expanded both geographically as well as in terms of human resources. At present, the JAG has been resourced with 40 advocate general officers and 22 advocate officer cadets and extended to all division headquarters (except the Valley Division), and four brigade headquarters.[15]

A Turning Point in the Military Justice System

The people's movement of 1990 reshaped Nepali politics, forcing the King to declare the multi-party system of governance and relegating the position of the King himself under the law. As a result, constitutional monarchism, parliamentary supremacy, and multi-party democracy became, at least in theory, the system of governance introduced by the Constitution of the Kingdom of Nepal, 1990.[16] The Constitution, however, kept the then Royal Nepal Army out of the jurisdiction of the Nepali apex court, stating that 'the Supreme Court shall not be deemed to have the power to interfere... with the proceedings and decisions of the Military Court...'[17]. This constitutional provision left the army immune to judicial review of its acts, including the decisions made by the courts-martial. The governing legislation further rendered immune the army personnel from being subjected to any civil action for acts undertaken in the course of duty, including the death of civilians.[18]

---

[14] Major Pyakurel A, *supra* note 6, p 49.

[15] *Supra* note 12.

[16] The Preamble of the Constitution of the Kingdom of Nepal,1990 reads:
Whereas it is expedient to promulgate and enforce this Constitution, made with the widest possible participation of the Nepalese people, to guarantee basic human rights to every citizen of Nepal; and also, to consolidate adult franchise, the parliamentary system of government, constitutional monarchy and the system of multi-party democracy by promoting amongst the people of Nepal the spirit of fraternity and the bond of unity on the basis of liberty and equality.

[17] Article 88(2)(a), The Constitution of the Kingdom of Nepal 1990.

[18] Sections 24A, the Army Act, 1959. The provision reads:
Defence for the Actions Undertaken in the Course of Discharging Duties: Notwithstanding anything contained in prevailing laws, in case any person dies or suffers any loss as a result of any action undertaken while discharging duties by any person to whom this act is applicable, no legal proceeding could be initiated in any court against such person.
Explanation: For the purpose of this section, the term 'any action undertaken while discharging duties' means any action to be taken for internal security or self-defence, including flag march, patrolling and guard duty.

The Constitution designated the King as the Supreme Commander of the Royal Nepal Army, who was vested with the ultimate power to use the Army.[19] This provision was designed arguably with the intention of giving parliament control of the military as the King would mobilise the military organisation only on the recommendation of the National Defence Council, of which the Prime Minister was the chair.[20] However, it proved to be wrong on at least two occasions: first, during the Maoists armed conflict,[21] the Prime Minister repeatedly failed in his attempt to mobilise the military to control the rebellion, especially because the King refused to order so, and second, on full military backing, King Gyanendra dissolved the cabinet and introduced himself as a *de facto* ruler of Nepal, revitalising the absolute monarchy in 2005. These incidents, for the first time in history, brought the army under enormous controversy, and its democratisation was felt indispensable to ensure the future of democracy in Nepal.[22] Consequently, the reinstated parliament[23] promulgated the new Army Act in 2006, and the following year was marked with the promulgation of the Interim Constitution, 2007, that brought military tribunals under the supervision of the Supreme Court of Nepal.[24]

Current Military Justice System of Nepal

The Army Act, 2006, is the main law that governs the military justice system in Nepal. As discussed earlier, this legislation was created with the intention of modifying the role of the army organisation in solidifying

---

[19] Articles 118-119.

[20] Article 118.

[21] The Communist Party of Nepal (Maoist) (CPN-M) launched an armed insurgency against the Government of Nepal in 1996 that lasted for ten years and claimed the lives of 17,000 people and came to an end after the signing of the Comprehensive Peace Accord in 2006.

[22] For detail, see: Bhandari C & Sharma R, 'Discourse of Civil Military Relations in Nepal', 1 *Unity Journal* (2020), 21-32.

[23] Upon the recommendation of Prime Minister Ser Bahadur Deuba, King Gyanendra dissolved the 205-member of House of Representatives of the Nepalese Parliament in October 2002. In 2005, the King took over the executive power and exercised absolute monarchy for 14 months, which, as a result of People's Movement II, ended with King's announcement of reinstating the Parliament on 24 April 2006. See: Reliefweb, Nepal: King ends direct rule, reinstates parliament, online posted on 25 April 2006. Available at: https://reliefweb.int/report/nepal/nepal-king-ends-direct-rule-reinstates-parliament

[24] Article 102(2), The Interim Constitution of Nepal, 2007.

the democratic governing system and making it accountable to the Nepali people.[25] The new legislation also laid down the reformed provisions of the military justice system in detail. The most significant of this was allowing the general courts (civilian courts) to try military personnel in at least two situations: first, if the military personnel commit such offences as homicide, rape, torture or enforced disappearance, the jurisdiction with respect to such a case will rest with the *other* court;[26] and second, if a dispute arises regarding the jurisdiction between the civilian and the military court, the proceedings have to be initiated at the civilian court.[27]

The judges in all military tribunals except summary courts-martial (SCM) are active military commanders. Though the SCM will be chaired by a civilian judge, the structure and formation will allow the executive to strongly influence the tribunal because the majority will be from the executive branch, and the government also nominates the judge.[28] This was the main reason that the question regarding the independence of military tribunals was seriously raised in the Supreme Court of Nepal.[29]

Iman Singh Gurung v. The HMG – Nepal's Supreme Court Considers Whether Military Courts Can Try Civilians

By the end of the twentieth century, Nepal was already a party to a number of international human rights conventions.[30] The socio-political

---

[25] The Preamble of the Army Act 2006 reads:
Whereas it is expedient to amend and consolidate the prevailing laws relating to the establishment, arrangement, control, use and mobilisation of the Nepal Army for making the Nepal Army accountable to the people of Nepal.

[26] Section 66(1), The Army Act, 2006 (Nepal).

[27] *Ibid*, Section 69(1).

[28] Pursuant to the Section 119(1)(a), on the recommendation of the Judicial Council, the Government of Nepal will nominate the judge of a High Court. The composition of the judicial council as per Article 153 of the Constitution of Nepal, is a) Chairperson – the Chief Justice; and members (b) The Federal Minister for Law and Justice, (c) The senior-most judge of the Supreme Court, (d) one jurist nominated by the President on the recommendation of the Prime Minister, and (e) a senior advocate or advocate to be appointed by the President on the recommendation of the Nepal Bar Association.

[29] *B.P. Niraula v. Constituent Assembly and Legislative Parliament*, NKP 2068 [2011], V10, DN 8692.

[30] For example, International Convention on the Elimination of All Forms of Racial Discrimination (ICERD), 1965 in 1971; International Covenant on Civil and Political Rights (ICCPR), 1966 in 1991; Second Optional Protocol to ICCPR aiming to the abolition of the death penalty (ICCPR-OP2-DP) in 1998; International Covenant on Economic, Social and Cultural Rights

openness and awareness of human rights further coincided with the decade-long armed insurgency that dragged the Nepal Army into human rights discourses.[31] The fairness and impartiality of the military tribunal was also questioned in some incidents,[32] which was absolutely unthinkable under the previous regimes. All these developments gave rise to the issue of jurisdiction and fairness of military tribunal, which became the subject matter of general public debate. One such debate concerned whether the military court can try a civilian person. This was the case of *Iman Singh Gurung v. The HMG*.

Whether a military tribunal can try civilians is a question of jurisdiction that has been a major issue of debate internationally. The UN Human Rights Committee has raised concerns that the trial of civilians in military or special courts may raise serious problems as far as the equitable, impartial, and independent administration of justice is concerned.[33] In 1995, the UN Committee against Torture had recommended that 'military courts should be regulated to prevent them from trying civilians and to restrict their jurisdiction to military offences by introducing the appropriate legal and constitutional changes'.[34] In Nepal, the previous legislation, the Army Act, 1959, contained a provision that empowered the courts-martial to also try a civilian.[35] This controversial provision was

---

(ICESCR), 1966 in 1991; Convention on the Elimination of All Forms of Discrimination against Women (CEDAW), 1979 in 1991; Convention against Torture and Other Cruel Inhuman or Degrading Treatment or Punishment (CAT), 1984 in 1991; Convention on the Rights of the Child (CRC), 1989 in 1990.

[31] For example, a UN body produced a report stating that 'unlawful killings occurred throughout the conflict in multiple contexts' and 'enforced disappearances were among the most serious human rights violations committed during the armed conflict in Nepal.' See, OHCHR, Nepal Conflict Report 2012: An analysis of conflict-related violations of international human rights law and international humanitarian law between February 1996 and 21 November 2006, p. 18, available at: https://www.ohchr.org/Documents/Countries/NP/OHCHR_Nepal_Conflict_Report2012.pdf

[32] For example, see above-cited OHCHR Report, at p. 24; also see generally *Devi Sunuwar v. District Police Office Kavrepalanchok*, NKP 2064(2007) V2, DN 7857; *Rabindra Prasad Dhakal v. Ministry of Home Affairs*, NKP 2064(2007), V2, DN 7817. The full text of these judgments, including other judgments on conflict-related cases, could be found in ICJ publication, Transitional Justice and Right to a Remedy: The Supreme Court Jurisprudence in Nepal, 2011 Kathmandu.

[33] Human Rights Committee, General Comment No 32, Article 14: Right to equality before courts and tribunals and to a fair trial, U.N. Doc. CCPR/C/GC/32 (2007), para 22.

[34] UN Document, A/50/44, 26 July 1995, para 73.

[35] Section 1(3)(d) of the then Army Act, 1959 read:

absent in the original text but was later inserted as Clause (d) in 1983,[36] and was ultimately declared *ultra vires* by the Supreme Court of Nepal in the case of *Iman Sing Gurung v. The HMG (His Majesty's Government).*[37]

The facts of the case are as follows: while prosecuting an incumbent major for an offence of smuggling and unlawful transaction of foreign currency, the general court-martial, pursuant to the Army Act, 1959, also prosecuted seven other civilians including the petitioner and awarded a sentence of imprisonment for eight years in October 1987. Against this judgment, a review petition was lodged before the Council of Ministers of His Majesty's Government, which failed to attract any consideration. In the meantime, the petitioner was also prosecuted at a special court (civilian court) for the same offence and was awarded a sentence of two years imprisonment and some penalty. Soon, the political system changed in Nepal, and the new Constitution was promulgated,[38] guaranteeing the fundamental rights of the people. The petitioner approached the Supreme Court of Nepal, invoking the equality and due process provision of the Constitution.

The main question before the Court was whether application of military law over a civilian like the petitioner was necessary to achieve the objective of the Army Act and whether such application would encroach upon the right to equality guaranteed to the petitioner by the constitution.[39] Answering these vital questions, the then Chief Justice, Biswanath Upadhyaya, authored a landmark judgment and held:

> [T]here is no proper and sensible ground of designing[40] and applying the impugned Clause (d) over a civilian, classifying him in the manner similar to an army personnel. If we consider it appropriate to apply

---

This Act will apply to any person without regards to whether that person remains or is residing in the Kingdom of Nepal or abroad ... the person who does not fall under the jurisdiction of the Army Act but involves in a crime as killing of a person whom this Act applies; or involved in a plot with the intention of killing of such person; or engages in activities that derelict a person or group of duty whom this Act is applied; or cause to damage military equipment, weapon or arsenal; or with intention of making such damages engages in an activity of inciting or causing someone to act against this Act.

36 The 3rd Amendment (1983) of Army Act, 1958.

37 NKP 2049 (1992), V8, DN4597.

38 The Constitution of the Kingdom of Nepal 1990.

39 *Iman Sing Gurung v. The HMG*, NKP 2049 [1992], V8, DN4597, para 18.

40 The judge was referring to the fact that Clause (d) was inserted by the third amendment of the Army Act in 1983.

> military law to a civilian just because that person was involved in a crime, along with an army officer or soldier, or was related to an army officer or soldier, then we have to realise the fact that our legal system has been embracing a military jurisprudence that is abnormal and abstract.[41]

Arriving at the conclusion that the provision set forth under the impugned Clause (d) was inappropriate and discriminatory, the learned judge further observed:

> [T]he fact that a certain act is considered a crime under military law attracting the military tribunal's jurisdiction just because it has some connection with the Army, may gravely affect the social relations of military personnel.[42]

The full bench of the Court that declared the legislative provision in question as null and void, also held:

> [D]ue to the institutional and procedural differences precipitated by the formation and operation of the military tribunal, there are qualitative differences between the justice delivered by a military tribunal and civilian court. Where a citizen is treated differently from other commoners placing him in the military category and deprived from seeking and obtaining justice from general courts, his rights would be adversely affected, ... [which] is discriminatory and contrary to the Article 11(1) of the Constitution.[43]

This judgement became a milestone from the viewpoint of judicial intervention in reforming the military justice system of Nepal, which brought the system of a military tribunal trying civilians to an end. Consequently, the Army Act of 2006 designated only three types of persons as falling under the jurisdiction of the Act: a person serving in the Nepal Army; other persons assigned or related to the Nepal Army's work or operations; and a person selected for recruitment in the Nepal Army.[44]

---

[41] Para 18.

[42] *Ibid.*

[43] Para 20. According to Article 11(1) of the Constitution of the Kingdom of Nepal, 1990, 'All citizens shall be equal before the law. No person shall be denied the equal protection of the laws.'

[44] Section 3(1).

A Greater Focus of the Supreme Court of Nepal on Independence of Military Justice, the *BP Niraula's* Case, and Conclusion

The continuous judicial intervention made by the Supreme Court of Nepal in the last three decades has forced the military justice system to modernise. The political changes and public awareness also contributed to making the Army more adherent to democratic norms, public security and human rights. Just within this span of 24 years, the Nepali people witnessed three Constitutions, and one of the positive changes it brought about was the progressive reform of military organisation by way of its configuration to a democratic governing system. The 1990 Constitution placed the military tribunal out of the supervision of the Supreme Court,[45] whereas the 2007 Constitution removed such a prohibition and guaranteed every person a fair trial by a competent court or judicial authority, and brought all other courts, except the Constituent Assembly Court, under the jurisdiction of the Supreme Court.[46] The 2015 Constitution also incorporated the same spirit and explicitly added that the Supreme Court may inspect, supervise and give directives to all other courts, including specialised courts – the term including military tribunals as well.[47]

The *Iman Singh Gurung v. The HMG* case gives a snapshot of competing concerns in Nepal's legal and military communities. Nepal's Supreme Court remains active in shaping the scope, jurisdiction and character of the country's military tribunals.[48]

---

[45] Art 88(2)(a).

[46] Art 102.

[47] Art 128(3). The Supreme Court of Nepal confirmed that military tribunals fall within the terminology of specialised courts, see *Krishna Bahadur Magar v. Patan High Court,* NKP2075 [2018], V10, DN 10115, para 6.

[48] For example, on the issue of fairness and independence of military tribunal, see: *BP Niraula v. Constituent Assembly and Legislative Parliament,* NKP 2068 [2011], V10, DN 8692; and on the issue of civilian court's jurisdiction on military personnel, see: *Krishna Bahadur Magar v Patan High Court,* NKP2075 [2018], V10, DN 10115, & *Hari Bahadur Dakal v. Patan High Court,* WN: 075-WF-0006, DJ 019-08-23.

The matter of *BP Niraula v. Constituent Assembly and Legislative Parliament*[49] was again a watershed moment as far as commentary by the Supreme Court of Nepal on the independence of military justice is concerned. The facts of this case were as follows: for violating military discipline, a court martial dismissed Corporal Bhakti Shah (Ms) from military service in 2008 – a decision she felt was grossly unfair. She approached the Supreme Court of Nepal with a writ petition seeking mandamus and also challenging several sections of the newly adopted Army Act of 2006. It was argued that even if courts-martial constitute a tribunal as conceptualized by Article 100 of the (then) Constitution,[50] they are not competent to conduct a fair trial as envisaged by Article 24(9) because they do not enjoy the required independence. The government however took a stand that taking out courts-martial from the regular military chain of command would affect the maintenance of military discipline.

The Apex court, in *BP Niraula*, observed that:

> ...the military justice system related provisions in the Army Act create a solo mechanism within the military that exercises powers of investigation, prosecution and also adjudication of a case. Similarly, there are provisions that make it mandatory for decisions of courts-martial to be approved at administrative level; that do not provide the accused with the right to be defended by legal counsel of his/her own choice during trial, except for cases at the Special Court Martial; that mandate disputes to be settled in Courts that are constituted on a temporary or ad hoc basis; that do not make available experts in the area of law & justice in the absence of a standing tribunal; and that mandate that persons constituting courts-martial would be drawn purely from the active military chain of command and who cannot liberate themselves from hierarchical military discipline even when administering justice.

Chief Justice Khilraj Regmi and Justice Kalyan Shrestha also did not agree with the argument that a military tribunal's independence would undermine discipline and readiness, and further observed:

> ...In order to uphold dignity and maintain discipline within military service, it is not necessary to compromise the aspects of military justice...maintaining chain of command of the military organization and

---

[49] *Supra*, note 29.

[50] The 2007 Constitution, available at https://constitutionnet.org/sites/default/files/interim_constitution_of_nepal_2007_as_amended_by_first_second_and_third_amendments.pdf

> ensuring discipline & honour of the armed forces is not the only subject matter that should be focused upon by the military justice system, but also providing military personnel with the opportunity to express their grievances in an appropriate manner and obtaining judicial remedy...

Finally, the court arrived at the conclusion that various provisions of the Army Act required immediate reform in line with the principles of human rights, justice and the rule of law. Accordingly, the court ordered the creation of a taskforce comprising representatives from the fields of law, justice and security sectors to conduct a thorough review of the existing provisions concerning military justice in the Army Act and take other necessary actions to facilitate the necessary reform after consulting experts in the fields of law & justice, military personnel of all ranks, civil society including human rights activists.

Regrettably the government failed to take steps towards the desired direction and such reluctance once again compelled the Supreme Court, after seven years, to touch the topic of independence and competence of court martial in yet another case, *Krishna Bahadur Magar v. Patan High Court*[51] wherein it observed:

> ...in order to ensure fair trial, there must be a judicial entity which is independent, impartial and competent, and these are the regular courts established under Article 127 of the Constitution...though the Constitution does not repudiate military tribunals, they only remain a special category of courts which also have to comply with instructions from the Supreme Court. The Constitutional provisions we have been adhering to, does not allow us to surrender judicial authority to a body which is unable to work as an independent, impartial and competent court.

This direction, respecting military imperatives but guiding the system towards independent, impartial and competent tribunals, further aids Nepal in moving towards a judicial system that inspires the confidence of its population and acceptance by the international community.

---

[51] *Krishna Bahadur Magar v. Patan High Court* NKP2075 [2018], V10, DN 10115.

Prem Chandra Rai has been teaching law at the Kathmandu School of Law (KSL) as an associate professor. He is also a practising lawyer in Nepal. After attaining a master's degree in International Human Rights Law from the University of Hong Kong, Mr Rai has served as the national legal advisor for the International Commission of Jurists (ICJ) in Nepal. While in the ICJ, Mr Rai edited several books relating to law and justice, including *Supreme Court Case Digest on Women's Rights (ICJ, 2013)*; *Witness Protection in Nepal: Recommendations From International Best Practices* (ICJ, 2011); *Transitional Justice and Right to a Remedy: Supreme Court Jurisprudence in Nepal* (ICJ, 2012); and was also a co-editor in the report, *Completing the Peace Process in Nepal: Implementing the Supreme Court Order to Reform Military Justice* (ICJ, 2013). As a human rights advocate, he has been involved in several related litigations, including the famous *BP Niraula* case, which resulted in the landmark judgment on military justice reform in Nepal.

The Colombian Constitutional Court's Role in Upholding Peace, Reconciliation, Justice and Differential Treatment to the State Forces Members

Marialejandra Moreno Mantilla

Constitutional Court Decision C-674 et al., Colombia

Introduction

In November 2016, after lengthy negotiations and a failed referendum, the Colombian Government and the *Fuerzas Armadas Revolucionarias de Colombia – Ejército del Pueblo* ('FARC-EP') signed the peace agreement that aimed to terminate more than 60 years of armed conflict in the country.[1] The 2016 Peace Agreement led to the establishment of the Special Jurisdiction for Peace (SJP),[2] tasked with the massive mission of adjudicating conflict-related crimes committed by both parties to the conflict. The 2016 Peace Agreement, which was given constitutional footing as a constitutional amendment, and the SJP's legal framework was reviewed by the Constitutional Court as per the Colombian Constitution. Due to these procedural and constitutional safeguards, other pieces of legislation setting up the SJP and its functioning have been constitutionally reviewed

[1] *Acuerdo Final para la Terminación del Conflicto y la Construcción de una Paz Establey Duradera,* 24 November 2016 [2016 Peace Agreement].

[2] *Jurisdicción Especial para la Paz.*

on several occasions, leading to a constellation of Constitutional Court's decisions. This constellation of decisions has scrutinized, assessed, tweaked and adjusted the new special jurisdiction and the implementation of military jurisdiction in the Colombian post-conflict scenario, providing for an accountability mechanism for those conflict-related crimes committed by State Forces members.

As enablers of the SJP's jurisdiction over State Forces members, these Constitutional Court decisions can be analyzed collectively around their impact on the prosecution of crimes such as 'false positives' cases. While, ultimately, these Constitutional Court's decisions will have facilitated the prosecution of these atrocious crimes, seeking to guarantee justice, truth, reparation and non-repetition for victims of crimes committed by the State Forces, their pronouncements also imply difficulties and challenges in its unfolding.

These challenges are crystallized in the differential treatment to be given to the States Forces members and the understanding of the notion of 'command responsibility' to be applied by the SJP. Despite these, the Constitutional Court has been essential in the establishment of the SJP and guaranteeing its jurisdiction over conflict-related crimes committed by the State Forces, such as 'false positives', towards the achievement of truth, justice, reparation and non-repetition in Colombia.

The Colombian Armed Conflict and the 2016 Peace Agreement

The Colombian armed conflict has spanned over more than 60 years, characterized by the confrontations between the State Forces and organized armed groups such as FARC-EP, *Ejército de Liberación Nacional* (ELN), *Ejército Popular de Liberación* (EPL), *las Autodefensas Gaitanistas de Colombia* (AGC) and other paramilitary groups [for example, the *Autodefensas Unidas de Colombia* (AUC), which demobilized in 2005], criminal bands (or BACRIM), among others.

The violence has taken its biggest toll on the civilian population, which has been a victim of grave human rights violations and crimes committed by all parties to the conflict, as well as other civilians (such as businessmen and politicians), and that includes murder, kidnappings, violations to personal freedom, enforced disappearance, forced displacement and sexual and gender-based crimes.[3] Against this backdrop, impunity in the country remains rampant, fueled by unjustifiable delays and lack of justice, truth and reparation for at least more than nine million victims.[4]

The 2016 Peace Agreement was not the first attempt to reach a peace accord after peace negotiations. In fact, Colombia has experienced multifarious (and, mostly, failed) peace negotiations and processes, which have included those with the ELN, AUC, and FARC.[5] However, the 2016 Peace Agreement marked a milestone in the history of peace negotiations in the country, as it sought to terminate hostilities and ensure guarantees for the demobilization of FARC-EP, the largest rebel group in Colombia, while providing for a transitional justice mechanism to address crimes committed both by rebels and military members. Concerning the crimes committed by the latter group, of particular relevance is the phenomenon of 'false positive' cases, whereby State actors – in some cases, along with paramilitaries and civilians – have purportedly murdered thousands of civilians to boost their rates of enemy killings. This boosting was allegedly encouraged by the military command, fostering the obtainment of monetary awards from State funds and other incentives for so doing.[6]

---

[3] According to different international institutions, including non-governmental organizations, international jurisdictional bodies such as those of the Inter-American System of Human Rights (the Court and the Commission) and the International Criminal Court. See, e.g.: International Criminal Court, Office of the Prosecutor, *Situation in Colombia - Interim Report*, November 2012 [www.icc-cpi.int/NR/rdonlyres/3D3055BD-16E2-4C83-BA85-35BCFD2A7922/285102/OTPCOLOMBIAPublicInterimReportNovember2012.pdf]. Inter-American Commission on Human Rights, Country Report, Colombia. Truth, Justice and Reparation' (31 December 2013) [www.oas.org/en/iachr/reports/pdfs/Colombia-Truth-Justice-Reparation.pdf].

[4] As of October 2021, with a population of approximately 54 million, the Colombian Victims' Registry records 9,189,839 victims. See: *Registro Único de Víctimas*: https://www.unidadvictimas.gov.co/es/registro-unico-de-victimas-ruv/37394

[5] See further: Woodrow Wilson International Center for Scholars, Latin American Program, *Los procesos de paz en Colombia: Múltiples negociaciones, múltiples actores*, January 2007, https://www.wilsoncenter.org/sites/default/files/media/documents/publication/LAP_PDF.indd.pdf

[6] Human Rights Watch, *On Their Watch: Evidence of Senior Army Officers' Responsibility for False Positive Killings in Colombia, Report*, 23 June 2015 [www.hrw.org/report/2015/06/24/their-watch/evidence-senior-army-officers-responsibility-false-positive-killings]. Fédération Internationale pour les Droits Humains, 'Colombia. The war is measured in litres of blood. False positives, crimes against humanity: those most responsible enjoy impunity' (June 2012) [www.fidh.org/IMG/pdf/rapp_colombie__juin_2012_anglais_def.pdf]. United Nations, *Informe anual de la Alta Comisionada de las Naciones Unidas para los Derechos* Humanos, UN Doc. A/HRC/19/21/Add.3., 31 January 2012.

Comprised of six main pillars, the 2016 Peace Agreement provides for comprehensive rural reform, political participation for former guerrilla members, termination of the conflict, solutions for the issue of illegal drugs and implementation and verification.

The fifth point revolves around the creation of an integral system aiming to provide truth, justice, reparation and non-repetition to the millions of victims of the conflict. In turn, this integral system is comprised of three main institutions: the Commission for the Clarification of Truth, Coexistence and Non-Repetition,[7] the Unit for the Search of Missing Persons in relation to the Armed Conflict,[8] and the Special Jurisdiction for Peace.

The Special Jurisdiction for Peace: Its Legal Framework and the Constitutional Court's Decisions Enabling its Functioning

As the judicial arm of the integral system aiming to provide truth, justice, reparation and non-repetition, the SJP is envisaged as the forum where those alleged perpetrators will be tried for conflict-related crimes committed until 1 December 2016. The SJP comprises a series of justice chambers, including one on amnesties, and a peace tribunal, to investigate and prosecute grave human rights violations and infractions to international humanitarian law. As a special jurisdiction, the SJP has personal jurisdiction over crimes committed by FARC-EP and State Forces members. However, it is intended to substitute neither the ordinary nor the military jurisdiction due to its temporary mandate.[9]

In line with Colombian law as a civil law system, the SJP is regulated by a legal framework developed to facilitate its establishment and operationalization, enshrined in constitutional amendments, statutory laws[10] and ordinary laws.[11] Among the most important pieces of legislation, the following are of particular relevance for the establishment and enabling

---

[7] *Comisión para el Esclarecimiento de la Verdad, la Convivencia y la No Repetición.*

[8] *Unidad para la Búsqueda de Personas Desaparecidas en el Marco del Conflicto Armado.*

[9] The SJP is vested with an initial mandate of 15 years, which may be extended.

[10] Statutory laws or *leyes estatutarias* are regulated in Article 152 of the Colombian Constitution and are those addressing fundamental rights and duties, the administration of justice, political participation, among other matters. Statutory laws enjoy a higher rank over ordinary laws.

[11] Colombian Constitution, Article 150.

of the SJP: Legislative Act 01/2017 (Legislative Act), Law 1820/2016 on amnesties and special treatments (Amnesties Law), Law 1957/2019 on the SJP's Statutory Law (SJP's Statutory Law), and Law 1922/2018 on its rules of evidence and procedure (SJP's RPE).

While the Legislative Act 01/2017 incorporates the 2016 Peace Agreement into the Colombian constitutional order,[12] Law 1820/2016 regulates the amnesties to be granted to those who submitted themselves to the transitional justice process, including the principles to be applied as well as the procedure before different SJP chambers. As the SJP's Statutory Law, Law 1957/2019 provides for its structure, mandate, guiding principles, the amnesty and sanctions regime, among others. Law 1922/2018 contains the procedural normative applicable to SJP proceedings, including the parties, evidentiary regimes, and precautionary measures.

The Constitutional Court, as the highest court with constitutional jurisdiction and ultimate guardian of the constitutional text, is tasked with guaranteeing the supremacy of the Constitution and the review of constitutional amendments and other pieces of legislation to ensure their compliance.[13] The constitutional review takes form in different procedures according to the nature of the legislation under examination. Either due to the automatic constitutional review or prompted by public action, namely, an unconstitutionality claim, the Constitutional Court has reviewed both the procedure and content of the Legislative Act in Decision C-674 of 14 November 2017, of the Amnesties Law in Decision C-007 of 1 March 2018, of the SJP's Statutory Law in Decision C-080 of 15 August 2018, and of the SJP's RPE in Decision C-112/2019 of 13 March 2019. Consequently, the Constitutional Court's decisions have provided both a procedural and substantial review of the SJP's legal framework, having an impact on its structure, jurisdiction and applicable law.

---

[12] Legislative acts are laws that may amend the Constitution. Colombian Constitution, Title 13.

[13] The Constitutional Court has the mandate to procedurally review constitutional amendments under Articles 241 and 379 of the Constitution. The Constitutional Court has developed the 'constitutional replacement doctrine' to justify its substantial review of constitutional amendments. See: Bernal-Pulido C, *Transitional Justice within the Framework of a Permanent Constitution: The Case Study of the Legal Framework for Peace in Colombia*, Cambridge Journal of International and Comparative Law, 2014, p. 1147.

The SJP, the Constitutional Court's Decisions and Military Jurisdiction: Two Steps Forward, One Step Back

The Constitutional Court's decisions positively impacted the jurisdictional scenario in Colombia, enabling the establishment and functioning of the transitional justice system in the country. As a step forward towards the materialization of the victims' rights to truth, justice, reparation and the guarantees of non-repetition, these pronouncements were generally positively acknowledged by the international community and civil society stakeholders at the national, regional and international level.[14] Special attention was given to the Court's recognition and upholding of the SJP's jurisdiction over crimes committed by the State Forces, such as 'false positive' cases. However, its pronouncements concerning the implementation of command responsibility and the sources to be applied were considered controversial as they seemed to neglect standards of international humanitarian and international criminal law.

On the SJP's Jurisdiction Over Conflict-related Crimes

Concerning the SJP's jurisdiction, the 2016 Peace Agreement referred to 'grave infractions to international humanitarian law and grave human rights violations, as well as those conflict-related crimes'.[15] The SJP's particular jurisdictional scope applicable to State Forces members was thus further developed by the Legislative Act, and the SJP's Statutory Law and RPE, which highlight the requirement of the nexus between the crime base and the armed conflict.[16] In analyzing this framework, the Constitutional Court took a broad approach to the concept of nexus of State Forces' crimes and the conflict, assessing whether such an approach would facilitate the fulfillment of the 2016 Peace Agreement's objective and implementation.[17] Consequently, it upheld the elements for this analysis, namely: a) that the armed conflict was the direct or indirect

---

[14] Several stakeholders supported the establishment and functioning of the SJP, including Colombian civil society and victims' organizations, international NGOs such as Human Rights Watch, and regional and international justice tribunals such as the Inter-American System of Human Rights and the International Criminal Court.

[15] 2016 Peace Agreement.

[16] SJP Statutory Law, Article 62.

[17] Constitutional Court, Decision C-674/17.

cause of the commission of the crime or, b) that it influenced the perpetrator, participant or accessory to the crime in terms of their capacity to commit the crime, resolve or willingness to commit it, the manner in which it was committed, and the objective which was intended with the commission of the crime.[18] Furthermore, the Court assessed the qualification of 'war crimes' under the SJP's jurisdiction, under which the waiver of prosecution excluded those 'grave war crimes', defined in the Amnesties Law as those grave infractions to International Humanitarian Law (IHL) committed in a systematic manner.[19] The Court declared the provision as unconstitutional, as it created an additional requirement – inexistent in IHL or International Criminal Law (ICL) – and potentially hampered the State obligation to investigate and prosecute all IHL infractions.[20]

Although the Colombian ordinary jurisdiction has competence over such grave human rights violations and infractions to IHL committed by State Forces, several of these cases have been traditionally examined by the military jurisdiction, casting doubt over the independence and impartiality of these judicial proceedings.[21] The Constitutional Court's broad understanding of the element of nexus between the crime and the armed conflict allowed for the SJP's jurisdiction to cover crimes that usually would not be assessed as conflict-related by either the ordinary or the military jurisdiction, while leaving it to the judges to implement a case-by-case analysis of these requirements.

Nonetheless, concepts such as the 'differential treatment' to be granted to State Forces members, as well as its impact on the implementation of command responsibility and international criminal law, raised concerns among international judicial institutions and civil society, and warnings that such a treatment would lead to State Forces receiving disproportionate legal benefits.[22]

---

[18] Legislative Act, Transitional Article 23.

[19] Law 1820/2016, Articles 46, 47, 52 and 57.

[20] Constitutional Court, Decision C-007/2018.

[21] See: Camila Andrea Santamaría Chavarro, Diana Isabel Güiza Gómez and Rodrigo Uprimny Yepes, *Colombia's Fuerza Pública (Security Forces) in the Special Jurisdiction for Peace: Special Treatment or Preferential Treatment?* in Patrick Mileham (ed.), *Jus Post Bellum*, Brill Nijhoff, 2020.

[22] *Ibid.*

On the Differential Treatment

The differential treatment is recognized in the 2016 Peace Agreement, which states that State agents who have committed conflict-related crimes will be subjected to differential treatment, meaning 'an equal, balanced, simultaneous and symmetrical treatment', considering 'the State's role as guarantor of rights'.[23] However, such treatment was reflected in the bills of the SJP's Statutory Law and RPE as a flexible understanding of command responsibility for State Forces' members, the proposal on the establishment of a special chamber for their prosecution, and the incorporation of 'operational law' as a source to be applied by the SJP.

The SJP's RPE provided for a 'special and differential procedure' for the prosecution of State Forces.[24] Seeking to uphold the appropriate fulfillment of the right to truth, justice and reparation, the Constitutional Court deemed the provision unconstitutional while arguing on the principles of judicial autonomy and independence.[25] Consequently, to ensure that the objectives of the transitional justice mechanism were achieved, it upheld the SJP's structure without such a special chamber and as provided for in the 2016 Peace Agreement and the Statutory Law.

On the Applicable Law

The Constitutional Court also assessed the tension between the differential treatment, the applicable sources and the notion of command responsibility since the Legislative Act bill included potentially conflicting provisions concerning these notions. On the one hand, it envisaged the Colombian Criminal Code, International Human Rights Law (IHRL), IHL and ICL as SJP's sources.[26] On the other hand, as part of the implementation of this differential treatment to State Forces' members, it stated that the SJP was to consider the Colombian Criminal Code at the time of the commission of the crime, IHRL and IHL, as well as the State Forces' 'operational law'.[27] Despite stakeholders' interventions in the constitutional proceedings highlighting the preferential treatment

[23] 2016 Peace Agreement.
[24] Law 1922/2018.
[25] Constitutional Court, Decision C-112/2019.
[26] Legislative Act 02/2017, Transitional Article 5.
[27] *Ibid*, Transitional Article 22.

that such a regime of applicable law could imply, for instance, notions on collateral damage or the understanding of legitimate targets, the Constitutional Court declared the provisions constitutional.[28]

Luckily, the scope of 'operational law' was further clarified by the Court, determining that it referred to State Forces' administrative rules 'intended to regulate the conduct of military operations in accordance with human rights and international humanitarian law'.[29] Thus, their evidentiary value to the SJP to qualify the responsibility of the State Forces members is subject to their congruence with 'international human rights treaties ratified by Colombia, national legislation and jurisprudence on human rights and IHL'.[30] Nonetheless, such a differential treatment and applicable law had an impact on the way the SJP was to interpret the command responsibility of State Forces members.

On Command Responsibility

Command responsibility is a mode of liability that allows for the recognition and prosecution of military commanders for the acts of their subordinates. Recognized by IHL and ICL, command responsibility is reflected in the Geneva Conventions of 1949 and Additional Protocols of 1977. It has been applied by the International Criminal Tribunals for the Former Yugoslavia (ICTY) and Rwanda, the Special Tribunal for Sierra Leone and by the International Criminal Court (ICC). Generally, the Rome Statute of the ICC incorporates the customary international standard for command responsibility, consisting mostly of:

(i) A superior-subordinate status,

(ii) The superior's effective command and control over the forces that committed the crime,

(iii) The crime was committed due to the superior's failure to exercise control properly over the forces,

(iv) The superior's failure to take necessary and reasonable measures to prevent or repress the crime, or to submit the matter to competent

[28] Constitutional Court, Decision C-674/2017.

[29] Constitutional Court, Decision C-080/2018.

[30] *Ibid.*

authorities for investigation and prosecution, and

(v) The superior knew or should have known that the forces were committing or about to commit the crime(s).[31]

Although the SJP's legal framework on command responsibility recognizes that it is not an objective responsibility solely based on authority,[32] it is contrary to the international standard, as it was highlighted by civil society organizations such as Human Rights Watch[33] and by the Office of the Prosecutor of the ICC[34] in their amicus curiae interventions in the relevant Constitutional Court proceedings.[35] The incongruence lies on the standard concerning the required superior's knowledge and *de jure* authority, and the effective control exercised.

First, concerning the superior's knowledge, the SJP legal framework conditions it to the 'information available to them before, during and after the commission of the respective conduct'.[36] Moreover, it relativizes the 'adequate measures to prevent or repress the crimes, as long as there is updated or easily updated knowledge' from the superior.[37] This assertion neglects the international standard on knowledge, namely that 'the superior knew or should have known', imposing a higher burden on the prosecution and the victims regarding the superior's knowledge.

Second, the SJP's framework adds as a requirement of command responsibility the *de jure* authority that the superior must have to limit their responsibility to those crimes committed 'in the superior's responsibility area and in relation to the activities under their responsibility' as well as to 'their legal and material capacity to issue, modify and enforce orders; their legal capacity to carry out operations in the area; and their material and direct capacity to take adequate measures to prevent or repress the

---

[31] Rome Statute of the ICC, Article 28.

[32] In line with international jurisprudence such as that of the ICTY in the *Kordić and Čerkez* case.

[33] Human Rights Watch, *Colombia: Amicus Curiae sobre la Jurisdicción Especial para la Paz*, 17 July 2017. [https://www.hrw.org/es/news/2017/07/17/colombia-amicus-curiae-sobre-la-juris diccion-especial-para-la-paz].

[34] International Criminal Court, Mr. James Stewart, Deputy Prosecutor of the ICC, *The Role of the ICC in the Transitional Justice Process in Colombia*, 30-31 May 2018, [https://www.icc-cpi.int/iccdocs/otp/201805 SpeechDP.pdf].

[35] Constitutional Court, Decision C-674/2017 and Decision C-080/2018.

[36] Legislative Act, Transitional Article 24; SJP's Statutory Law, Article 68.

[37] *Ibid.*

crimes'.[38] These *de jure* authority conditions to the superior's responsibility are not included in the international standard, which only requires the existence of 'effective command and control over the forces'.

Third, regarding the 'effective control', the SJP's normative misapplies the element and requires the superior to have effective control over the crime,[39] and not simply over the subordinates as required in ICL and IHL. Thus, it mixes this notion up with another mode of liability: 'perpetration-by-means'.

Despite these concerns and incongruences between the transitional justice framework and the internationally recognized standards, the Constitutional Court decided in favor of the provisions' constitutionality, stating that such understanding of command responsibility did not hamper the State's obligation to investigate and prosecute grave human rights violations and infractions to IHL. Taking a broad understanding of the 'general prohibition on impunity', the Court analyzed the other applicable law and determined that, since the Colombian Criminal Code included a compendium of different modes of liability which could assist the SJP in its proceedings, the notion of command responsibility as included in its framework did not hamper the investigation and prosecution of crimes.[40]

Looking Forward: Prospects of Justice, Truth, Reconciliation and Guarantees of Non-repetition for Conflict-related Crimes Committed by State Forces

The 2016 Peace Agreement constituted a milestone in transitional justice in Colombia, as well as the materialization of the rights to truth, justice, reconciliation and guarantees of non-repetition of the victims of crimes committed both by FARC-EP and the State Forces. While the 2016 Peace Agreement provided for the transitional justice mechanisms, these required a normative framework to regulate their structure, jurisdiction, and applicable law. Amidst this process, the Constitutional Court had a

---

[38] *Ibid.*

[39] *Ibid.*

[40] Constitutional Court, Decision C-674/2017 and Decision C-080/2018.

crucial and often controversial role in enabling the unfolding of the transitional justice mechanisms in the country.

The Constitutional Court delineated the material jurisdiction of the SJP, clearly elaborating on the required nexus between the crime and the armed conflict. It was essential in outlining the definition of IHL infractions under the SJP's jurisdiction and amnesties regime, removing the requirement of systematicity of war crimes in line with international law. Additionally, while upholding the differential treatment to State Forces' members granted under the 2016 Peace Agreement, it repealed the establishment of a special procedure and chamber within the tribunal and clarified the content of the applicable law, seeking to sustain independence or impartiality within the transitional justice process.

However, in implementing such differential treatment, the Constitutional Court misapplied internationally recognized notions and concepts, such as command responsibility, confirming a strict standard that might imply an additional burden for the prosecution of State Forces' crimes. Although the Court highlighted other legal regimes that might assist the SJP, these regimes often focus on the direct or material perpetrators, providing little room for the required linkage analysis to connect the crime base to criminal organizational structures and those 'most responsible'. Considering that State Forces' crimes in Colombia, such as those of 'false positives' have been allegedly committed under State policy, a restrictive interpretation of command responsibility might hamper the disclosure of the military and political structures involved, those most responsible, and the scope of this criminal phenomenon.

Nonetheless, despite what can be considered missteps from the Constitutional Court in assessing the constitutionality of the SJP's legal and normative framework, its judgments were essential in pondering the tension between peace and justice and providing a space for Colombian society to move forward towards reconciliation. As the SJP continues to disclose the magnitude of the crimes committed by the State Forces, particularly the 'false positives' phenomenon,[41] the Constitutional Court's

[41] As of February 2021, the SJP established that at least 6.402 persons were illegally murdered as part of the 'false positive' cases between 2002 and 2008. See: SJP, Chamber on the Recognition of truth and Responsibility, Case 003, *Order 033 of 2021* [https://www.jep.gov.co/Sala-de-Prensa/Paginas/La-JEP-hace-p%C3%BAblica-la-estrategia-de-priorizaci%C3%B3n-dentro-del-Caso-03,-conocido-como-el-de-falsos-positivos.aspx].

constellation of decisions must be highlighted as an enabler of the transitional justice process in Colombia.

Marialejandra Moreno Mantilla is a qualified Colombian lawyer currently working as a Project Officer at the International Nuremberg Principles Academy. Marialejandra has previously assisted the Defence at the International Criminal Tribunal for the Former Yugoslavia and the Chambers of the International Criminal Court. She has extensive experience working for civil society organizations, such as the *Comisión Colombiana de Juristas* and Human Rights in Practice. More recently, she has worked for Case Matrix Network, Centre for International Law Research and Policy (CILRAP-CMN), where she was responsible for the development and implementation of capacity-building programs in Colombia and the monitoring of other project activities in Latin America, seeking to strengthen the application of international criminal and human rights law in the region.

Marialejandra studied Law and International Relations at Universidad del Rosario (Colombia) and holds an advanced master's degree in Public International Law, specializing in International Criminal Law from Leiden University (The Netherlands).

The Thunder Road to Justice: Ukraine's 2001 Constitutional Court Opinion on the Rome Statute

Kateryna Busol

Case No 1-35/2001, Ukraine

'What's past is prologue'[1]

The International Criminal Court (ICC), founded by the Rome Statute, may consider the gravest crimes under international law, namely war crimes, crimes against humanity, genocide and, potentially, the crime of aggression. Having signed the ICC's Rome Statute in 2000, as of June 2021, Ukraine has still not ratified it. In 2001, Ukraine's Constitutional Court released a controversial opinion in a case concerning the constitutional request of the President of Ukraine to provide a conclusion on the correspondence of the Constitution of Ukraine to the ICC's Rome Statute (Opinion),[2] which trumped the ratification. Based on its misunderstanding of the ICC's complementarity to national criminal jurisdictions, the Constitutional Court found that the Rome Statute contravened

---

[1] William Shakespeare. *The Tempest,* Act 2, Scene I http://www.online-literature.com/shakespeare/tempest/3/

[2] Opinion of the Constitutional Court of Ukraine in a case concerning the constitutional request of the President of Ukraine to provide a conclusion on the correspondence of the Constitution of Ukraine to the Rome Statute of the International Criminal Court (the Rome Statute case) №3-v/2001 of 11 July 2001, para 1 of the conclusion https://zakon.rada.gov.ua/laws/show/v003v710-01#Text

Ukraine's Constitution, which did not envisage any additional components to its domestic judiciary. At the time, only a handful of Ukraine's international lawyers were dismayed at such misreading of the ICC's founding treaty and Ukraine's drop-out from the important international movement to narrow the atrocities impunity gap. However, Ukraine's stance on the Court has acquired new and far wider connotations when Russia occupied parts of the country in 2014. Since then, the ICC's possible intervention into Ukraine's situation became a sought-after and often over-idealised justice option for some and a hybrid threat for others. In some important aspects, the modalities of Ukraine's engagement with the Court now are still shaped by the Constitutional Court's 2001 Opinion and the lingering misunderstandings it generated.

The Constitutional Court's 2001 Opinion

Beams of Reason and Reasoning

Ukraine signed the Rome Statute on 20 January 2000. Ukraine may not become a party to an international treaty that contravenes the Constitution unless the necessary amendments to the Constitution have been introduced and the contravention is no longer in place.[3] Given the ICC's novel nature, before the ratification, the President of the country requested the Constitutional Court of Ukraine to assess the Statute's compatibility with the Constitution. The President was concerned with a number of the treaty's provisions; among them was the ICC's complementarity to domestic courts, the removal of immunities of state officials, the surrender of persons to the Court, the functions of the ICC's Prosecutor and their compatibility with the rules of public prosecutions in Ukraine and the possible serving of the punishment by those convicted by the Court in other states party to the Rome Statute.

The Constitutional Court of Ukraine issued its Opinion on 11 July 2001. The Court found the majority of the Rome Statute's provisions raised in the President's request compatible with the Constitution. It ruled that although Ukraine's legislation did not allow the extradition of

[3] Constitution of Ukraine of 28 June 1996 No 254k/96-VR, art. 9 part 2 https://zakon.rada.gov.ua/laws/show/254%D0%BA/96-%D0%B2%D1%80#Text (Constitution of Ukraine)

its nationals for criminal proceedings in other states, that did not necessarily apply to surrender to international courts.[4] Concerning the terms of punishment, the Constitutional Court saw an option for Ukraine to declare its readiness to accept its own convicted citizens.[5] And as regards the ICC's Prosecutor, the judges pointed it out to the President that, first, this position was part of the international and not Ukraine's domestic legal and institutional framework, therefore, the expectations of the post's full compatibility with the rules of Ukraine's public prosecution were unjustified. Second, should Ukraine become a party to the Rome Statute, it will be able to participate in the election of the Prosecutor and, thus, have a say on the qualifications and stature of the persons it deems most appropriate for the job.[6]

The Constitutional Court's pronouncement on immunities was particularly important. The judges concluded that the Statute's non-recognition of immunities of state officials did not affect the regulation of the issue under Ukraine's domestic law[7] and, thus, did not prevent the ratification. However, the relevance of the argumentation on this point transcended the issue of the Rome Statute. The Court stressed that responsibility for a considerable spectrum of conduct regulated by the Statute was already envisaged by numerous international treaties, including those binding upon Ukraine. In particular, the Court listed the 1948 Genocide Convention, the 1949 Geneva Conventions, the 1954 Hague Convention on the protection of cultural property in armed conflict, the 1973 Apartheid Convention, and the 1984 UN Torture Convention. The Constitutional Court recalled the customary and treaty rule *pacta sunt servanda*[8] – treaties must be performed in good faith.[9]

Under Ukraine's domestic law, the rules of Ukraine's international treaties prevail over those of domestic legislation regulating the same issue.[10] The non-applicability of immunities under some such treaties ratified by Ukraine indicated its obligation to apply its domestic rules on

---

[4] Opinion, paras 2.3.2–2.3.3.

[5] Opinion, para 2.7.1.

[6] Opinion, para 2.8.

[7] Opinion, para 2.2.1.

[8] Vienna Convention on the Law of Treaties (1949) UNTS, vol. 1155, p. 331, art. 26 https://legal.un.org/ilc/texts/instruments/english/conventions/1_1_1969.pdf

[9] Opinion, para 2.2.

[10] Law of Ukraine on the International Treaties of Ukraine No 1906-IV of 29 June 2004, art. 19.2 https://zakon.rada.gov.ua/laws/show/1906-15#Text

immunities pursuant to these instruments.[11] The judges went even further and reminded in the Opinion that both the prohibition of and the responsibility for the crimes of genocide, aggression, crimes against humanity and war crimes had acquired customary nature. Therefore, their criminality had already been established for Ukraine pursuant to existing customary rules and treaty obligations and irrespective of the (non-)ratification of the Rome Statute.

However flawed and stumbling the 2001 Opinion turned out to be for the relationship with the ICC, paradoxically, it still contained the sections which were relevant for addressing atrocity crimes, albeit on a domestic level. The above-mentioned discussion on immunities stressed that, by joining a range of treaties, Ukraine understood the danger that international crimes posed to the international rules-based order and recognised the need to prosecute them. The Opinion further noted the guiding relevance and obligatory nature of international customs.

The above reasoning and findings from the Constitutional Court became important 13 years later when, for the first time since World War II, Ukraine prosecuted alleged war crimes and crimes against humanity perpetrated in the context of Russia's aggression. Building such domestic proceedings was tricky, partly due to the poor domestic criminal legislation with its patchy incorporation of war crimes and the complete absence of crimes against humanity. When respective amendments to the Criminal Code were developed,[12] arguments were made that the post-factum application of such detailed provisions properly criminalising war crimes and crimes against humanity to past events breached the principles of legal clarity and legality. The drafters of the amendments refuted by referring to the 2001 Opinion and rightly pointing out Ukraine's long-existing non-recognition of atrocity crimes and obligation to prosecute them.[13] References to the customary nature of certain such obligations and custom were also crucial. Due to a very restrictive legalistic tradition of applying domestic law, references to international treaty law, let alone

---

[11] The Constitutional Court referred to the 1948 Genocide Convention prescribing that perpetrator of genocide shall be punished, whether they are constitutionally responsible rulers, public officials or private individuals, Opinion, para 2.2.1.

[12] Draft Law Amending Certain Legislative Acts of Ukraine concerning the Implementation of the Rules of International Criminal and Humanitarian Law №2689 of 27.12.2019 http://w1.c1.rada.gov.ua/pls/zweb2/webproc4_1?pf3511=67804 (IHL/ICL Draft Law).

[13] IHL/ICL Draft Law, Explanatory Note.

customs, are often met with overcautiousness, lack of insight and resistance. The gradual normalisation of such references, especially through the opinions of the Constitutional Court, is a positive transition to a more informed and holistic application of international law in Ukraine.

The Complementarity Confusion

The majority of the above-mentioned promising aspects of the 2001 Opinion have been eroded, however, by the Constitutional Court's misreading of the ICC's complementarity. Under the Rome Statute, the ICC's jurisdiction is complementary to national criminal jurisdictions, which leaves the primary right to address atrocities effectively and efficiently with the states. The Constitutional Court read this provision very literally, stating that nothing in Ukraine's legislation provided for the ICC's positioning in the fabric of the state's judiciary. The judges of the Constitutional Court were further concerned about the ICC's right to step in when national systems were unable or unwilling to prosecute and the alleged encroachment of such a right on state sovereignty.

As per the judges, the above-mentioned powers marked a difference between the ICC and, for instance, the European Court on Human Rights (ECHR). The judges described the ECHR's role in domestic systems as auxiliary, whereas the ICC's complementary positioning was more invasive. Drawing a contrasting comparison, Ukraine's judges claimed that the ECHR was the court of last resort, which accepted the claims only once all available domestic justice options had been exhausted.[14] The right to refer to such courts after trying all national mechanisms of redress is enshrined in Ukraine's Constitution,[15] whereas, as of 2001, nothing in Ukraine's principal law provided for the ICC procedures. As the Constitution did not explain the relationship of Ukraine's justice system with the ICC and its frameworks, the Constitutional Court found that the complementarity provisions of the Rome Statute contravened Ukraine's Constitution of the time and that the Statute only could be joined after the Constitution was amended to allow that.

Ukraine's Constitutional Court's reading of the complementarity

---

[14] Opinion, para 2.1.

[15] Constitution of Ukraine, art. 55.

provision as an infringement on the country's sovereignty is the opposite of how the provision has been contemplated and used.[16] The first ICC Prosecutor stressed that:

> [a]s a consequence of complementarity, the number of cases that reach the Court should not be a measure of its efficiency. On the contrary, the absence of trials before this Court, as a consequence of the regular functioning of national institutions, would be a major success.[17]

Indeed, positive complementarity aims to mobilise domestic efforts to investigate and prosecute the Rome Statute crimes that fall within the respective national jurisdiction and leave only exceptional cases that have not been addressed due to the lack of access to the territory, lack of political will or other factors indicating inability or unwillingness, to the ICC.

The application of the complementarity principle in practice and the case-selection dynamics of the ICC might eventually be more nuanced. However, the foundation of complementarity, especially at the time of the drafting of the Opinion, was to provide more options to states to diligently prosecute atrocities themselves, not deprive them of that right as the Constitutional Court of Ukraine was concerned.

However profound the Constitution Court's misreading was, its limitations on the ratification of the Rome Statute could be bypassed only by amending Ukraine's Constitution to expressly allow the country to join the ICC's founding treaty. The initiative to do that was reinvigorated more than a decade later.

Lingering Effects and New Beginnings

Since 2001, four important developments related to the 2001 Opinion, which called for the reconsideration of Ukraine's engagement with the ICC, have happened.

---

[16] Mykola Gnatovsky. Ukraine and the International Criminal Court: A Constitutional Matter (Democracy Reporting International, Briefing Paper 60, 2015), p. 3 https://democracy-reporting.org/wp-content/uploads/2016/03/briefing_paper_ukraine_and_the_international_criminal_court_a_constitutional_matter_en.pdf

[17] Statement by Mr. Luis Moreno-Ocampo, 16 June 2003 Ceremony for the Solemn Undertaking of the Chief Prosecutor in The Office of the Prosecutor, International Criminal Court, Informal expert paper, *The Principle of Complementarity in Practice* (2003), p. 3 https://www.icccpi.int/nr/rdonlyres/20bb4494-70f9-4698-8e30-907f631453ed/281984/complementarity.pdf

First, in 2014 Russia occupied Ukraine's Crimean Peninsula.[18] The mounting evidence about Russia providing military, financial and organisational support to armed separatist groups in eastern Ukraine also started to appear.[19] In both situations, alleged war crimes, crimes against humanity and grave human rights violations have been reported.[20] The demand for qualitative criminal proceedings concerning such incidents has been increasing.

Second, the Ukraine-EU Association Agreement, signed in 2014, stressed Ukraine's obligation to ratify and implement the Rome Statute.[21]

Although the two developments appeared as self-evident wake-up calls to amend the Constitution and ratify the ICC's founding instrument without delay, the actual progress has been alarmingly slow.

Instead, third, in 2014 and 2015, Ukraine recognised the jurisdiction of the Court to consider the violence perpetrated in the country, especially its temporarily occupied and non-government-controlled territories and falling under the ICC's jurisdiction. However, it was done by the adoption of the special *ad hoc* declarations and not by the ratification of the Court's founding treaty.

Finally, in 2016 Ukraine made a long-overdue step and enshrined its right to 'recognise the jurisdiction of the International Criminal Court pursuant to the conditions defined by the Rome Statute' in its Constitution.[22] However, such a right became effective only in 2019.[23] No reasonable explanation of this three-year postponement was provided. Even with such a controversial option to ratify the Statute, which came into

---

[18] UNGA Resolution 68/262 *Territorial Integrity of Ukraine*, A/RES/68/262 (2014) https://www.securitycouncilreport.org/atf/cf/%7B65BFCF9B-6D27-4E9C-8CD3-CF6E4FF96FF9%7D/a_res_68_262.pdf; UNGA Resolution 'Problem of the Militarization of the Autonomous Republic of Crimea and the City of Sevastopol, Ukraine, as well as Parts of the Black Sea and the Sea of Azov', A/RES/75/29 (2020) https://digitallibrary.un.org/record/3895282? ln=fr

[19] Parliamentary Assembly of the Council of Europe, Resolution 2198 (2018) http://assembly.coe.int/nw/xml/XRef/Xref-XML2HTML-en.asp?fileid=24432

[20] For example, see the Office of the United Nations High Commissioner for Human Rights, Report on the human rights situation in Ukraine (16 November 2016 to 15 February 2017) https://www.ohchr.org/Documents/Countries/UA/UAReport17th_EN.pdf; for more see: Ukraine – OHCHR Reports https://www.ohchr.org/EN/Countries/ENACARegion/Pages/UAReports.aspx

[21] The Association Agreement between the European Union and its Member States, of the one part, and Ukraine, of the other part, art. 8 https://trade.ec.europa.eu/doclib/docs/2016/november/tradoc_155103.pdf

[22] Constitution of Ukraine of 28 June, art. 124 part 6.

[23] Constitution of Ukraine, Note to art. 124.

force in mid-2019, Ukraine still has not proceeded with the ratification two years later, as of June 2021.

Apart from the postponement controversy, the very wording of the constitutional amendment is alarming. As it is framed around the recognition of the jurisdiction and not merely the ratification of the Rome Statute, it opens the doors to misinformed or intentional challenges to the constitutionality of the 2014 and 2015 declarations, which recognised the Court's jurisdiction allegedly before the Constitution expressly allowed it to do so. From the international law perspective, such possible arguments will not impact the ICC's power to conduct a preliminary examination and a potential investigation into the situation in Ukraine. However, they might receive a dangerous welcome domestically and, depending on the national political conjuncture, disrupt Ukraine's cooperation with the ICC and undermine the international perception of Ukraine's commitment to the rule of law.

Unlike Georgia, which has also suffered from an armed conflict with Russia and a temporary loss of control over its certain territories, Ukraine still appears to be misinformed about the ICC and, thus, reluctant to ratify its Rome Statute. Such a stance appears even more surprising given that the armed conflict with Russia is, as of June 2021, in its eighth year and still ongoing. Certain domestic experts have gone as far as to label the ICC as 'one of the threats to Ukraine in a hybrid war'.[24] One of the main concerns is that the Court might not be able to get hold of alleged Russian top perpetrators, and might thus focus exclusively on the Ukrainian side and lead to a distorted narrative about the armed conflict with little contribution to either justice or reconciliation.

Such opponents of the ICC do not realise three crucial things. First, Ukraine's declarations have already entitled the ICC to consider all those allegedly implicated and oblige Ukraine to cooperate with the Court. Second, to retain the local ownership, Ukraine can, and should, owing it to its own war-affected people, develop its own qualitative criminal proceedings concerning the perpetrators it can get hold of. If such proceedings live up to international standards, including adjudications by military tribunals, the ICC will potentially focus on other incidents, which Ukraine

[24] Ukrainian Institute for the Future, Report *International Criminal Court as One of the Threats for Ukraine in Hybrid Warfare* (2021) https://uifuture.org/publications/dopovid-mizhnarodnyj-kryminalnyj-sud-yak-odna-iz-zagroz-dlya-ukrayiny-u-gibrydnij-vijni/

is unable to investigate or prosecute due to the lack of access to the territory, Russia's non-cooperation, or other reasons. Finally, the ratification of the Rome Statute will only benefit Ukraine. It will entitle Ukraine to nominate and elect new ICC judges and the Prosecutor, as well as negotiate and vote on the amendments to the Rome Statute and, thus, contribute to eradicating impunity for the gravest crimes and comply with its international obligations, including under the Association Agreement with the EU.

Such a state of affairs proves that Ukraine crucially needs a clear strategic communication policy regarding the ICC. Such a policy should have two key aims. First, it should debunk the misinformed and intentionally constructed myths around the Court. Second, it should provide clear arguments why the ratification of the Rome Statute, finally allowed by the Constitution, will catalyse Ukraine's justice efforts for atrocities perpetrated in the Russia-Ukraine armed conflict. These two strategic communication streams should be tailor-made for the most varied audiences – state officials, military, journalists, think tanks and the general public. Most importantly, like the majority of the most meaningful and successful policy initiatives in Ukraine recently, such strategic communication should be developed jointly by the state and the civil society, whose human rights groups have been the most active-reasoned proponents of the ICC's involvement in Ukraine and advocates of justice initiatives for the war-affected country for years now.

Dr **Kateryna Busol** is a Ukrainian lawyer specialising in international human rights, humanitarian law, criminal law, transitional justice, gender and cultural heritage law. Currently, she is a UN Women National Consultant on Transitional Justice and Prevention of and Response to Conflict-related Sexual Violence. Kateryna is a consultant for Ukraine with the Global Survivors Fund, the initiative of the Nobel Peace Prize laureates Denis Mukwege and Nadia Murad, on a study on the needs and opportunities for conflict-related sexual violence survivors in Ukraine.

Previously, she was a fellow at the Royal Institute for International Affairs (Chatham House), a legal consultant with the Global Rights Compliance and a visiting professional at the Office of the Prosecutor of the International Criminal Court. She is the founder of the *#InternationalLawTalks* media rubric and a board member of the Cambridge Society of Ukraine.

Dr Busol has contributed to this publication in her private capacity.

Supreme People's Court Services and Safeguards for China's Defense and the Military

Susan Finder

Supreme People's Court Opinion on Military 2014/2017/2021, China

This brief article explains how China's political leadership uses the court system to achieve some of its national defense policy objectives. Improving China's national defense and modernizing its military is what in Chinese is called a national strategy (国家战略). China's national strategies include diplomacy, economics, science and technology, and military affairs. They are focused on the medium-term rather than on the long-term. A national strategy is embodied in the formal planning documents formulated and major official speeches articulated by the paramount leader or set of senior leaders at the apex of power.[1]

Under the leadership of the President (and the General Secretary of China's Communist Party) Xi Jinping, China is seeking to modernize and professionalize its armed forces. Among the strategic goals are to make military service an honored profession, terminate the involvement of the armed forces and armed police in civilian commercial operations, and improve the workings of China's military-industrial complex. Other policy objectives relevant to this article include improving military morale

---

[1] Andrew Scobell, Edmund J. Burke, Cortez A. Cooper III, Sale Lilly, Chad J. R. Ohlandt, Eric Warner, J.D. Williams – *China's Grand Strategy: Trends, Trajectories, and Long-Term Competition* (Rand Research Report) (2020) at ix, 10-11.

and conditions for veterans, particularly the 300,000 or so military personnel demobilized by the end of 2017. This article shows how the Supreme People's Court (SPC), China's apex court, mobilizes the court system to do its part to achieve the leadership's policy objectives concerning national defense and the military.

National defense is not the only national strategy for which the Chinese courts have provided services and safeguards. The political leadership has decided that the Chinese courts are a necessary force in accomplishing their policy goals, and for that reason, President Xi Jinping has demanded that the courts (and other legal institutions) provide services and safeguards for many Communist Party (CCP or Party) policies.[2] For those unfamiliar with the Chinese court system, China has a separate military and civilian court system. Under military reforms, the status of the military courts (and procuratorates) has been elevated.[3] The PLA Military Court has the status of a provincial higher people's court, with basic level and intermediate level courts.

An official definition of 'services' and 'safeguards' (guarantees) is lacking, but the phrase has been a critically important concept in Chinese political discourse since Xi Jinping became the General Secretary of the CCP in 2012. It is used to convey the concept that the relevant institution will fully fulfill its function (职能) in Chinese governance, implement the relevant policies or initiatives of the Party and government in its specialist area, to ensure that it advances the goals of the Party and the state's initiative or policies. The legal basis for the SPC's role is a clause in Article 2 of the Organizational Law of the People's Courts, calling on the courts to 'safeguard (guarantee) the legal uniformity, dignity, and authority of the State and guarantee the smooth progress of the building of socialism with

---

[2] Over the years, slightly different phraseology has been used: 2013: http://www.gov.cn/ldhd/2013-01/28/content_2321165.htm ; 2014: http://cpc.people.com.cn/n/2014/0109/c640942 4065903.html; 2015: 习近平：把政法工作摆到经济社会发展全局中谋划 履行好维护国家安全和社会安定重大责任 http://111.205.184.229/2015-01/20/content_11170812.htm; 2016: http://news.12371.cn/2016/01/22/ARTI1453471166051925.shtml ; 2017: http://politics.people.com.cn/n1/2017/0113/c1024-29019620.html ; 2018: this uses services and guarantees http://www.xinhuanet.com/legal/2018-01/22/c_1122296147.htm; 2019: http://www.xinhuanet.com/politics/leaders/2019-01/16/c_1123999899.htm； 2020: https://www.chinacourt.org/article/subjectdetail/id/MzAwNMhJM4ABAA.shtml

[3] China's National Defense in the New Era, 25 July 2019, https://www.chinadaily.com.cn/a/201907/25/WS5d38f349a310d83056400dc1_5.html

Chinese characteristics'.[4]

The policies described in this article have been recently codified in military-related legislation promulgated in June 2021. The first is the Law of the People's Republic of China on the Protection of the Status, Rights and Interests of Military Personnel (Law on Protecting the Military and its Personnel).[5] At the same time, the national legislature, the National People's Congress (NPC) Standing Committee amended the counterpart law directed towards providing legal protection for military facilities, the 1990 Military Facilities Protection Law of the People's Republic of China, previously amended in 2014.[6] These laws together act as a skeletal legal framework for institutions of the Party and government to provide special protections and preferential treatment to the military and its personnel, including veterans. In relation to the Chinese courts, these two laws do not 'make new laws' but instead place in legal form Party policy that has long existed but is made more workable through codification.

To illustrate the accomplishments of the court system in achieving its goals of providing 'services and guarantees to national defense and the military', Zhou Qiang, SPC President, stated in his March 2021 report to the National People's Congress:

> [The courts] strengthened military rights protection work...served the building of national defense and military reform and promoted the unity of the military and government and the military and civilians...10,418 military-civilian-commercial cases were concluded, resolutely defending the dignity and honor of military personnel, and safeguarding the legitimate rights and interests of military personnel. Continued to do a good job in providing judicial services for the next phase of the cessation of military business operations and safeguarded the legitimate rights and interests of the military and the legitimate interests of the masses [ordinary people] in accordance with the law. In conjunction with the Ministry of Veterans Affairs, etc., issued an opinion to increase the degree of assistance in judicial relief for retired soldiers... Other courts took the initiative to send law into the military camps,

---

[4] Article 2, Organic Law of the People's Courts, last amended in 2018, bilingual version available at: https://npcobserver.com/legislation/peoples-courts-organic-law/

[5] See https://npcobserver.com/legislation/law-on-the-protection-of-the-status-rights-and-inter ests -of-military-personnel/

[6] See https://npcobserver.com/legislation/military-facilities-protection-law/

opening up green channels for military rights protection....[7]

The SPC has issued several policy documents, not linked to any dispute, to implement leadership policy as expressed in Party and government documents that relate to national defense and the military. This type of SPC policy document is not unique to the area of national defense and the Chinese military but is a type of soft law document issued by the SPC. Under the leadership of Xi Jinping, the SPC has issued many more of these documents that provide 'judicial services and safeguards' of the type that SPC President Zhou Qiang mentioned in his speech. As this author has written elsewhere, these documents create and transmit to the lower courts new judicial policy, update previous judicial policy, establish new legal guidelines that may be eventually crystallized in judicial interpretations and direct the lower courts, but cannot be cited in judicial judgments or rulings.[8] They are generally linked to an important Party or state strategy or initiative, in this case, national defense.[9]

It is generally recognized, particularly within China, that its political leadership uses documents as an expeditious way of governance. As a professor of politics and law in the Party's Central Party School wrote:

> By comparison [with law], with documents, matters are handled economically...In general, however, while there are corresponding procedures for documents, these are not hard and fast procedural requirements, so adjustments can easily be made in them as the situation requires. For China, which is ruled by an exemplary advanced political party, this means that this is still essentially rule by the elite. China's primary goal remains becoming a rich country with a strong military (富国强兵) All other values must be subordinated to this goal.[10]

As shown in this article, the Party leadership rarely communicates

---

[7] See http://www.gov.cn/xinwen/2021-03/15/content_5593012.htm

[8] Judicial interpretations are issued by the SPC and sometimes together with the Supreme People's Procuratorate, not linked to a specific case or controversy, that have the appearance of legislation. See more at: Susan Finder, The Supreme People's Court and Interpreting the Law Revisited, 10 July 2015, https://supremepeoplescourtmonitor.com/2015/07/10/the-supreme-peoples-court-and-interpreting-the-law-revisited-part-one/

[9] Susan Finder, *The Soft Law of the Supreme People's Court,* 16 November 2020, https://supremepeoplescourtmonitor.com/2020/11/16/the-soft-law-of-the-supreme-peoples-court/

[10] Zhang Xuebo,文件治国的历史观察: 1982—2017, 学术界 No 9 September 2017, (translated by David Cowhig) https://gaodawei.wordpress.com/2021/01/09/2017-zhang-xuebo-observations-on-the-history-of-rule-by-document-1982-2017/

directly with the SPC, but instead, the intermediate Party (and sometimes the state) institutions communicate new policies in the form of documents, most often issued to multiple Party and state organs of which the SPC is one. At the same time that this indicates to the observer the status of the SPC and the court system in Chinese governance, it also shows that the SPC and the court system have a unique role in it. One of the most important goals of these documents, listed below, is reshaping and reorganizing fragmented Party and government policy across many Party and state institutions. The goal is to implement better policy related to national defense and the military, called 'protecting military rights', (涉军维权), as President Zhou Qiang mentioned in his speech. The term 'military rights' does not have a specific definition but includes better protecting the rights of the People's Liberation Army (PLA), the armed police (now under PLA command), military personnel, and veterans.

The remainder of this article examines how the SPC seeks to achieve the political leadership's policy goals. The next section describes the documents by which Party and state policy relevant to protecting military rights is transmitted to the SPC. The section following it lists and summarizes the documents that the SPC has issued or is drafting to implement these goals and concludes with the author's thoughts on the significance of these documents and the work of the SPC in this area.

Party and Government Policy Related to Better Legal Protection of Military Interests

I have been able to identify several Party and government policy documents that inform the SPC that the courts need to take measures to better protect military interests. The authorities did not release the full text of most of these documents to the public, although the official Chinese press issued detailed summaries. There is no legal requirement to release such documents. It is generally recognized both in China and abroad that there is a high degree of secrecy related to military matters.

In April 2014, Central Political Legal Committee and the General Political Department of the PLA (the PLA's highest Communist Party organization) issued 'Improving the protection of the rights of the military, military personnel, and military dependents' (关于加强维护国防利益

和军人军属合法权益工作的意见）(PLA Legal Protection Opinion).

This document is directed towards improving the legal protection of China's national defense, military, military personnel, and military dependents. The SPC was only one of the lists of many institutions to which the document was issued. Among the others were:

Supreme People's Procuratorate

Ministry of Public Security

Ministry of Civil Affairs

Ministry of Justice

Ministry of Finance

Ministry of Human Resources and Social Security

Ministry of Land and Natural Resources

National Civil Air Defense Office

National Leading Group on Double Support

(On the military side, presumably, the General Political Department issued it to the military counterparts of many of the above authorities, including the PLA Military Court and PLA Military Procuratorate, but the press release did not specify)

Although the specific details of the PLA Legal Protection Opinion are unavailable, the principal objectives are clear from press summaries. One principal objective of the Party leadership was to coordinate better institutional policies related to protecting the interests of the military and its personnel, including policies of the courts.

As is usual practice in the drafting of multi-institutional documents, the SPC was consulted on its content.[11] It is likely that the SPC internally consulted specific substantive departments or tribunals. Through the mechanism and specific policies, the SPC was tasked to find methods of improving or resolving significant issues related to the siloed military and civilian systems. The siloed systems meant that civilian courts faced dif-

[11] See https://supremepeoplescourtmonitor.com/2014/04/18/will-new-supercommittees-resolve-the-plas-complicated-legal-problems/

ficulties in resolving a range of legal issues involving the military authorities, and PLA institutions and personnel also had difficulties relating to the civilian court system.

Related to the PLA Legal Protection Opinion was a Fall 2014 State Council and Central Military Commission policy document on improving legal aid work to military personnel and their families. In China, legal aid is provided to those who pass a means test in a limited category of civil cases, and more recently, much more broadly in criminal cases.[12] To implement the broad requirements of the PLA Legal Protection Opinion and the Fall 2014 document, the SPC issued its own policy documents to guide its own work and that of the lower courts, described in the following section.

In February 2016, the Central Military Commission issued a notice ordering the Chinese military and armed police to stop providing all paid services within three years with the Central Military Commission. The full text of the document (Notice on the military and armed police forces stopping entirely compensated services) (关于军队和武警部队全面停止有偿服务活动的通知) has not been made public, only summaries have been shared.[13] The SPC established a leading small group (equivalent to a project team) headed by one of the senior leaders of the SPC soon thereafter.[14]

In 2016, the Central Committee and Central Military Commission issued a document on military-civil fusion. Although it did not specifically mention intellectual property rights, a State Council notice on reforming intellectual property rights institutions called for the promotion of military-civil fusion of intellectual property rights.[15] In 2018, the Notice of the General Office of the Equipment Development Department of the Central Military Commission of the Office of the State Intellectual Property Office on the Pilot Work of Military-Civilian Fusion of Intellectual Property included provisions on resolving defense-related patents. The link to the SPC and patent rules is found in a 2020 notice of the

[12] Fu Hualing, Pro Bono, Legal Aid, and the Struggle for Justice in China (2020), https://papers.ssrn.com/sol3/papers.cfm?abstract_id=3743658

[13] See http://www.mod.gov.cn/shouye/2017-05/31/content_4781764.htm

[14] *Id.*

[15] Notice of the General Office of the State Council on Issuing the Overall Plan for the Intellectual Property Right Comprehensive Administration Reform Pilot Program, http://lawinfochina.com/display.aspx?id=26068&lib=law

Inter-Ministerial Joint Conference on the Implementation of the Intellectual Property Strategy of the State Council, headquartered at the China National Intellectual Property Administration. Article 25 of that Notice designates the SPC, along with the Equipment Development Department of the Central Military Commission, the National Defense and Technology Bureau, and the State Intellectual Property Office, to amend the Defense Patent Regulations and start work on a judicial interpretation on defense patent matters. The SPC is one of many members of the Inter-Ministerial Joint Conference. An official definition of an inter-ministerial joint conference states:

> … is established to negotiate and handle matters involving the responsibilities of multiple departments of the State Council. It is established with the approval of the State Council. The member units communicate in a timely manner and coordinate differing opinions. It is a work mechanism for enabling the smooth implementation of a task (responsibility). It is the highest-level joint meeting system of administrative agencies.[16]

As described below, the SPC is one of many institutions issuing a document to improve legal aid to veterans. The SPC policy document on providing legal aid and judicial assistance to veterans is based on prior documents of a Party organization focusing on legal matters: the SPC, Ministry of Justice, and the Supreme People's Procuratorate, including:

> The 2014 Note of the CPC Political-Legal Commission, the Ministry of Finance and the SPC on Issuing the Opinions on Establishing and Improving the System of State Judicial Aid (for trial implementation);[17]
>
> The 2016 Opinions of the SPC on Strengthening and Regulating the State Judicial Relief Work of the People's Courts[18] and the experience of the courts in providing better legal assistance to soldiers and their families.

[16] See https://supremepeoplescourtmonitor.com/2021/03/05/how-the-supreme-peoples-court-coordinates-with-other-party-and-state-organs/

[17] See https://www.spp.gov.cn/spp/zdgz/201512/t20151208_109020.shtml

[18] See http://www.lawinfochina.com/display.aspx?id=26011&lib=law&EncodingName=big5; http ://www.legaldaily.com.cn/index/content/2021-01/19/content_8411167.htm

How the SPC Provides Judicial Services and Guarantees

The SPC has issued three principal documents to provide better judicial services and guarantees to China's national defense and the military. The fourth document appears to still be in the draft. The SPC released the full text of only one of these documents, which is not unusual for military-related documents:

October 2014: Opinion on Expanding Capacity in Safeguarding the Interests of National Defense, Guaranteeing the Rights and Interests of Military Personnel, and Military Dependents (关于进一步发挥职能作用维护国防利益和军人军属合法权益的意见)(Expanding Capacity Opinion) (public);

January 2017: Notice on Doing Well Work in Providing Judicial Safeguards for the Stopping of Paid Services by the Military and Armed Police (Stopping Paid Services Notice)《最高人民法院关于做好为军队和武警部队全面停止有偿服务提供司法保障工作的通知 (confidential);[19]

January 2021: Opinion on Strengthening the Provision of Judicial Assistance to Retired Military Personnel (关于加强退役军人司法救助工作的意见), a multi-institutional document (confidential);

(A judicial interpretation on defense patent issues does not appear to have yet been promulgated).

The discussion below will summarize these SPC documents and include some brief analyses.

Expanding Capacity Opinion

Although not entitled a 'Services and Safeguards Opinion', the Expanding Capacity Opinion has many commonalties with other such documents, starting with the structure. It starts with a description of the relevant political documents and concepts, which are relevant to the lower

[19] See http://www.court.gov.cn/zixun-xiangqing-37782.html

courts. The second section notifies the lower courts about current relevant judicial policy. The third section provides guidance on operational mechanisms, and the last section relates to institutional and personnel matters. The policies and notification from the SPC give a glimpse of the broad range of legal issues facing the military and military personnel.

The purpose of the initial section is two-fold. The first is to notify the lower courts of the political goals, background and principles of the Opinion. The second is to signal to the political-legal hierarchy that the policies that the SPC sets out in the body of the Opinion are harmonized with the latest policies of the Party and the Government. During the Xi Jinping era, harmonization with the latest Party policy is particularly important.

The second section informs the lower courts of court policy to be implemented in support of the particular goal. It informs the courts of any changes from previous policy and what the lower courts must do in support of that policy goal. That section is the longest. This one contains a reminder about relevant law, as is common, about criminal and civil jurisdiction in military-related cases, indicating that the SPC believes that the lower courts needed this reminder.[20] The SPC provides new guidance for the lower courts to be more hospitable to military-related parties and provide some advisory services to members of the military. Courts with many military-related parties are encouraged to create a special window in the litigation services hall where potential litigants can be advised on their claim, to give these cases preference ('green light') on procedures, and are given guidance on to deal with the dispute more rationally. That latter language indicates that too many military-related disputes are resolved through physical fights. For military members who have a valid legal claim, courts are encouraged to designate a team of judges to deal with those cases. Soldiers stationed in remote locations are encouraged to use online or other methods to file their cases. Provincial High Courts and their regional military commands have jointly issued documents to make this possible.[21]

One important aspect of the 2014 Expanding Capacity Opinion was to give PLA soldiers better access to legal services in the area of ordinary

---

[20] *Id.*

[21] See http://eng.mod.gov.cn/news/2017-12/25/content_4800757.htm

civil matters and, in particular, improving and broadening legal aid systems. It is for matters like this that the PLA Protection Opinion was needed because without the involvement of the Ministry of Justice, the regulator of lawyers, there would be no mechanism for ensuring that lawyers would provide pro-bono legal services to soldiers. As to why better legal services to soldiers are needed, among the reasons is that ordinary soldiers are generally confined to their military bases, have few holidays, and have little way to access lawyers or other personnel that could provide legal advice. Most ordinary soldiers in the PLA are recruited from the countryside, although more recent recruitment is targeting urban and more educated recruits.[22] The Opinion explains that judicial assistance means exempting or reducing court fees for poor military families in civil cases such as:

Support payments (to the elderly);

Child support;

Compensation payments (to the disabled or families of the deceased).

The 2014 Expanding Capacity Opinion, for example, directs the lower courts to take the initiative to assist soldiers and military dependents who qualify in receiving legal aid. What this means is that courts should reach out to local justice bureaus. In some provinces or municipalities, such as Zhejiang and Shenzhen, the local judicial bureau, or bureau, has worked detailed regulations with the local military district to establish legal aid centers for military personnel and their dependents, under which local law firms have concluded agreements to provide legal advice[23] and lawyers who can assist them with legal-related problems.

The Expanding Capacity Opinion directs lower courts to punish crimes related to national defense and the military harshly, such as harming military weapons and equipment, military installations, military communications, gathering hostile crowds to disrupt military facilities, and committing fraud by impersonating military personnel or creating fraudulent military documentation. Military-related civil cases that the SPC

---

[22]Marcus Clay, https://www.airuniversity.af.edu/Portals/10/CASI/Books/Understanding_the_People_of_the_PLA.pdf

[23] See http://sft.zj.gov.cn/art/2017/1/16/art_1229107411_439870.html; http://sf.sz.gov.cn/ztzl/mssszt/flyz/msssskzqk/content/post_8371493.html

considers, requiring special treatment, are ones involving military land, the construction of new military facilities and the administration of areas with military installations properly, to avoid or resolve disagreements with the civilian population, especially those that could cause public protests and to ensure that superior resources are truly used in accordance with laws and regulations to enrich the core national defense capabilities.

A long section of the Opinion addresses mediating military-related disputes in the first instance, to maintain the principle of unity between the military and civilians. The Chinese legal system has a long tradition of stressing the importance of mediating disputes. The SPC has specific recommendations for courts mediating military and civilian parties, with special instructions for military parties, enable dispute settlement and involve more senior military personnel if the dispute is considered major. The objective is to achieve a resolution that is an organic unity of legal, social and political results (法律效果、社会效果和政治效果). This latter phrase is an important one in the Chinese judiciary.

Other content in the Opinion addresses how to improve the enforcement of civilian judicial decisions, with a separate section on civilian courts providing information about the law and exercising rights to the military.

The third section of the Opinion is directed at improving how the courts achieve the above goals and improving the quality and positive impact of the courts' work in the form of specific guidance. First, the SPC advised the lower courts to designate a group of judges to handle these cases who are both capable politically and professionally. In the Chinese context, these skills are particularly needed to deal with military-related legal matters. Next, the SPC advised improving the working relationship between the civilian and military courts. One article directed local civilian courts to contact local military courts to establish a mutually beneficial relationship. The SPC directed the civilian courts to provide training and other expertise to their military colleagues. Local courts, particularly in areas with many military bases and disputes involving the military, have concluded memoranda of understanding with local military courts. Other guidance includes encouraging local courts to designate certain personnel to work on military-related cases, lower-level courts to report on military-related cases to higher-level courts, and working with the local Party leadership to smooth relationships between civilian and military authorities. For local courts, cases involving the military can be troublesome because military institutions may or may not turn over evidence or otherwise cooperate with civilian courts, so establishing a working relationship is helpful.

Stopping Paid Services

The 2017 SPC Notice on Doing Well Work in Providing Judicial Safeguards for the Stopping of Paid Services by the Military and Armed Police (Stopping Paid Services Notice), as mentioned above, is available only in summary on the SPC's website. The notice provides guidance to the lower courts on facilitating the decision to stop paid services by the military and armed police. Much of the guidance is related to the 2014 Opinion but focused on stopping within two years commercial arrangements in which the military and armed police were involved. This decision led to a great deal of litigation, particularly by commercial parties that had leased military real estate. Therefore, the judicial policy section of the Stopping Paid Services Notice required courts to resolve conflicts and disputes promptly and properly at all stages: case filing, trial, and enforcement. 'Promptly and properly' meant giving the cases a priority in case acceptance and hearing, and ease the process of enforcement, to do its part to achieve the goal of stopping paid services by the military and armed police. In the course of these cases, the courts need to achieve the Party and state's multiple goals – extracting the military and armed police from commercial arrangements, maintaining the prestige of the military and armed police while doing so, compensating civilians for their business losses, maintaining the image of the army and ensuring that ordinary people think that the army and armed police serve the people and the courts have provided justice.

In the section with guidance on achieving the above policy goals, the Notice directed lower courts to increase specialized judicial measures and cooperate with other authorities, using the multiple functions of the Chinese judiciary to achieve goals of the national leadership in the local environment. The guidance recommends research on related cases and summarizing prior work to guide their own future work and that of others.

Similar to the 2014 Opinion, the Notice recommends cooperating with the local Party and state leadership and using mediation and other alternative dispute mechanisms for resolving social conflicts and disputes. Analogous to the 2014 Opinion, the goal is to achieve the organic unity of legal, political, and social effectiveness.

In 2017, the official press published an article praising the work by the Beijing No 1 Intermediate People's Court in protecting military rights and indirectly holding it up as a model.[24] It is one of the Beijing courts with the most military-related cases. The cases relate to military institutions, military personnel, military structures, and military-use land so that the court hears major military-related cases in the first instance and many military-related appeals. The court, therefore, was facing a large increase in cases when the military exited business operations. The court followed general guidance to designate a special collegiate panel (three-judge panel) to hear military rights cases, who have proper political qualifications (all are Party members), are highly educated, and have more than five years of trial experience. The court and its counterpart military court, the Military Court, directly under the headquarters of the PLA, concluded a joint cooperation agreement after several rounds of negotiation.

The content of the agreement (according to press reports) followed the principles in the 2014 Opinion. The civilian court agreed to establish special arrangements for the military to file cases with designated personnel, compile military-related statistics, designate dedicated personnel to hear these cases, with simple cases heard quickly, complicated cases considered carefully, and make more use of mediation to ensure that disputes are resolved. As this author has written elsewhere, case closing numbers are one of the important metrics for courts.[25] The agreement calls for greater exchanges between the two courts on dealing with military-related petitioning (petitioning related to a military-related matter) and includes provisions related to criminal, civil and administrative cases and the entire judicial process from case acceptance to enforcement.[26]

These types of arrangements are becoming more and more common,

---

[24] See http://rmfyb.chinacourt.org/paper/html/2017-01/15/content_120859.htm?div=0

[25] Susan Finder, *Supreme People's Court Gears Up for the 19th Party Congress*, 25 September 2017, https://supremepeoplescourtmonitor.com/2017/09/25/supreme-peoples-court-gears-up-for-19th-party-congress/

[26] Susan Finder, *Two Beijing Courts Cooperate on Military-Related Cases*, 4 August 2018, https://globalmjreform.blogspot.com/2018/08/two-beijing-courts-cooperate-on.html

with regional arrangements between military areas and relevant civilian courts and other institutions in political-legal institutions, more recently including the recently established veterans' affairs bureaus.[27]

In July 2019, SPC President, Zhou Qiang, announced that the first phase of this work had been successfully completed.[28] A search of the SPC's case database, which shows partial statistics on the number of court decisions related to extracting the military and armed police from the business shows that the peak of about 2,400 cases was in 2018 but continued into 2019 (about 391) and 2020, with some cases (22) decided in the first half of 2021. It is likely that many cases were settled, but of the ones that when to judgment, most of the cases were decided on the intermediate or basic level court level, but the SPC heard at least thirteen related cases.

Strengthening Judicial Assistance to Veterans

As of this writing, the latest SPC policy document to support the military is the January 2021 Opinion on strengthening the provision of judicial assistance to retired military personnel. As described in detailed press reports, the Opinion requires courts to take measures to improve judicial assistance to veterans, focusing on eight types of veterans. The policy document promotes coordination among institutions to better assist veterans, designating financial support from the state as a last resort, with a preference for compensation obtained through civil or administrative proceedings, to better improve the status of veterans and promote social harmony and stability. Local governments have resettlement and other obligations to veterans, depending on their rank in the military. The complicated regulations are explained in the footnoted article.[29]

Similar to the earlier documents, the Opinion calls for establishing a judicial assistance work mechanism for veterans to enable better coordination, requiring the courts, administrative institutions in charge of lawyers, and other organs to link with local veterans affairs departments and

---

[27] See http://www.moj.gov.cn/Department/content/2020-09/10/612_3255791.html

[28] See https://www.chinacourt.org/article/detail/2019/07/id/4204573.shtml

[29] See generally, Ma Chengkun and John Chen, *System Overload? The 2015 PLA Force Reduction, Military-Locality Relations, and the Potential for Social Instability* (2019) https://ndupress.ndu.edu/Portals/68/Documents/Books/Chairman-Xi/Chairman-Xi_Chapter-17.pdf?ver=2019-02-08-112005-803

other relevant institutions to deliver relevant services.

Only a few press reports can be found of cooperation between local courts and veterans affairs bureaus on enabling veterans to receive judicial assistance (a type of legal aid), but that is likely to increase over time.

Civil-Military Fusion: Intellectual Property Issues

The 2014 Expanding Capacity Opinion contained one line relating to the national leadership's decision to promote civil-military fusion: provide judicial support for the scientific development of military core industries and military industry enterprises in accordance with the law. One small aspect of that relates to intellectual property.

Chinese legislation has created a separate military intellectual property system, with a separate defense intellectual property office. The legislation itself and related issues mean that defense inventions cannot be easily marketized. It also requires a high degree of secrecy. The dispute resolution mechanism to resolve disputes over rights to defense-related intellectual property cannot be easily resolved. Due to the closed-off military intellectual property system, the civilian courts have great challenges in hearing-related cases. The SPC has been tasked with working with the Central Military Commission to issue a judicial interpretation of the amended Defense Patent Regulations.[30] A partner at one of China's leading law firms commented on the intellectual property issues relating to national defense:

> Intellectual property rights are unclear, and interests are unclear. Especially for R&D units or individuals that have technological achievements, the possession and use rights enjoyed by them are not exclusive. The technological achievements are not liquid, so there is no profitability, so R&D units and individuals are easily discouraged. The individual's enthusiasm for technological innovation and achievement transformation [into something marketable] are not incentivized.[31]

[30] *Advancement Plan for the In-Depth Implementation of the National Intellectual Property Strategy and Accelerating the Building of an Intellectual Property Right Power in 2020*, http://www.lawinfochina.com/display.aspx?id=33330&lib=law

[31] See https://www.chinalawinsight.com/2018/04/articles/corporate-ma/%E6%B5%85%E6%9E%90%E6%88%91%E5%9B%BD%E5%86%9B%E6%B0%91%E8%9E%8D%E5%90%88%E5%8F%91%E5%B1%95%E6%B3%95%E5%BE%8B%E5%88%B6%E5%BA%A6%EF%BC%88%E4%B8%80%EF%BC%89/

Conclusion

Through this brief analysis of how the SPC protects military rights, some of the special characteristics of the Chinese court system and its interactions with the national defense and military system can be seen. It is a court system with commonalities and differences with other Party and state institutions and also with courts in other jurisdictions. The analysis has shown that the Chinese political leadership views the courts as useful in its social governance. As the article hints, the Chinese public is increasingly conscious of its rights under the law and is willing to go to court to defend them, even against an institution as powerful as the military. Too many soldiers and military personnel appear to be unaware of the need to comply with the law, or the SPC would not encourage 'bring the law into the military bases' activities. This analysis also provides small glimpses into the challenges of the PLA in achieving its long-term goal of becoming a modern professional army.

It is difficult to make an informed, independent assessment of the effectiveness of the policy documents described above, except to say that it seems to be a work in progress and that many civilian judges would rather not be involved in military-related cases because of their political sensitivity, difficult nature, and limited skills transferability in case the judge resigns. Three civilian court judges published a rare assessment on their court's website:

> ...the actual effectiveness of military-related rights protection regulations is limited. Most of the laws and regulations on the protection of military rights and interests provide broad principles and are not specific enough.... The handling of military-related cases has become increasingly complicated. With the continuous deepening of social and economic development and reforms to strengthen the army, the legal issues involved in the field of national defense and army building have shown an increasing and diversified development trend year by year...The working mechanism of military rights protection is not operating smoothly... [32]

It appears that much work is needed to create a legal framework that will meet the needs of China's political leadership, military officers, and

---

[32] See http://xzzy.chinacourt.gov.cn/article/detail/2020/08/id/5426566.shtml

soldiers and civilians, one piece of which is making military service a viable career option for some of China's law graduates. It is particularly necessary as the PLA becomes more involved with the world outside China's border. It also appears that further development is needed to make competent and low-cost legal services available for China's veterans. It is only if trained legal personnel are better integrated into China's military services will many of the measures described above no longer be necessary.

Susan Finder is the Distinguished Scholar in Residence at the Peking University School of Transnational Law (STL), Shenzhen, China. She is a scholar of China's judicial system (in comparative perspective). Her current research concentrates on Supreme People's Court and Chinese judicial reforms, much of which is published on her blog, the Supreme People's Court Monitor (最高人民法院观察). The blog is widely cited in books, academic journals, PhD theses and government reports. This is Susan's second career in academia, and she comes to STL after twenty years in China-related practice at Freshfields Bruckhaus Deringer (and other firms), in legal publishing and (briefly) as a securities regulator. In her first academic career (at what is now the City University of Hong Kong) she published the first comprehensive study of the operations of the Supreme People's Court. The author would like to express her appreciation to Mark Jia for commenting on an earlier draft of her essay.

The Elor Azaria Case and the Murderer or Hero Dilemma

Amos N Guiora

Elor Azaria, Israel

Introduction

On Thursday morning, 24 March 2016, Sergeant Elor Azaria of the Israel Defense Forces killed a severely wounded Palestinian terrorist, Abdel Fattah al-Sharif, who was incapacitated when mortally shot. For this act, Azaria was convicted of manslaughter by a military court and sentenced to 18 months' imprisonment. Subsequently, the sentence was reduced by the IDF Chief of Staff, General Gadi Eizencot.

While much attention was focused on the trial, the examination in this chapter will expand beyond what occurred in the courtroom. In the subsequent chapter, Colonel (Retired) Maya Heller – the judge who presided over the trial – will discuss the implementation of the principle of judicial independence during the trial despite the public atmosphere surrounding the case. In that vein, our chapters are intended to provide the reader with different perspectives of the trial, addressing distinct issues. Colonel Heller focuses on the period during the trial while I address the broader societal implications of the case. We wrote our chapters independently of each other, without collaboration, as we explored distinct themes. It is our hope that by reading the two chapters back-to-back, the reader will gain a broader insight into a matter that dominated the Israeli news cycle and became the focal point of extraordinary public attention. The intersection, or confluence, of the two chapters is intended to enable the reader to gain an understanding of both the inside (the courtroom) and the outside (the public arena).

For this chapter, I interviewed a range of individuals, including senior former Israel Defense Force commanders and individuals directly involved in the trial. While some of the interviews were on the record, I have decided to treat all the interviews as off the record.[1] The extent to which the Azaria matter made an indelible impression on all those interviewed was obvious in every conversation. That was true regardless of when they served in the IDF and what positions they held during their service.

Background

The decision to prosecute Azaria, his subsequent conviction, and incarceration rocked Israeli society reflecting deep fissures on powerful issues, including, but not limited to, what is the normative moral standard expected of soldiers in a non-traditional conflict. Azaria's actions were captured on film by a Palestinian.[2] The dissemination was immediate, with powerful consequences for the IDF, the public, politicians, and Azaria.

Outrage focused on the decision to prosecute a soldier who had killed a Palestinian terrorist. For some Israelis, Azaria became a hero and was referred to as 'our soldier' and 'king'.[3] For others, Azaria was a soldier who killed a helpless Palestinian and had to be punished accordingly, regardless of the fact that al-Sharif had stabbed an Israeli soldier prior to being killed by Azaria.

The key of the title of this chapter, *Murderer or Hero*, is intended to reflect the wide chasm that defined the debate in Israel, which extended well beyond the specific action in the streets of Hebron in the West Bank where Azaria killed al-Sharif.

---

[1] Interview notes are in my records; I am grateful to those who chose to engage with me, their insights and honesty are deeply appreciated. In full disclosure, I served with the majority of those interviewed and was referred to others, some who agreed to discuss the matter with me, others begged off.

[2] See https://www.youtube.com/watch?v=b4s2CrVvgpw

[3] See https://www.youtube.com/watch?v=Lh_8Y4fwG1I

That is not to diminish the importance of Azaria's actions but rather to highlight other aspects of the case that demand our attention. By broadening the scope of issues pertinent to the Azaria case, the intent is to provide a glimpse both into Israeli society and the IDF culture. Both are important when considering the broader consequences of a misbegotten decision by one soldier, highlighting the impact of one military trial. The incitement by politicians, the cacophony from the public, and the constant media attention became a story onto themselves, perhaps overshadowing the actual trial. Covering the trial required addressing its implications and ramifications on Israeli society. There, thus, came to be two stories.

What was complex and challenging were the larger issues. It is those issues that will be this chapter's primary focus without minimizing the trial's importance. In this chapter (distinct from Colonel Heller's chapter), we shall focus on three issues distinct from the judicial proceedings: actions of Israeli politicians, questions regarding morality in armed conflict, and the public outcry. Nevertheless, there is a need to set the stage with respect to Azaria's actions and the question before the Court with the understanding that Colonel Heller's chapter will focus on the trial itself. In that vein, this chapter will be divided into the following sections: I. Introduction; II. Murderer or Hero; III. 24 March 2016; IV. What Crime did Azaria Commit? V. Political Involvement; VI. Normative Behavior-Standards of IDF Morality; VII. The Costs; VIII. Final Word.

History and precedent are important, facts and circumstances notwithstanding. The question of whether and where to prosecute an IDF soldier was previously confronted by the public, the judiciary, and senior commanders. In short, the then Judge Advocate General, Brigadier General Amnon Strashnov, decided not to prosecute (then) Colonel Yehuda Meir for his actions in 1988 during the early stages of the Palestinian *intifada* but rather to bring Meir before a disciplinary hearing. In response to a petition filed by a human rights organization to the Supreme Court (sitting as the High Court of Justice), the Court ordered Meir's prosecution before a military court, which subsequently convicted him and lowered his rank to private.[4]

---

[4] 425/89, *Tzopan v. The Judge Advocate General*, https://www.latimes.com/archives/la-xpm-1990-06-23-mn-359-story.html, https://www.jta.org/1991/04/25/archive/idf-colonel-conv

Murderer or Hero?

The phrase 'murderer or hero' applies not only to the legal questions facing the prosecutor, defense attorney, and court but also the IDF, the public, and politicians. Answering the question, as became quickly apparent, was directly related to the significant political divide in Israel, focusing on the IDF's presence in the West Bank, whose population is overwhelmingly Palestinian.

As a result of the 1967 Six-Day War, Israel gained control of the West Bank (from Jordan) and the Gaza Strip (from Egypt). While the 1994 Oslo Peace Accords between Israel and the Palestinian Authority (the successor to the Palestine Liberation Organization) were intended to result in the establishment of a Palestinian state in the West Bank and the Gaza Strip, the conflict has yet to be resolved. While Israel disengaged from the Gaza Strip in 2005, the IDF still has a military presence in the West Bank as Israel has security (as compared to police) responsibility and power. Therefore, Azaria (and his unit) was stationed in Hebron, a major city in the West Bank. In broad strokes, Israelis of the political left opposed IDF's presence in the West Bank, favoring the establishment of a Palestinian state, whereas Israelis of the political right opposed the establishment of a Palestinian state and favored the continued presence of the IDF in the West Bank.

Both sides of the spectrum have consistently sought to separate the actions of units and soldiers from the broader political question. Nevertheless, as quickly became apparent, the decision to prosecute Azaria dramatically brought to the surface the consequences of assigning blame to a soldier sent by the State to serve in the West Bank. For those on the right, Azaria was a hero who justifiably killed a Palestinian who had sought to murder a soldier. That position was rejected by those who focused solely on Azaria's actions, rejecting the defense offered by his supporters who sought to legitimize the killing of al-Sharif.

Public reaction literally exploded in the streets where the Military Court was located. Demonstrations were so loud, sometimes so profane, the judicial process was hard-pressed to hear itself. The trial became a

---

icted-of-brutality-will-be-discharged-but-not-jailed; for a similar case in the UK please see https://www.gq-magazine.co.uk/politics/article/marine-a

critical part of the Israeli domestic dialogue, the decision to prosecute inflaming passions and emotions. Lost in the noise, perhaps deliberately, was that Azaria had killed al-Sharif long after the threat he posed had dissipated. We came to learn this because of the video of the event that went viral immediately.

The video depicts the following: al-Sharif lying prone on the ground, soldiers milling about in his presence in a manner clearly suggesting he is not perceived as posing a threat, Azaria exchanging words with a fellow soldier, taking a few steps toward al-Sharif, loading-cocking his rifle, taking aim and firing one shot directed at the head of the wounded terrorist. Careful viewing of the video does not suggest al-Sharif posed a danger to Azaria or the other soldiers, certainly not to Azaria when he approached al-Sharif from behind him while he was lying on his back.[5]

If not for the presence of Aymad Abu-Shsia, a photographer for the human rights organization, Bet'se'lem, the facts as captured in the video would not have been so accurately and graphically known. The video made clear the time gap between the stabbing of the soldier by al-Sharif and Azaria's criminal action that did not take place in the context of operational engagement when the latter posed a direct threat to the former, his fellow soldiers, or others. This was not a case of a soldier acting in self-defense.

When al-Sharif *had* posed such a threat, that had been neutralized when Azaria shot him, as clearly depicted in the video. It is not an exaggeration to suggest that Mr Abu-Shsia's video had the same impact Ms Darnella Frazier's video had in the conviction of Derek Chauvin for the murder of George Floyd.[6] Arguably, if not for Ms Frazier and Mr Abu-Shasia, neither Chauvin nor Azaria would not have been convicted.

The response in Israel was immediate.

Blame for that must be put squarely at the feet of right-wing Israeli politicians, ranging from low-level members of the Knesset (Parliament) to (then) Prime Minister. The rush to defend Azaria, facts notwithstanding, was in accordance with the right-left debate referenced above, whereby Azaria was portrayed as a hero, defending his fellow soldiers and others. The rush to weigh in on social media, radio and TV reflected a

---

[5] See https://www.youtube.com/watch?v=w4O6eRssOjs

[6] See https://apnews.com/article/video-dominates-derek-chauvin-trial-explained-f7608641d2fdbd6a8443691fd7ca1625

determined effort to frame the issue in the broader political context and to proactively influence a possible decision to prosecute Azaria. The original 'noise' did not abate over the course of time; the vilification of the IDF Chief-of-Staff Gadi Eizenkot was particularly heinous. Incitement best describes the chant repeated electronically and in the street, 'Gadi, Gadi, be careful Rabin is looking for a friend'[7] referencing assassinated Prime Minister Rabin. This is but an example of the tone and tenor in the aftermath of the decision to prosecute Azaria.[8]

24 March 2016

In and itself, what happened in the streets of Hebron is not particularly unique in the context of IDF soldiers stationed in the West Bank. In the morning hours of Thursday, 24 March 2016, Abdel Fattah al-Sharif, stabbed an Israeli soldier. Immediately thereafter, IDF soldiers shot and critically wounded al-Sharif. From an operational perspective, the decision to open-fire in immediate response to the stabbing fell well within IDF Rules of Engagement.[9] Neither the stabbing nor the shooting was noteworthy, no different from innumerable similar attacks/responses inherent to the interaction between IDF soldiers and Palestinians who live in the West Bank.

It is what happened when Elor Azaria 'swung' into action, firing the single shot that killed al-Shari whilst he lay on his back, critically wounded, that is our focus. That is when the situation, which until then had been under control, dramatically shifted. Were it not for Azaria's unilateral decision, al-Shari would have been yet another Palestinian who stabbed an Israeli soldier.

Other soldiers who were in greater immediate proximity to al-Shari, displayed no indication of operational readiness, concern, or preparation to open fire. In fact, it was quite the opposite. There is no indication of

---

[7] See https://www.youtube.com/watch?v=AnyjykLugt8

[8] This was brilliantly captured on the Israeli TV show, *Eretz Nehedert*, https://www.youtube.com/watch?v=F7gruBQX2QI

[9] See https://www.timesofisrael.com/revisiting-the-idfs-rules-of-engagement-in-light-of-hebron-shooting/, https://www.washingtonpost.com/world/middle_east/israeli-veterans-say-permissive-rules-of-engagement-fueled-gaza-carnage/2015/05/04/ab698d16-f020-11e4-8050-839e9234b303_story.html, https://www.jstor.org/stable/43946931

any of the soldiers, as seen on the video, sensing any danger from al-Sharif. Nonchalant would aptly describe the body language and conduct of the other soldiers in al-Sharif's immediate vicinity. Some retired IDF commanders interviewed for this chapter were critical of the soldiers' demeanor, noting the lack of operational readiness and lack of military bearing.

Azaria did not have any operational role or command responsibility during the incident or in its immediate aftermath. Azaria was not engaged in the initial neutralizing of al-Sharif. More than that, he was not present when the stabbing occurred and only arrived after al-Shari had been wounded by soldiers in the immediate response and who acted in accordance with IDF Rules of Engagement. That is distinct from Azaria's actions which took place well after the stabbing when no danger was posed and when the Rules of Engagement did *not* (italics intended) justify shooting al-Sharif.

Any effort to portray otherwise is not reflected in available evidence, whether in the video or in testimony before the Military Court. Azaria's decision to open fire was his alone; there is no evidence that an officer so commanded. Azaria's action took place well after the incident had been contained.

These are two distinct events, albeit occurring in the same location. To view al-Shari's death as a natural continuation of the initial stabbing is to misconstrue and misperceive the facts as Azaria's defenders did. To do so reflects, whether in whole or in part, the politicization of the event, adroit legal arguments by defense counsel, or 'spin' by various interested parties. As we shall come to see, that was the primary effort of defense counsel and politicians alike. Fortunately, the rule of law prevailed.

What Crime Did Azaria Commit?

We begin with the following premise: Elor Azaria committed a crime whose resolution had to come before the Military Court.

Precedent and policy indicate no disciplinary action would have been taken had the killing occurred as a reasonable response to the stabbing by a soldier present in the immediate moment. Had al-Sharif died when initially shot, the matter would not have been brought before the Military

Court, for there would have been no justification to court-martial the soldier who shot al-Sharif in the *immediate* (italics intended) aftermath of the stabbing.

That was not the case regarding Azaria. The distinction-separation between the initial shooting and the subsequent shooting-killing of al-Sharif is essential to understanding the title of this chapter. Elor Azaria was no hero; his action was unrelated to the attack response. Therefore, the only question was whether he should be charged with murder or manslaughter. Any attempt to frame the question in a different light does not square with the facts. Had Elor Azaria been an integral component of the unit that responded to the stabbing and opened fire in accordance with IDF Rules of Engagement, his name would not have been in the public domain. IDF soldiers are trained to respond in such situations; that is the reasonable expectation commanders have of soldiers who serve in a combat unit. From all perspectives, the soldier/s who opened fire in the immediate aftermath of the stabbing acted in accordance with IDF regulations. There was no consideration given to bringing them before commanders for disciplinary purposes; an operational 'after action' review was deemed sufficient, given the event. That is, in all probability, the outcome that would have awaited Azaria had he acted in accordance with IDF regulations. As the video depicts, Azaria acted well after the threat posed by al-Sharif had dissipated. It is for that reason, then, to equate Azaria's actions to decision making in the context of operational decision making must be rejected. The only question, then, regarding Azaria was whether to indict on the charge of murder or manslaughter.

The former IDF commanders interviewed were in near-unanimous agreement Azaria had to be prosecuted; with one exception, all believed the appropriate charge was manslaughter. Two commanders were of the opinion the Azaria should not have been charged, arguing a disciplinary hearing before a senior commander was sufficient. The commander who believed Azaria should have been charged with murder was harsh in his criticism of the manslaughter decision. The commanders who agreed with the manslaughter decision were more concerned with the question from a military unit discipline perspective rather than a legal dilemma. Their primary focus was how the case would impact the willingness of combat soldiers to open fire when operational circumstances are not black and white. This concern has been raised previously in response to courts-martial or disciplinary actions taken against combat soldiers.

Those involved in the legal decision-making process emphasized the 'close call' in assessing whether to indict manslaughter or murder. The primary question was whether Azaria's actions were premeditated; if so, that would justify indictment for murder.

This is not the 'classic' murder scenario whereby an individual carefully plans in advance, purchases necessary weapons, tracks the victim, lies in wait, and acts in a premeditated manner. However, it is also not the 'classic' manslaughter vignette where a person comes home, only to find his/her partner romantically engaged with another person, killing them in an 'act of passion', devoid of forethought and planning. Azaria's actions do not reflect that scenario. There is no evidence either from the video or from others that this was an instinctive act, reflecting a spontaneous decision and action. Actually, quite the opposite, for there is a coolness, a sense of deliberateness to Azaria's conduct as depicted in the video.

It is for this reason that both the decision-makers and I define this as a 'close call', and why commander opinions were not unanimous, albeit heavily tilting strongly in favor of manslaughter. However, from a narrow legal perspective, based on my understanding of criminal law, a decision of murder would have been jurisprudentially justifiable. The elements of murder were met with a slight tweak, which perhaps is what ultimately led to the manslaughter decision – this was not pre-planned as murder is traditionally understood, but also not impulsive as manslaughter is defined in the criminal code.[10] As there was time for Azaria to reflect, as clearly depicted, and given that al-Shari did not pose a threat to Azaria or others, I would have voted to indict on murder. The fact that this is not the classic pre-emptive model does not sufficiently dissuade me from viewing the killing of al-Sharif as an act of murder.

Political Involvement

Israeli politicians rushed into the arena. Their actions and words galva-

[10] For a further discussion of this, see Col (Retired) Heller's chapter in this book; for additional reading see, https://www.idf.il/en/minisites/military-advocate-generals-corps/the-idf-military-justice-system/, https://en.idi.org.il/articles/12244, http://www.knesset.gov.il/review/data/eng/law/kns2_militaryjustice_1_eng.pdf

nized the Israeli political right; demonstrations, rallies, angry voices, incitement, cheap politicking became the norm. Elor Azaria was turned into a hero, referred to in some quarters as 'our son'. It was as if he had been adopted by a segment of the population, seizing a moment to attack the left, the media, the judiciary, and the Chief of Staff. In other words, the right was attacking the usual suspects who have drawn their wrath for unrelated events over the years.

As is widely known, even mainstream politicians got involved,[11] many of whom labeled Azaria as the new national hero.[12]

While disagreement, loud and direct, is integral to the Israeli national psyche, there was something different in how leading politicians, and subsequently the public, attacked the IDF. There are very few sacred cows in Israel. Political correctness is an anathema to the culture, but for decades attacking the IDF was considered off-limits amongst much of the Israeli public. While the fawning, almost obsequious interaction between the public and IDF leadership that defined the relationship after the 1967 Six-Day War had turned critical in the aftermath of the 1973 Yom Kippur War, this was different. Never had an IDF Chief of Staff been called a traitor – a word with dangerous connotations in contemporary Israeli society.

While words are casually bandied about in Israel, the failure of the political establishment to condemn those voices illuminates the extent to which politicians seized the moment. Azaria became the code-word for Israelis seeking to castigate the judiciary and political left. The demonstrations were emboldened and incited by politicians who quickly reached conclusions regarding the events that transpired in Hebron.

Whether they watched the video is an open question; whether the facts as presented in the Court mattered to them is a foregone conclusion. In the context of Israeli politics, there is nothing particularly striking about this. What is important, for our purposes, is the willingness of politicians, including high offices, to cast aspersions on the Chief of Staff specifically and the IDF in general, casting doubt in the public's mind regarding the legitimacy of the decision-making process regarding Azaria.

---

[11] See https://www.haaretz.com/israel-news/why-the-hebron-shooter-trial-is-dividing-israel-1.5481805

[12] See https://www.haaretz.com/israel-news/.premium-hebron-shooter-elor-azaria-released-from-prison-after-nine-months-1.6070371, https://www.timesofisrael.com/hebron-shooter-gets-heros-welcome-after-serving-term/

That is dangerous in a democracy predicated on the rule of law. More than that, as the former commanders emphasized, failure to prosecute Azaria could have negative consequences on the unit's discipline. While there is no doubt regarding the importance of discipline, there is also no doubt this was an issue politicians paid no heed to. Fortunately, at the end of the day, the loud, cacophonous external noise had no impact on the Chief of Staff, the prosecutor, or the Court. That is to their credit. The same cannot be said regarding those who deliberately sought to undermine the legal-judicial system.

With that, we turn our attention to the way the IDF instructs soldiers regarding requirements to act both in accordance with the rule of law and accepted norms of morality. The discussion is particularly important both because of Azaria's actions and the efforts of his defenders to frame al-Sharif's killing as legitimate self-defense. The retired IDF commanders placed particular importance on the need to directly address this issue when meeting with combat soldiers. While there was disagreement amongst them regarding the murder-manslaughter debate, there was unanimity regarding the need to reinforce training imbuing normative standards.

Normative Behavior Standards of IDF Morality

On a personal note, relevant to this section: From 2001–2004, I served as Commander, IDF School of Military Law. Officers under my command created a sophisticated, interactive video teaching an 11-point code of conduct.[13] The purpose was to confront soldiers with legal-moral-operational dilemmas akin to what transpired in Hebron on 24 March 2016. The scenarios in the video were based on events that had occurred in the West Bank. The video included an international law test.

The impetus for creating the video was a culmination of events, including specific actions by soldiers, complaints filed by non-governmental organizations, and an understanding that addressing these issues was essential to ensuring that soldiers conduct themselves in accordance with recognized laws of armed conflict. While 'why now' was a question some posed, its relevance was minimal. What was important was the decision

---

[13] See https://papers.ssrn.com/sol3/papers.cfm?abstract_id=783985

to directly confront these critical issues. That was confirmed when then-Deputy Chief of Staff, Major General Gabi Ashkenazi, mandated the video be incorporated in both training courses and operational units. Following Ashkenazi's decision, thousands of soldiers viewed the video.[14]

While empirical data was not gathered regarding the video's effectiveness, anecdotal evidence strongly intimated its positive impact. More than that: combat unit commanders requested their soldiers view the video, after which discussions would be held when soldiers voiced complaints that the application of the code of conduct unnecessarily exposed them to danger. Commanders were uniformly adamant that respecting the codes was essential to ensuring both unit discipline and operational effectiveness.

The IDF is closely monitored by domestic and international human rights organizations that report misconduct, whether minor or egregious.[15] The reporting primarily focuses on the interaction between soldiers and Palestinian residents (non-combatants) of the West Bank and Gaza Strip, rather than the manner in which the IDF conducts operational counterterrorism. The extent to which these organizations influence decision-making is an open question. What is clear, however, is that sensitivity to respect for human rights is embedded into the IDF culture with the understanding that mistakes have occurred and, in all probability, will again. That is not to excuse misconduct but, rather, to state what is largely the obvious.

This brings us to Elor Azaria. Distinct from the soldiers who responded to the stabbing, Azaria's actions, in addition to their criminal nature, do not reflect the IDF's code of conduct, as captured in the video. Azaria's unilateral decision to open fire when al-Sharif did not pose a threat is in direct contradiction to the requirement to protect the wounded, their actions notwithstanding. While al-Sharif was a terrorist, when killed by Azaria, he was lying prone on his back, critically wounded.

Distinguishing between a terrorist shot while committing an act of terrorism and a neutralized terrorist, posing no danger to those in the vicinity, is at the heart of the code of conduct. It is the difference between legitimate use of force and an act that fails on two different fronts: legal

[14] *Ibid.*

[15] During the course of my career, I met with a number of these organizations.

and moral. While the Military Court addressed the former, the second is also of great importance from both a strictly moralist perspective and a utilitarian approach to unit discipline and command influence. The commanders emphasized Azaria's unilateral decision, made without any operational justification, violated the IDF's principles regarding the use of force. For them, this was an issue of great importance because of their decades-long commitment to an IDF predicated on normative behavior. That is not to suggest they are naïve, viewing the world through rose-colored glasses; based on my professional experience with them, I know that not to be the case.

Similarly, I am aware that during their decades-long careers, they have been faced with complex challenges that formed their approaches to morality in armed conflict and the obligations it imposes. While nuances are inherent to operational dilemmas, and the decision to open fire must be viewed through that prism, normative standards articulated through a code of conduct must not brook Azaria's actions.

The Costs

The incitement and politicization of the decision to prosecute Azaria were not cost-free. Those involved in the decision and its implementation paid a personal price that, unfortunately, did not impose a subsequent cost on those responsible.

We begin with the following: because of threats against them, the prosecutor and judge were provided 24-hour security protection. To define that as 'outrageous' is to minimize its importance. While it is a direct result of the actions of several politicians, its importance goes beyond that.

To fully appreciate the positioning of the Azaria trial in contemporary Israeli society, one must recognize the deep fissure emanating from the inability (unwillingness?) to resolve the Israeli-Palestinian conflict. At its deepest root, when the legal question regarding Azaria is relegated to the back seat, the case brought to the surface questions that deeply divide Israeli society today. While there are innumerable issues on the national 'plate', the question that has been at the 'front and center' is how and whether to resolve this decades-long matter. Issues come, issues go, but this matter is, depending on one's political perspective, stuck in the throat like a bone.

Regardless of one's political leanings, the Azaria matter forced Israelis to address this question. While terrorist attacks in the West Bank are frequent and violent, they are largely accepted as part of the national heartbeat. The same accepting of reality applies to instances when Israeli soldiers respond to terrorist attacks, whether killing or injuring the terrorist. Soldiers who serve in combat units understand terrorism/counterterrorism is part and parcel of the experience. That also holds for the broader public, which understands the reality of the situation, regardless of their political leanings. It is not an exaggeration to suggest an attack such as the one addressed in this chapter would have barely registered a blip on the collective radar screen of an Israeli public saturated with news.

That changed once the video went viral.

From that moment, all bets were off as the standard responses to terrorism/counterterrorism were swept by political incitement and public clamor. It was as if the lid blew off whatever restraints had been acceptable – the rush to judgment, the race to score points, the gallop to dictate the news cycle, the unquenchable need to be heard was so overwhelming. While the video was clear in its depiction, the extraordinarily irresponsible castigation of those involved in deciding to bring Azaria to trial in the Military Court was extraordinary.

Facts be damned.

Our 'hero' had killed a Palestinian terrorist, and the IDF wants to prosecute him? He should receive a medal. He should be lauded. He exactly did what we train and expect soldiers to do. How can they prosecute 'our son'? It was as if Elor Azaria now had hundreds of thousands of parents, ready to embrace him, warding off the evil IDF Chief of Staff, prosecutors, and the Court. If they were not evil, there would be no need to protect them.

Yet they were evil, determined to prosecute a soldier who had protected his fellow soldiers while serving the state. It was, after all, the State that sent him, that endangered him, that demanded his military service and was now prosecuting him. For what? For heroically killing a Palestinian terrorist who, only a few minutes before, had stabbed another soldier and was, any minute, going to detonate himself with the suicide bomb that he surely had under his coat, or would stab other soldiers with the knife lying on the ground within arm's reach of him.

In a nutshell: It was temerity to prosecute this brave soldier. Our son. Our hero.

The narrative, driven by political involvement, was black-white, devoid of gray, and ignoring the facts. While, perhaps, we can excuse the public from taking its lead from the politicians that tolerance does not extend to the politicians. They were playing with fire, deliberately exacerbating a situation to suit their needs and agenda. While that is the essence of politics, in a tinderbox such as Israel, with an assassination fomented by incitement in its history, that is the height of irresponsibility, if not dangerous. What demands attention was the failure of politicians to condemn the incitement that marked the response to the decision to prosecute Azaria. That failure must be understood in the context of the assassination of Prime Minister Rabin in November 1995 that can be directly attributed to the unfettered political incitement. The same words and phrases used against Rabin, particularly 'traitor', reared their ugly head again. It is in that context that the demonstrations outside the courthouse and elsewhere must be understood. Elor Azaria was merely becoming an impetus, or perhaps a 'political tool' is the correct phrase.

The danger inherent to the incitement against Eizenkot must be understood in a broader context. Not only was he under attack, but the moral standards the IDF seeks to imbue its soldiers were assaulted. The consequences from the perspectives of IDF commanders were potentially dangerous. It is not by chance that the retired officers unanimously articulated their deep concern regarding the impact of the political clamoring on IDF units. Some were deeply angry at the politicians; while criticism is legitimate, calling the Chief of Staff a 'traitor' crossed the Rubicon.

Lost in the shuffle was the following: While not indicted for murder, Elor Azaria was far removed from being a hero.

Final Word

Azaria, whose sentence was shortened by Eizenkot, is today a private citizen, working as a baker. His moment in the sun has, perhaps, passed. The fleeting talk of him going into politics has, seemingly, passed. The star power that embraced his family has also moved on. There was a sense his family enjoyed the moment or at least did not shy from it. Those involved in the trial have retired from the IDF and entered the civilian workplace. The demonstrations have moved onto other issues and causes. The politicians have also gone on to other issues and endeavors.

That is the nature of affairs that capture headlines and then recede into the dustbin of history. Israel is chock-full of such examples. There are too many to recount.

However, there are certain lessons that demand our attention from both an Israeli-specific and from a broader military justice perspective. In the lines ahead, I shall seek to address both, at times separately, at times merging.

From an Israeli perspective, the fault lines we came to see in the street reflect the powerful divisions in society. The vociferousness with which they rose to the surface was both telling and disturbing. The threat of violence was visceral and cannot be easily dismissed; the decision to prosecute Azaria angered a sector of the public in a way few previous events had. The sustained embrace of the soldier was powerful and telling in how the Israeli-Palestinian conflict burns under the surface. The cynicism of the politicians was extraordinary. Fortunately, those entrusted with decision-making ignored threats and personal danger and were, at the end of the day, loyal to two things: the rule of law and the moral code by which the IDF lives. The public owes them its gratitude.

However, more than anything, IDF commanders – past, present, and future – must ensure moral codes by which the IDF defines itself, be at the forefront of operational decision making.

We must recall the following: while al-Shari was lying wounded on the ground, awaiting medical attention, the soldiers who had been engaged in response to the terrorist attack conducted themselves in accordance with IDF norms. The attack/response was over, and therefore, from an operational perspective, there was nothing to do. The incident was over. The terrorist was critically injured; there was no need for operational engagement. That is exactly what combat soldiers are taught.

Azaria, and Azaria alone, did the exact opposite, and for that, he was appropriately court-martialed.

From the perspective of military justice, public and political clamor notwithstanding, the system worked. The three actors – prosecution, defense, and the Court – fulfilled their obligation as demanded of officers of the Court. All three conducted themselves in accordance with their duties and responsibilities. While critical voices were heard, whether on specific issues or broader themes, it would be hard to criticize the way witnesses were heard, rulings rendered, arguments made. I believe the prosecution could have indicted for murder. However, the decision to indict for manslaughter falls well within the boundaries of reasonableness and can be, and has been, eloquently explained to me.

The old saw that 'reasonable minds can reasonably disagree' can be applied here. What is, however, not in dispute is that the prosecution of Azaria was the absolute correct decision, and the way the judicial system conducted itself stands in stark contrast to the way the public and certain other personalities conducted themselves.

The dignity of the former is only matched by the untethered cynicism, incitement, and dangerous anger of the latter. Fortunately, the rule of law ultimately won.

Full circle: as we know from the initial viewing of the video, Elor Azaria was no hero but rather a soldier who killed a mortally wounded terrorist when there was no justification for opening fire.

This is the crux of the matter of *IDF v. Elor Azaria.*

Amos N Guiora is Professor of Law at the SJ Quinney College of Law, the University of Utah. He is a Distinguished Fellow at The Consortium for the Research and Study of Holocaust and the Law at Chicago-Kent College of Law, and a Distinguished Fellow and Counselor at the International Center for Conflict Resolution, Katz School of Business, University of Pittsburgh. He is also the Inaugural Chair of the University of Utah Independent Review Committee. He served in the Judge Advocate General Corps of the Israel Defense Forces (IDF) from 1986 to 2005 and was the Commander of the IDF School of Military Law from 2001 to 2004.

Professor Guiora has an AB in history from Kenyon College, a JD from Case Western Reserve University School of Law, and a PhD from Leiden University. He has published extensively both in the United States and Europe on issues related to national security, limits of interrogation, religion and terrorism, the limits of power, multiculturalism, and human rights.

His most recent book is *Armies of Enablers: Survivor Stories of Complicity and Betrayal in Sexual Assaults* (2020). His previous books include *Populist and Islamist Challenges for International Law* (2019); *Earl Warren, Ernesto Miranda and Terrorism* (2018); *The Crime of Complicity: The Bystander in the Holocaust* (2017); and *Tolerating Intolerance: The Price of Protecting Extremism* (2014).

Professor Guiora's research contributed to legislation ratified by the Utah Legislature, signed into law by Governor Cox on 23 March 2021, that criminalizes bystanders who do not intervene on behalf of children and vulnerable adults.

Views are personal.

The Trial of the Hebron Shooter, Judicial Independence, and Personal Reflections

Judge Maya Heller

Elor Azaria, Israel

Prologue

Nothing in the succinct and factual description appearing in the indictment filed against Sergeant Elor Azaria even hinted at the public uproar surrounding the incident, which was referred to by the general public as the 'Hebron Shooting Incident'.

That single shot, fired by Sergeant Azaria from his personal weapon, which tore through the head of terrorist Abdel al-Sharif, also threatened to tear apart Israeli society. It seemed that one single moment had a profound impact on the country. The entire public, including its leaders, demonstrated unprecedented involvement in the legal proceedings. The trial, from beginning to end, triggered reactions and controversies, both within the Israeli society and throughout the world.

Immediately upon the soldier's arrest, there were those who called for his immediate release.[1] Some believed that even if Sergeant Azaria

---

[1] Rami Amichay, thousands rally to call for release of Israeli soldier who shot Palestinian assailant, *Reuters* (19 April 2016), https://www.reuters.com/article/us-israel-palestinians-soldier-idUSKCN0XG2N2; Peter Beaumont, Most Israelis support soldier accused of shooting Palestinian, says poll, *The Guardian* (29 March 2016), https://www.theguardian.com/world/2016

shot a terrorist lying wounded on the ground in the head, he acted properly since a terrorist who intended to kill soldiers deserved to die. Others argued that he acted in self-defense and the defense of others, in light of a concern that the terrorist was wearing an explosive belt and – despite his condition – could detonate the explosives. There were those who argued that even if he did exercise flawed judgment, legal proceedings should not be initiated against him given the circumstances of him being a soldier who was serving by virtue of a statutorily mandated duty, who was entrusted with defending the relevant area and who therefore was putting himself at risk to protect local residents and state citizens. At a later stage, upon the filing of the indictment, there were those who, based on various reasonings, argued against the decision to charge him of the offense of manslaughter (pursuant to Section 298 of the Penal Law, 5737-1977, as was worded at the time). Some demanded a more severe charge, while others demanded a lenient one. There were also those who demanded to immediately pardon him while his trial was still being held.[2] It seems that only very few believed that one should wait until the legal proceeding was over before determining his fate one way or the other.

On the day the ruling was delivered, mass protests took place next to the Kirya (Rabin) base in Tel Aviv, during which threats were voiced against the Chief of General Staff.[3] Even after Sergeant Azaria's conviction and after the factual and legal findings had been reached, the uproar did not subside. As we discovered while hearing evidence regarding the sentencing, even at this stage, attempts were made to influence the legal proceeding.

The public clamor continued even after the Defendant was sentenced, by a majority opinion, to eighteen months imprisonment as well

/mar/29/most-israelis-support-soldier-accused-of-shooting-palestinian

[2] Gil Hoffman, Bennett calls for pardoning Hebron shooter, *The Jerusalem Post* (8 October 2016), https://www.jpost.com/israel-news/bennett-calls-for-pardoning-hebron-shooter-469712; Peter Beaumont, Netanyahu backs calls for convicted Israeli soldier to be pardoned, *The Guardian* (4 January 2017), https://www.theguardian.com/world/2017/jan/04/israeli-soldier-guilty-manslaughter-shooting-palestinian-elor-azaria-abdel-fattah-al-sharif

[3] ToI Staff, AG orders police investigation into threats to IDF chief, The Times of Israel (5 January 2017), https://www.timesofisrael.com/ag-orders-police-investigation-into-threats-to-idf-chief/ ; Itay Blumenthal, Hundreds of Azaria supporters' riot outside courtroom, Ynet (4 January 2017), https://www.ynetnews.com/articles/0,7340,L-4902933,00.htm

as a suspended sentence and a demotion in rank to private.[4]

Despite the public uproar, and perhaps to its credit, I believe now, as I believed then, that this was the military justice system's finest hour.

The media and public clamor, despite its intensity, did not substantively or conceptually penetrate the proceedings of the military court. Moreover, although the case was of concern to the senior echelons of the defense establishment, among others, and despite the Military Courts Unit being an integral part of the Israel Defense Forces, there was no intervention in how the Hebron shooter's trial was conducted and certainly not in its outcome.

One of the overarching principles of the Israeli legal system, which is anchored in law, is the principle of judicial independence and the independence of judicial discretion. In Sergeant Azaria's trial, we implemented this principle in letter and spirit, and I shall expand on this below.

The Bench

According to Section 202 of the Military Justice Law, 5715-1955 (hereinafter: the 'Military Justice Law' or the 'Law'): 'The President of a District Military Court ... who selects a court bench, shall include therein at least one military judge and at least one legally-qualified military judge'. Hence, this is a unique judicial model of a bench that combines legally qualified military judges alongside military judges.[5] The former are officers with legal training who were appointed as judges by the President of the State of Israel, after being selected by a judicial selection committee (Section 186 of the Law), and who, upon their appointment, pledged 'to be in allegiance to the State of Israel and its laws, to dispense justice fairly, not to pervert the law and to show no favor' (Section 190 of the Law). The latter are military officers who do not have any legal

---

[4] See: Central (District) 182/16 *Military Prosecutor v. Sergeant Azaria* (Nevo, 21 February 2017) (hereinafter: the 'Sentence'). The appeals that were filed against the convicting ruling and against the punishment that had been sentenced were denied, see: A/17/18,21 *Sergeant Azaria v. Chief Military Prosecutor* (Nevo, 30 July 2017).

[5] For a review of the military courts' judicial model, see: *History Will Judge – 70 Years of Military Justice*, Ministry of Defense Publications (2019), page 13.

training and bring their military and command experience to the military court and subsequently assist in formulating the army's required behavioral norms. The prerequisites for the judges' appointment as members of the bench are that they are not involved in the incident, are not versed in its details, are not personally familiar with the witnesses listed on the prosecution's witness list, and have no command relationship whatsoever with any of them. This is all meant to ensure that there be no concern that they could be biased with regard to testimonies.

It follows that sitting on the bench of any procedural instance is at least one legally qualified judge and at least one military judge. The 'character' of the third judge can be chosen. The law further provides that when a president of a military court is one of the members of the bench, he shall serve as presiding judge.[6]

In the framework of Sergeant Azaria's trial, factual arguments were heard that *inter alia* addressed the causal connection between the shooting and the terrorist's death, the motive that led to the shooting, and the *mens rea* accompanying his actions. Legal arguments, asserting that the mere fact that criminal proceedings were being held allegedly prejudices the sense of justice and fairness, were also voiced. It was argued that the decision to instruct that a criminal investigation be launched and the decision to file an indictment were only reached after heads of the military had intervened. In addition, arguments were raised regarding the applicability of criminal liability defenses, such as 'mistake of fact', together with 'justification', 'necessity' and 'self-defense', and allegations were also voiced regarding selective enforcement as it was argued that by merely being prosecuted, Sergeant Azaria was being discriminated against compared to soldiers, commanders, or policemen who were involved in similar cases.[7] Therefore, considering the factual and legal issues that the military court was expected to address during the trial and in light of the complexity and sensitivity of the case, it was decided to

---

[6] Section 221 of the Military Justice Law; also see Section 188 of the Law that provides that a president of a district military court is appointed by the Chief of General Staff, at the recommendation of the President of the Military Court of Appeals, from among the legally qualified military judges of the courts of the same instance. At that time, I served as the President of the Central District Military Court, and therefore, once I included myself on the Court's bench in Sergeant Azaria's trial, I was the presiding judge of the appointed bench.

[7] The judicial rulings regarding all the arguments that were raised appear at length in the ruling, Central (District) Case 182/16 *Military Prosecutor v. Sergeant Azaria* (Nevo, 4 January 2017) (hereinafter: the 'Ruling'), and shall not be detailed here.

appoint an additional legally qualified military judge who had significant judicial experience as the third judge on the bench. As for the military judge, it was decided to appoint a senior officer with relevant command and operational background, who would be able to contribute from his experience when hearing the evidence and examining the law.

Although all the judges on the bench were senior officers in the IDF, which is a distinctly hierarchical organization, while sitting on the bench, we judged the Defendant's case based solely on the evidence that was presented to us and on the law, in keeping with the principle that grants judges complete judicial independence.

The Principle of Judicial Independence

The principle of judicial independence was already anchored in the early days of the state. Section 41 of the Military Justice Regulations 5708 (September 1948),[8] stated:

> Every judge in a military court, including any commander sitting as a judge – while sitting on the bench – is independent and is not subject to any authority whatsoever of his commanders, it is his duty to judge the matter before him to the best of his understanding and conscience and in accordance with the army's laws.

It shall be noted that in the early days of the military justice system, there was no obligation to include people with legal training on the military court's bench. The command echelon in the IDF was given extensive powers, which granted it significant influence on how the judicial proceeding was conducted.

In 1955, the Military Justice Law was legislated, and it regulated both the professional and independent nature and the military character of the military justice system – the Military Courts Unit. Over the years, the law was amended several times. The significant amendment, which is relevant to the case at hand, was meant to reinforce the judges' judicial independence and to establish the status of the Military Courts Unit as an integral part of the judicial authority in Israel, alongside being an IDF unit. This was Amendment No 17 of the Military Justice Law (1986),

---

[8] See review appearing in note 6 above.

which prescribed, in Section 184 of the Law, titled *Judicial Independence*. It is as follows:

> In judicial matters – a military judge is not subject to any authority save that of the law and is not subject to any authority whatsoever of his commanders.

Sergeant Azaria's case was heard in the spirit of this overarching principle. Accordingly, and for the sake of removal of all doubt, we stated at the beginning of the ruling,[9] as follows:

> This case, which has been presented to us, has raised significant public interest and has led to extensive public debate, the likes of which have not been seen by the military justice system in recent years. It is not for us to interpret the reasons that have led to this. For the purpose of this ruling, we shall address certain aspects of the 'public' controversies, all within the framework of the legal and factual allegations that were raised in the trial. Given the above, we have found it appropriate to already clarify now that the ruling in the Defendant's case is based solely and exclusively on the evidence that was presented and heard within the Court's walls, since "a judge has only what his eyes see" (*Bavli, Bava Batra,* 131a). He is guided by his judicial discretion and the command of his conscience. This is the essence of the principle of the judicial system's independence. Its integrity and its power derive therefrom. And it has already been held: "The presumption is that the courts will ... stand firm and will not consider anything other than the evidence before them. This is the judges' test. This is the heart and soul of the judicial system". [HCJ 5699/07 Jane Doe (A) v. The Attorney General, IsrSC 62(3) 550, 648(2008)]

Open Court

One of the principles of law in a democratic regime is that the judicial proceeding must be public so that justice shall not only be done but also be seen.[10] Sergeant Azaria's trial was also held in open court. In light of the public interest that the trial aroused, journalists and photographers who wished to cover the trial and publish photographs of all those who

---

9 Paragraph 4 of the ruling.

10 Section 324 of the Military Justice Law.

were involved inundated the courtroom every day of hearings. The Defendant's relatives attended the hearings and even passers-by who chose to express support and solidarity. From time to time, public figures and politicians who felt the need to express support for the Defendant and to stand by him would also appear. The military court was, therefore, required to make appropriate logistical adjustments which were meant to guarantee the principle of an open court on the one hand and to ensure the personal safety of the Defendant, his family, the parties' attorneys, and the witnesses (some of whom were Palestinians) on the other hand. Indeed, there were a small number of cases in which we were informed by the Courts Guard that the force maintaining public order had to calm the atmosphere and restore order inside the courtroom (before the hearing began or after it was over) or outside it. However, generally speaking, by and large, it was my impression that despite the fact that the hearings were emotionally charged, those who attended understood the role of the military court and the litigating parties in the judicial proceeding and showed respect for the proceedings.

Freedom of Protest

While public order within the military court compound, in general, and within the courtroom, in particular, was maintained, this cannot be said with respect to the public space outside the 'Green House'[11] camp in Jaffa. The military court in Jaffa is located in the middle of a civilian neighborhood and is bordered by two main streets in the center of the city. Since Israel is a democratic country, freedom to protest is a basic right that derives from freedom of expression. Consequently, on more than one occasion, the evidence and the parties' attorneys' arguments were heard against the background of the sound of the voices of protesters who assembled on nearby streets. At times, these were moderate voices, expressing support for the Defendant and seeking to encourage him. At other times, these were cruder voices, personally attacking my colleagues and me on the bench or the military prosecutors. However,

[11] The building which houses the Military Courts Unit in Jaffa is called the 'Green House', named for the building's color. See: The Green House (Jaffa), Wikipedia, https://commons.wikimedia.org/wiki/Category:Green_house,_Jaffa

as stated, in terms of how the judicial proceeding was conducted and in terms of its outcome, the voices resonating from the protesters' megaphones remained nothing more than background noises. This was also the case when the vitriolic voices became stronger in public protests, in talkbacks to media items, and on social networks, to the point where some believed that I was facing a concrete threat and a personal security detail was assigned to me.

The Witnesses – All Equal Before the Law

Every defendant is entitled to his day in court. Therefore, all the witnesses whom we were asked to summon were obligated to fulfill their duty under the law and to report to deliver their testimony, even when some of the witnesses sought to evade this duty.

Accordingly, dozens of witnesses testified before us. Some of them had been present on the scene of the incident, and some had not. There were eyewitnesses, and there were expert witnesses. Some of the witnesses were ordinary civilians, and some were holders of senior positions in Israel, including two politicians. One of them was summoned as an expert witness on behalf of the defense due to his military past.[12] The other was summoned to testify at the sentencing hearing stage in connection with an 'abuse of process' argument that alleged that he had acted, along with senior military commanders, to influence the Defendant's father to replace the defense team and to convince him to reach a plea bargain regarding the punishment.[13] Military personnel holding a wide variety of ranks, ranging from corporal to major-general,[14] also appeared before us. Some of them were in regular service, and some were in the reserves.

All the witnesses were questioned in direct examination and cross-examination. Some of the examinations lasted many hours. A few of them went on more than a day. For the lion's share of the witnesses, this was the first time they had ever been on the witness stand, and it was

---

[12] See paragraphs 157, 159 and 253 of the Ruling.

[13] See beginning from paragraph 31 of the sentence.

[14] The rank of a major-general in the Israel Defense Forces is a senior officer rank, second in the hierarchical order only to the rank of the lieutenant-general, held only by the Chief of General Staff.

evident that the situation was not easy for them – not because the duty to tell the truth was foreign to them, but because they appreciated the burden of responsibility on their shoulders to be precise in their responses. Some of the examinations were uncomfortable for the witnesses. For example, when they were required to face direct questions relating to their own actions or omissions or when they had difficulty properly establishing conclusions in their field of expertise.

As is known, all are equal before the law. Therefore, when the time came to make a ruling, and we were required to determine findings regarding reliability and facts, expertise, relevance, and evidentiary weight, nothing in the status of the witnesses or the positions or ranks they held tilted the scales. Naturally, the testimonies were examined on their merits, using customary criteria. For example, when we examined the testimonies of three expert witnesses who had been senior commanders in the IDF and were convinced that no findings could be established based on their testimonies, we wrote as follows:[15]

> Defense witnesses, Major-General (Res) Dayan, Major-General (Res) Biton and Brigadier-General (Res) Zakai, are undoubtedly officers who have long and rich experience, whose contribution to the state's security is invaluable. However, their testimonies with respect to the incident raise a few difficulties, both because they were not present at the scene of the incident and because at the relevant time they were not entrusted with that arena and did not bear responsibility for what was happening there. Naturally, these witnesses are not familiar with the concrete threats present in the arena at the relevant time and are not versed in the updated threats, as defined by the command echelon. Given that, it is doubtful whether their statements could assist the Court in exposing the truth in the case before us.

Moreover, at the stage of the sentencing hearing, the defense raised an argument that the Defendant's punishment should be mitigated since:

> [he] suffered extensive damage due to his public condemnation, in the media, shortly after the incident, by the Minister of Defense at the time and by the Chief of General Staff and the IDF spokesperson.

[15] Paragraph 157 of the Ruling.

As we were of the opinion that labeling the Defendant's acts as contrary to the IDF's values – before the investigation was exhausted – could have harmed him, we saw it fit for this to be taken into certain consideration when determining the Defendant's sentence, and with respect to the remarks of such senior figures, we noted as follows:

> ... After examining the publications that the defense presented to us, we have found that indeed shortly after the incident, the Minister of Defense at the time, the Chief of General Staff and the IDF spokesperson voiced remarks that expressed a strong opinion as to the meaning of the Defendant's acts and the moral flaw attached thereto. At this stage, the military police's investigation of the incident had just begun. There can be no dispute that the senior military echelon is permitted, and on occasion is even obligated, to express an immediate and clear position with respect to matters on the agenda. However, when at issue are matters that are subject to a criminal investigation, it is fitting to wait until the factual picture emerging from the investigation becomes clear, and if, and to the extent it is necessary to issue a command statement at such an early stage, then the statement should be restrained and qualified pending the outcome of the investigation. However, we posit that this is applicable to all remarks that are voiced with respect to proceedings that are being held before a judicial forum, including by public electees, the most senior thereof included. Indeed, while sitting as judges, the judges are not subject to any authority other than the authority of the law, and yet, remarks that are voiced by senior public figures have a very broad impact on the public's positions and on the public's trust in the judicial authority. Respecting the principle of separation of powers thus requires expressing oneself with restraint and caution with respect to matters that are pending in court and breaching this duty could severely harm the principles underlying the democratic regime in the State of Israel.[16]

Criticism of this kind, directed at the Minister of Defense, the Chief of General Staff and 'public electees, the most senior thereof included', also reflects the nature and character of our legal system, which rests on a solid foundation of judicial independence, and which allows, and even demands, when required, that truths be spoken without reservation or qualification. Also, this too must be said: In my opinion, a strong army

[16] Paragraph 85 of the Sentence.

is an army that can easily absorb such criticism, as in the case before us.

Personal Security Detail

As mentioned above, as the proceeding progressed, more testimonies that were heard and more evidence that piled were covered extensively by the press and on social media. Concurrently, reactions against both the judges on the bench and the military prosecutors escalated among a small minority of the public. These reactions became vitriolic, threatening and violent, and climaxed on the day the ruling convicting the Defendant was delivered.[17] At that time, I was subject to curses and expletives; I was called a Nazi, with my picture decorated with Hitler's mustache. There were those who wrote that I am the sister of Tali Fahima,[18] a radical left activist, and called me a traitor and a hater of Israel. I was at the receiving end of much name-calling.

I do not know the exact reasons for this escalation. I can only guess. Perhaps this public was disappointed by the fact that despite the remarks and statements by public electees, the legal proceeding was getting closer to a ruling without the trial having been canceled or the Defendant having been pardoned. Perhaps the mere fact that a trial was being conducted against a soldier offended their personal, social and political beliefs, and perhaps the vitriolic behavior stemmed solely from a sincere concern for the soldier and his fate.

At that time, I was not on social media. Also, I had removed myself from WhatsApp groups, so I would not be exposed to conversations

---

[17] *ToI* Staff, Man who threatened Azaria judges released to house arrest, *The Times Of Israel* (5 January 2017), https://www.timesofisrael.com/man-who-threatened-azaria-judges-released-to-house-arrest/; Yael Freidson, Police arrests two suspected of inciting against Azaria judges, *Ynet* (5 January 2017), https://www.ynetnews.com/articles/0,7340,L-4903364,00.html; *ToI* Staff, Two Israelis arrested for calling for attacks on Azaria judges, *The Times Of Israel* (5 January 2017) https://www.timesofisrael.com/two-israelis-arrested-for-calling-for-attacks-on-azaria-judges/

[18] See: SCC (District) 1229/04 *The State of Israel v. Tali Fahima* (22 December 2015), from which it emerges that Tali Fahima was convicted, based on her admission, of offenses relating to delivering information to an enemy and for its benefit, pursuant to the middle part of Section 111 of the Penal Law, 5737-1977 (hereinafter: 'the Penal Law'), contact with a foreign agent, pursuant to Section 114(a) of the Penal Law, and violation of a lawful instruction, pursuant to Section 287(b) of the Penal Law, and was sentenced to three years imprisonment and a suspended sentence.

regarding the incident and to allow others to express themselves freely, I completely refrained from reading any 'talkbacks', so I was not exposed to the full intensity of the incitement and the derogatory statements against me. However, I was aware of the general mood and, therefore, when a decision was made to assign a security detail to me, I accepted the letter and spirit of the professional opinion of those charged with such matters. On a personal level, I was not concerned about me or any of the members of my family being harmed. I assumed the chances of that happening were not high, even after my daughter found that someone had written 'Elor the Hero, The *Lehava*[19] Organization!' on the cover of her school notebook that had been left on her desk when she left her classroom for recess.[20] It may have been naïve on my part to believe that the chances that the threats would materialize were low. In any event, since it was explained to me by the security experts that when incitement to violence exists, it is enough that one single person is influenced and attempts to carry it through to fruition, I followed the directions vigilantly. For a while, every time I left my home, I was accompanied by a security guard. So, I limited my daily movement primarily to driving from home to the military court and back. The exceptions were my early morning runs (also joined by a security guard), which I continued as part of maintaining my daily routine.

However, as I stated above, the issue of the threats and of having a security detail did not penetrate the courtroom or the judicial craft. These were background matters, and as significant as they may have been, they were not, at any stage, something that the bench addressed in its discussions.

[19] See https://en.wikipedia.org/wiki/Lehava

[20] Moshe Cohen, Dispute regarding Azaria's conviction has penetrated to the trial's judge's children's classrooms, *MA'ARIV* (8 January 2017), https://www.maariv.co.il/news/israel/Article-569480 (in Hebrew).

Summary

The Hebron shooter's trial presented the military court with a significant challenge. However, it was primarily a complicated logistical challenge that required meticulous, precise, and appropriate preparation to hear the trial without any snags. When determining the findings and the facts, based on the evidence presented in trial, when interpreting the law, when delineating the boundaries of what is permitted and forbidden with regard to use of firearms in the IDF, and when prescribing the standards required of commanders and soldiers in accordance with moral values – there was no special challenge. This has always been the bread and butter of the military justice system since its establishment, and *a fortiori* following the adoption and internalization of the 'Spirit of the IDF'[21] document, which is the 'Ethical Identity Card' of the IDF. This is the daily routine of the military courts' judges, myself, and my colleagues in Sergeant Azaria's trial included.

Ultimately, by convicting the Defendant of the offense of manslaughter after having found that he had shot a terrorist who no longer posed a threat, and had done so from motives of vengeance which was contrary to the law, and then sentencing him, we had the privilege of taking part in shaping the binding norms of the army, in the spirit of the principle of the 'sanctity of life' and the value of the 'purity of arms'. These norms are repeated by soldiers day and night, and their importance, even vis-à-vis the enemy, is clear. By doing so, we were able to make our contribution to the strengthening of the IDF's resilience and its moral character.

---

[21] See https://www.idf.il/en/who-we-are/

Colonel **Maya Heller** (Retired) served as a judge in the Israel Defense Forces Military Court of Appeals. Prior to that, she was the President of the Military Court for the Central Command and the Air Force Military Court. She presided over the court-martial of Sergeant Elor Azaria, which is the topic of her contribution. She has an LLB from the Hebrew University of Jerusalem, and a Master's in Law, with distinction, from Tel Aviv University. She wishes to thank Professor Amos Guiora, Professor of Law, SJ Quinney College of Law, University of Utah, her former commander (1997), who requested her to share her personal reflections from the Hebron shooter's trial.

Views are personal.

Acknowledgements

We would like to acknowledge with gratitude the hard work of all contributors to this book.

We would also like to thank, for their full support, assistance and inputs, the BluOne Ink team, who have published this book.

Major Navdeep Singh would like to thank his associates, Mr Pankaj Thakur and Ms Ananya Sharma, Advocates, for giving him space, mind and time for this project, and his *munshis*, Mr Jai Singh and Mr Ashok Bisht, for secretarial and administrative assistance.

Major Singh would also like to spare a moment of remembrance for Justice RN Aggarwal, former Chief Justice of the Delhi High Court, and Justice JS Narang, former Judge of the Punjab & Haryana High Court, who passed away in recent times, and who were a source of strength in such projects.

Thanks also to all brave women and men in uniform who valiantly defend their respective nations, for inspiration.

Le Petit Journal

Le Petit Journal
CHAQUE JOUR 5 CENTIMES
Le Supplément illustré
CHAQUE SEMAINE 5 CENTIMES

SUPPLÉMENT ILLUSTRÉ
Huit pages : CINQ centimes

ABONNEMENTS

	TROIS MOIS	SIX MOIS	UN AN
PARIS	1 fr.	2 fr.	3 fr 50
DÉPARTEMENTS	1 fr.	2 fr.	4 fr.
ÉTRANGER	1 50	2 50	5 fr.

Sixième année — DIMANCHE 13 JANVIER 1895 — Numéro 217

LE TRAITRE

Dégradation d'Alfred Dreyfus